DENBY & DISTRICT

From Pre-History to the Present

Aerial view of Upper Denby showing Denroyd Farm in the foreground heading off towards the Greenacre estate to the south west. 1997. *Author's collection*

Denby & District

FROM PRE-HISTORY TO THE PRESENT

CHRIS HEATH

Wharncliffe Books

By the same author:

The History of the Denby Dale Pies
(J R Nicholls, 1998)

First edition published in 1997 by Richard Netherwood Limited

This completely revised and updated edition published in 2001 by
Wharncliffe Books in association with Chris Heath

ISBN: 1-903425-11-5

A CIP catalogue record of this book is available from the
British Library

Cover design: Artwork by Jon Wilkinson
        Photograph supplied courtesy of 'Old Barnsley'

Printed in the United Kingdom by
CPI UK

Contents

Dedication

For my Dad, with love and thanks.

For my Mum, for her love, support and so much more.

For my brother Paul, for technical wizardry, friendship, support

and good humour.

And finally,

For Karen, for putting up with it all and for her love.

From: *Whites 1838, Gazetteer and Directory*
of the West Riding of Yorkshire.

DENBY is a scattered village in two divisions, called Upper and Lower Denby, occupied chiefly by woollen weavers, extending from 3$\frac{1}{2}$ miles to 4$\frac{1}{2}$ miles north of Penistone and including in its township the neighbouring hamlets of Denby Dale, where there are several manufacturers of fancy goods, on one of the tributary streams of the river Dearne; Upper and Lower Bagden, Exley Gate, Dryhill and High Flatts.

It has 1295 inhabitants and 2870 acres of land, forming a hilly district, all enclosed, though part of the common is still uncultivated.

The Earl of Scarborough is Lord of the Manor, but the soil belongs to a number of proprietors. An eminence called Castle Hill is said to have been a Roman encampment.

The Church or Chapel of Ease at Denby is a small ancient structure, and comprises within its chapelry the townships of Denby, Gunthwaite and Ingbirchworth. It has a perpetual curacy, worth £98 per annum, and was augmented in 1739, with £200 of Q.A.B. (Queen Anne's Bounty); in 1816, with a parliamentary grant of £1200; and in 1738, with £200 given by the Reverend Jonothan Perkins. The vicar of Penistone is the patron, and the Reverend Brice Bronwin, the incumbent. The Wesleyan and Primitive Methodists have each a chapel in Denby Dale, and the Society of Friends have one at High Flatts.

In 1731, Francis Burdett bequeathed £200 for the school and poor of Denby township, and in 1769 it was laid out in the purchase of a cottage, barn and 10A of land, in Hoyland Swaine, now let for £12 6s a year, half of which is paid to the schoolmaster, for six free scholars.

Acknowledgements

✧

Grateful thanks must be given to the following, without whom this book would have been significantly thinner, in no particular order:

Alan Burdett, Annie Heath, Ava Newby, Betty Springer, Bryan Heath, Carol Heath, Christine Martin, David and Keeley Whittaker, Doug and June Fisher, Frank and Lynn Burdett, George Wilby, Harry Heath, Jane Helliwell of Huddersfield Local History Library, Jane Whittaker of Canon Hall Museum, Jim Barber, Joe Price, John Gaunt, John Goodchild, John Rumsby-Curator of Tolson Museum, Huddersfield, John White, Johnny White, Karen Heath, Lena Nicholson, Mabel Pickford, Margaret Peace, Paul Heath, Phillip Parker, Richard Peace, Ronald Heath, Rupert Gill Martin, Stella Crossland, Stella Kenyon, Steven and Jill Slater, Wendy Hawkins and Gillian Nixon at Barnsley Local Studies Library, Mike Baldwin, Julia Landon, Shirley Wilson (for proof reading the manuscript), Richard Netherwood, Tony Turton, Paul Wattenburger, Mr W Broadhead, John Slater, Charles Crossland.

And also, Harry Meadowcroft and Guy Hirst both of whom know far more about the Burdet family than I. Also, I am very grateful to Sir Savile Burdett for agreeing to wade through a difficult, error ridden manuscript to be able to write the foreword.

My thanks go to all those at Wharncliffe Books - Charles Hewitt (Managing Director), Barbara Bramall (Production Manager), Jon Wilkinson for the cover design and Sylvia Menzies for design and setting of the book.

Finally, a special mention for the historians now passed away, who not only provided the foundation for my work but also the inspiration;

Reverend Joseph Hunter, Henry Moorhouse, Fred Lawton, John Ness Dransfield and William Herbert Senior.

(Joseph Hunter (1783-1861) was born in Sheffield and is buried in Ecclesfield churchyard. In 1833 he was appointed Sub-Commissioner of the Records Commission in London, becoming Assistant Keeper in 1838 when the Public Record Office was established. His two volumes on the History of South Yorkshire were published in 1828 and 1831).

Any errors or omissions in this book are entirely my own. None of the above are responsible in any way for the thoughts and opinions expressed by the author herein.

Whilst every effort has been made to locate the copyright holders of all illustrations within this book, the author apologises to anyone who has not been acknowledged.

Throughout this book, the spellings of personal and place names varies. Ancient spellings of these names was not an exact science, therefore I have endeavoured, as much as possible, to use the spelling most commonly associated to the period in question.

Forefathers
by Edmund Blunden

Here they went with smock and crook,
Toiled in the sun, lolled in the shade,
Here they muddied out the brook
And here their hatchet cleared the glade:
Harvest supper woke their wit,
Huntsman's moon their wooings lit.

From this church they led their brides,
From this church they themselves were led
Shoulder-high ; on these waysides
Sat to take their beer and bread.
Names are gone - what men they were
These their cottages declare.

Names are vanished, save the few
In the old brown Bible scrawled;
They were men of pith and thew,
Whom the city never called;
Scarce could read or hold a quill,
Built the barn, the forge, the mill.

On the green they watched their sons
Playing till too dark to see,
As their fathers watched them once,
As my father once watched me;
While the bat and beetle flew,
On warm air webbed with dew.

Unrecorded, unrenowned,
Men from whom my ways begin,
Here I know you by your ground
But I know you not within -
There is silence, there survives
Not a moment of your lives.

Like the bee that now is blown
Honey - heavy on my hand,
From his toppling tansy-throne
In the green tempestuous land
I'm in clover now, nor know
Who made honey long ago.

Foreword

Sir Savile Aylmer Burdett Bt

Many are the people who would like to know more about their antecedents - a few set about the tortuous journey of finding out at least the names of their forebears. Generally, the track is lost and the searchers left wondering.

In this respect, I feel greatly privileged - not only have I had to do little to collect the various events together - Chris Heath has done much more than I would have even attempted - but so much more is recorded or at least inferred about our family that I feel especially thankful. I am disappointed that the second half of the family, of which Sir Francis was the most famous member, died out recently and I hope that we can continue with just the finest patters set.

The wise learn from their parents; both their winning ways and their less desirable characteristics can be used for both positive and negative guidance. Some manage to remember their grandparents and learn from them too. However, few have the skill, the patience or the resolve to dig any deeper. In this book Chris Heath has dug up from the past a history which shows how little we have learnt over the past years; the modes and details have changed but the people still have the same nature with thwarted ambitions and great goodness.

In this book he includes much more detail which only the diligent will manage to assimilate, but the less assiduous still have the opportunity to learn from the past as well. One can only hope that many will realise how significant the individual personal contribution can be to the world around and take opportunities to emulate the best and avoid the petty pride and jealousies which can so easily distract from such an objective.

Birthwaite Hall near Kexborough, Barnsley. 1998.
Author's collection.

Introduction

The worlds of family history and local history have been likened to an 'interchangeable jigsaw puzzle, without any straight edges, and constantly missing various important pieces or having pieces which do not fit'.

This book is a by-product of my research into my own family, who by their close connections with Denby and its environs caused me to look into the background of the settlement to help understand how they lived, loved and died. This was the acorn.

Unfortunately, all previously published material was disjointed and fragmentary, sometimes ambiguous and always insufficient. What I needed was a book solely concerned with the settlement, which included all the important previously published material and the fruits of my own enquiries presented in a logical, cohesive, and accessible narrative. The Reverend Joseph Hunter was the first to attempt the task, back in the mid-nineteenth century. His work has formed the basis for all subsequent historical research into the village, including that of John Ness Dransfield, who reproduced, word for word, Hunter's narrative, adding only his own notes concerning Denby workhouse.

Fred Lawton's notes on the Spanish Armada, the District Militia and Witchcraft added to the tale. Finally William H. Senior continued the task until he died last year, adding notable features from the nineteenth and early twentieth century and frequently giving lectures utilising his excellent memory to continue to breath life into this ancient foundation. The work of these four men inspired me to attempt to learn not only all that they knew, but also to build on their discoveries and attempt to write the 'logical, cohesive and accessible narrative' that I required.

The book begins in the late Stoneage period, with the settlement at High Flatts, which in historical terms is only a stones throw from the village. Although this chapter appears at first glance to be a fairly general overview of the country up until the Norman Conquest, it does form a pivotal role in setting the scene for the rest of my narrative. For instance, to be able to understand that the site which was to become Denby formed part of the ancient lands known as Elmet, and subsequently part of Northumbria, I believe it prudent to know why these two ancient Kingdoms existed at all.

In essence, it would be very difficult to prove that there was any activity on the site of the village before the coming of the 'Vikings' in the ninth century. Yet there must have been tribes living locally and familiar with the topography of the lands here before that time. Further evidence from this 'Dark Age' is unlikely, unless serious archeological excavation is undertaken in the future; therefore, it is down to individual speculation as to the truth of the site before historical documentation.

Cumberworth and Burnt Cumberworth are both ancient British settlements and are on the boundaries of the present day villages of Upper and Lower Denby. Do they have connections with the settlement on Castle Hill at High Flatts? Were the lands at Denby used by them for hunting, or was there a settlement here before 'Viking' activity? Speculative conversation can realise some quite wonderful possibilities!

The narrative moves on from 1066 to the first settlement of the Lords of the Manor, the Burdet's who from at least the thirteenth century until 1643 raised the township's stature and instituted the basis for the modern village of today. Throughout this time and the following 150 years, I have endeavoured to intermingle their story with the available details of the lives of the peasants that worked on their lands. Of course, once we reach the nineteenth century a rich wealth of source material still survives to provide a far more detailed picture of the lives of these ordinary folk.

The chapters concerning occupation and leisure and celebration span both the nineteenth and twentieth centuries, and reduce the content in the chapter on the twentieth century by a large degree. Though I believe the narrative in these chapters sits comfortably together.

The book is somewhat 'introverted', much has already been written concerning Denby Dale and Penistone, therefore I was determined to concentrate my attention on the villages of Upper and Lower Denby, both sadly neglected in most modern publications.

In recent years the pursuit of Local History as a pastime has grown immensely and judging by the number of books available and locally organised lectures and exhibitions I believe that the time is now right for Denby to have at least its first, certainly not the last, history of its own.

Introduction to Second Edition

The second edition of this book has been made possible because of the success of the first. The large quantities of new information have come in part from letters received from contacts who read the first edition and supplied the answers to many of the questions I raised. Naturally, my own researches have continued and the resulting manuscript is now more than twice the length of the first. Needless to say, I thank all those who purchased the first edition for their support and interest in a small, anonymous, but nevertheless, important and influential district.

During the stimulating task of re-writing much of the original manuscript I have learned much along the way. First and foremost being the size of the original area of the places we now call Upper and Lower Denby. The manor of Denby included sizeable lands in Clayton, Bagden and High Hoyland, not to mention the whole of the then non-existent Denby Dale, then known as Denby Milne. When considering a phrase such as 'lands at Denby' in the context of the fourteenth century, one has to always remember the above geography. The importance of Nether Denby in ancient records has also surprised me somewhat. The notable and influential families that lived there making this tiny hamlet of today their home and workplace, though its site and situation almost midway between today's Upper Denby and High Hoyland does seem to lend it a strategic role.

I have discussed the possible locations of these early sites and areas, and also the gritty problem as to the true location of the original Denby Hall. My conclusions are by no means the last word on the matter, particularly with regard to the Hall, but I hope to stimulate more argument which will hopefully uncover the truth that I am searching for.

I was accused in the first edition of not presenting my own opinions on subjects to which there are few or no known facts to provide the answers. Here again I have tried to remedy the problem, though again I must stress that hypothetical scenarios can only be as close to the truth as the existing records will allow.

The new details on the Turton families connections to a Bishop of Ely and the Civil War coins dug up in a field somewhere near the church are wonderful examples of records which have come to light since the publication of the first book. Of course, I know that shortly after the publication of this manuscript more evidence will be unearthed that I will only be able to wish had been available for inclusion.

I have consciously endeavoured to expand the history of Denby and its environs to cover some of the more notable local villages. This is not a history of the township of Denby as to be true to its title it would have to contain far more about the villages of High Hoyland, Clayton West, Ingbirchworth and Denby Dale and to do this would render the whole manuscript far too long for any publisher to undertake. Yet, a wealth of material is contained in this book about these places. For instance the

Bosville and Gunthwaite families have been expanded upon as the nearest and most prominent neighbours of the village. Indeed they held land at Denby and to consider the history of the village without them would be to create an isolation which just did not exist. The village of Denby Dale was nothing until the Industrial Revolution, subsequently, its history is always recorded under the heading, 'Denby' and can be taken to be exactly the same, until the early nineteenth century. It is only when we reach the late eighteenth and early nineteenth centuries that I have had to scale down in terms of scope. The trades and occupations are based very firmly in Upper and Lower Denby, or at least, very close to. They are representative samples of the kind of lives our forebears had. Yes – the names and sites vary from place to place but the fundamental arts and practices remain the same. This is not to undermine the crucial aspects of village identity which are so strong in this part of the world. The recreation of our ancestors also varied from village to village but essentially, only Denby Dale has any tradition which varies enormously from the norm, this being of course, the famous Pies. What would be ideal, at some stage in the future, are a series of follow up volumes on the other major villages in the township. Looking at their people, buildings, occupations, disputes, industries, leisure, religion, the list is endless.

There will never be a book entitled, 'Denby – The Truth, The Whole Truth, and Nothing but the Truth', we are dealing with a vast time period and many lives are already forgotten altogether. Their absence from these pages can be attributed to any number of disasters involving our recorded heritage, e.g. the destruction caused during the civil war between Stephen and Matilda in the twelfth century, Henry VIII's monastic clampdown and religious upheaval in the sixteenth century, even the Second World War bombs dropped by the Germans. Of course, the lower the class the less the likelihood that anything was ever written down about them in the first place.

We can only have a glimpse of the lives of these long forgotten people, records are only instants in time. When reading this book, try to remember that every new name you read was, in his or her own time, your equal. They loved and lied, fought and lost, cried and laughed, experienced pain, heartbreak and every emotion you or I have ever had, within the England that they then inhabited. Some were bad, some were worse, but many were just ordinary people, going about their lives in an orderly fashion, the very people upon which the foundation of this country has long been based.

Chris Heath
August 2001

The author with his Border Collie, Charis, sat at the top of Bank Lane, Upper Denby.
Author's collection.

Chapter One

Early Origins

✦

The village unit now known as Denby was probably first created soon after the Viking invasion of York in 866 AD. Denby, or Denebi means simply; 'Farmstead of the Danes'. Whether this name was created by the Viking settlers or was given to the village by neighbouring Anglo-Saxons is now impossible to tell.

Fortunately the history of the locality stretches back somewhat further and we are able to trace Iron Age and possibly Neolithic (late Stone Age) settlement in and around what is referred to in the *National Sites and Monuments* record as an 'Iron Age Hill Fort' on Castle Hill at High Flatts.

Table of Early Time Periods

Mesolithic	(Middle Stone Age)	8000 BC – 4000 BC
Neolithic	(Late Stone Age)	4000 BC – 2200 BC
Bronze Age		2200 BC – 650 BC
Iron Age		650 BC – 43 AD
Roman		43 AD – 410 BC

NB: All dates are approximate

Brigantes

The modern area of Yorkshire was once part of a much greater territory populated by the ancient British Celtic tribe known as the Brigantes. These were not only warrior people but also skilled craftsmen and traders. Gone were the 'hunter gatherers' of the Stone and Bronze Ages. These people now farmed the land and kept livestock for subsistence and made pottery and metalwork, not only for themselves but also for export to the continent. The tribe's most famous daughter was Queen Cartimandua, who allowed her kingdom to become a client of Rome during their conquest of the country. She surrendered her countryman, Caratacus to them after he was defeated in battle resisting the Romans and had fled to her for shelter in AD 51. The tribal capital was at Isurium Brigantia, modern day Aldborough near Boroughbridge, and it is likely that she ruled from here when she fought a civil war against her estranged husband, Venutius.

Although it makes sense to mention her in the context of this chapter, it would be a romantic notion to connect her with Denby's modest earthwork. A more or less common Celtic language linked these Britons before the Romans, which is the forerunner of today's Welsh and Cornish.

It is generally accepted that it is from this group of people that we owe the construction of the High Flatts 'Iron Age Fort', but can this be challenged?

The *Victoria County History of Britain* suggests that the site is of, 'not exactly a defensive situation' and Henry Morehouse in his *History of Kirkburton* was able to suggest only that the earthworks were probably of British origin (though he was writing before excavations were carried out). In the early 1970s John Gilks of the Tolson Museum, Huddersfield examined the site, (which is 1025 feet above sea level), in response to work undertaken by Mr. B. Spence and his pupils from Birdsedge Junior School, who had discovered large quantities of flint after the field in which the enclosure lies was ploughed. Though they were not the first to dig here, I have been told of other local teachers taking classes onto

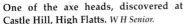

One of the axe heads, discovered at Castle Hill, High Flatts. *W H Senior.*

A selection of flints found during field work undertaken at Castle Hill, High Flatts in 1972. *Courtesy of the Tolson Museum, Huddersfield.*

the hill in the nineteenth century and setting about it with shovels! Archaeology has not always been the science it is today. Also in 1845 workmen labouring on a new drain recovered a stone axe head from the property of Herbert Dickinson of High Flatts. Described by Henry Morehouse as a 'British Celt' (or stone battle-axe) it weighed two pounds nine ounces and measured nearly seven inches long, three and a half inches on the cutting edge tapering to approximately two inches.

Gilks examined the finds, which included scraping tools, fragments of knives and leaf shaped arrow heads, and over the course of the next few years added numerous others, though the site was never properly excavated. He also noted that large quantities of the underlying rock had also been thrown up to the surface through deep ploughing. Approximately ninety Neolithic flints were recovered, 80% of which were collected from a fourteen square metre area of the plough reduced rampart on the south side of the enclosure. Two fragments of stone axe heads were also found. Flint is not found locally, therefore it was brought here by human hands, upon this basis it is reasonable to assume that the site had Neolithic origins, which could give an earliest date of 4000-2200 BC, for activity in the area. The site itself lies on the southern side of a low hill, and the remains extant today have been greatly reduced by ploughing. According to the West Yorkshire Archaeology Service, a slight lowering of the inner bank on the west side may have been an entrance, but cattle could also have caused this! What is almost immediately apparent is the site's poor defensive position. It is overlooked from both the north and east and would have afforded scant protection to its inhabitants against a strong external attack, even with a three to four metre wide ditch below the ramparts and a strong wooden palisade around the top perimeter.

It would appear more likely that the area was a settlement rather than an 'out and out' military fort, probably a Neolithic site in origin which was re-fortified and occupied by the people of the Iron Age and probably abandoned as the Roman legions were spreading north in their invasion of Britain, and local inhabitants fled to safer strongholds.

I must stress that the site's Iron Age origins would seem to be an assumption and that the Neolithic or early Bronze Age activity would at present appear to be fact. The projected size of the enclosure would seem to be the only evidence for Iron Age activity, it being typical of the period. But, can we accept that this was just an isolated farmstead or has other evidence survived to give us a clearer picture of the area. A chance association with two young archaeology students has certainly opened up the possibilities after they visited the site and surveyed the area lying around it.

It is now that I must proceed with some caution, because until a serious archaeological examination of the area is undertaken much of what follows will be hypothesis and speculation. To remain rooted to already well established theories, based on scant evidence, would be to stick ones head in to the sand and shy away from controversy which could lead to a far better appreciation of the site, its size and its relationship to local topography. Perhaps, by sticking out ones neck and being prepared to be wrong we may well achieve more illumination than ever before.

Utilising aerial photography and features in the landscape, the first new site that the team discovered was a possible settlement area in the fields below the ramparts. This would indicate that perhaps the ditch and bank were associated with a hill fort and that a civic settlement had grown up, around the foot of the hill. This caused them to re-examine the possible extent of the earthwork at the top of the hill. They believe that the earthwork could have originally been much larger than at present thought, probably crossing over today's road, Windmill Lane, and encompassing the higher point of the hill, which we have already noted would have overlooked the settlement as it stands today. If this theory is correct then we are certainly looking at a large, well defended enclosure, of reasonably high status, a site that was not overlooked from any direction, which seems to make far more sense.

To add to this we also have at least five possible ring ditch burial sites, south of the fort, lying on the side of a hill, but facing towards the fort, just behind the Blackwater Dyke. These were only visible because of the shadows cast by late evening summer sunshine. Burials were constructed away from settlements because of ancient superstitions and beliefs about the souls of the dead, and also because of the smell as the corpses interred in the mounds began to rot. These at High Flatts appear to be in exactly the right place. The population size of the site could only be guessed at when the exact area has been discovered, but we can at least say with confidence that accommodation in the form of round houses would have been present. We can go little further without actually digging the site to prove or disprove these academic theories, though attempts to preserve these other sites will be made alongside possible archaeological excavation.

Two other local sites, contemporary with the settlement at High Flatts should be mentioned at this point. The first is an area of land known as 'Burnt Cumberworth' which lies to the north of High Flatts, behind the *Sovereign* public house. I reported in the first edition of this book that this area was in danger of being lost for good unless the quarrying activities, which border it, were discontinued. Unfortunately, quarrying continued and the site is now lost for ever. Remains of a floor, and a number of ridges in the ground were noted by Henry Morehouse back in the nineteenth century, though when I last saw the ridges they were not so clear, but the settlement was thought to be of British Celtic origin, and is only a stones throw from Castle Hill at High Flatts.

The second is the hillfort at Almondbury. First occupied by Neolithic man, it could have connections with the High Flatts activity at this time. Later the site was abandoned, until, as at High Flatts, it was re fortified during the Iron Age, circa 590 BC. This new settlement was then destroyed by fire, apparently caused by spontaneous combustion inside the ramparts, sometime around 550 BC. It is possible that Almondbury had direct links with High Flatts, but it is almost certain that, throughout their respective periods of occupation the inhabitants of the two sites would have been well known to each other. Pevsner, suggests that Almondbury could well have been the tribal capital of the Brigantes before they adopted the more northerly site at Aldborough.

Castle Hill at Almondbury is still very prominent today, sited on a 900 foot high bluff with three very steep sides. After the Roman invasion the site was abandoned until the reign of King Stephen (1135-1154). At the orders of the de Lacy family in approximately 1150, a great ditch was dug across the interior and the spoil was piled up to form the base of a great keep, this castle surviving until the reign

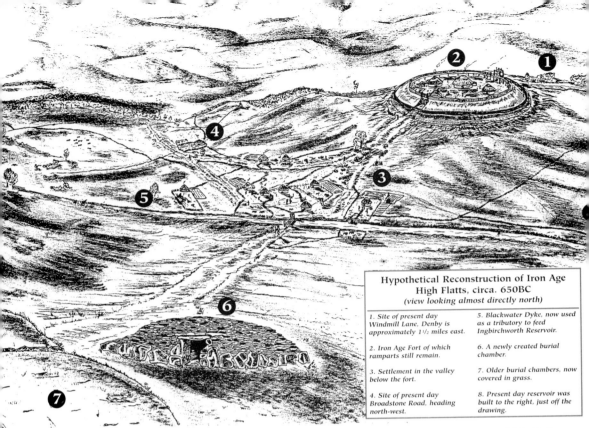

Hypothetical Reconstruction of Iron Age High Flatts, circa. 650BC *(view looking almost directly north)*	
1. Site of present day Windmill Lane, Denby is approximately 1½ miles east.	5. Blackwater Dyke, now used as a tributory to feed Ingbirchworth Reservoir.
2. Iron Age Fort of which ramparts still remain.	6. A newly created burial chamber.
3. Settlement in the valley below the fort.	7. Older burial chambers, now covered in grass.
4. Site of present day Broadstone Road, heading north-west.	8. Present day reservoir was built to the right, just off the drawing.

Hypothetical reconstruction of Iron Age, High Flatts (circa 750BC). The view is looking almost directly north. *Author's collection.*

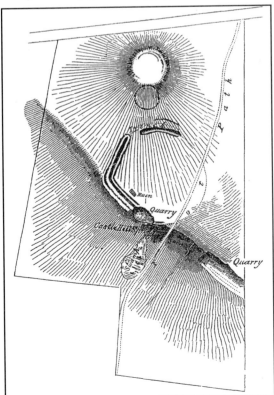

of King Henry III who dismantled it. The only stonework to be found today is comprised in the Victoria Tower which was erected in 1897.

Naturally, far more archaeological evidence lies buried under today's modern villages and field systems, but these latter two sites do at least suspend the feeling of isolation created whilst considering the settlement at High Flatts as a single unit.

A coin hoard dating from the Iron Age was discovered at Almondbury, Neolithic finds have come from Farnley Tyas and New Mill, Bronze Age material from Netherthong and Kirkburton, Iron Age material in Denby Dale and from Upper and Lower Whitley Edge, Mesolithic and Bronze Age relics have been discovered. There was an incredible amount of activity taking place around High Flatts, from the middle Stone Age to the Iron Age, people were living here, importing and

Plan of the Castle Hill remains as drawn by the antiquarian Henry Morehouse in 1861. *Author's collection.*

Ivar the Boneless died in 873, leaving his brother Halfdan as King of Jorvik. Halfdan abandoned the conquest of Wessex for pursuits elsewhere, notably trying to retain his brother's authority in Ireland. By 876 his fighting men must have been around forty years old, by Medieval standards too old and as was a king's duty Halfdan was obliged to grant gifts to them in return for their loyal service, a little like the retirement presents of today:

Extract from the Saxon Chronicle:

AD 876 : And in this year Halfdan apportioned the land of the Northumbrians and from that time they (the Danes) continued ploughing and tilling them.

Halfdan was not for settling, ultimately entering Valhalla in battle off the coast of Ireland in 877 whilst many of his men lived out the rest of their lives working on the farmsteads that he had granted to them. It is possible that Denby was created at this time, although Scandinavian settlement in the area continued for over another century. As the name suggests Denebi was the farmstead of the Danes and it could be that its original occupants were former members of Halfdan's army. Perhaps the first settlers of Denebi, fought alongside Halfdan and Guthrum against Alfred the Great and his brother Aethelred. Though this notion could be tarnished when we remember that they could also have been sons or grandsons of these early warriors and that they were born locally, did not arrive in dragon crested longships, and founded Denebi a generation or two later. Unfortunately, all we may do is speculate. Life is not made any easier when one considers the fact that, to date, not one artefact relating to the Viking period has been discovered in or around Denby or indeed in the whole Kirklees area. It is now impossible to suggest where the original site of the settlement in Denby was. Many successful farmsteads became medieval villages and now both lie buried under their modern counterparts. I would speculate that the medieval pot (examined later) dated 1150-1250 discovered in the field above the modern day village green suggests occupation in this area 600 years ago. If the latter theory is correct then the Danish farmstead could not have been far away.

The farmstead itself was probably enclosed amidst an associated field system. Buildings would have included a long house (living quarters) and perhaps a bakery, a grindstone, an oven, a simple smithy, or indeed any variation thereof.

So by now the country was populated by many diverse peoples, Saxons, Angles, Friesans, Jutes, Danes, Celts, Scotti, Picts, Irish, Roman, Norse and the original Britons. All originally practising differing ways of life and religion – though initially all were predominantly pagan. Now living alongside each other, embracing Christianity, inter-marrying and creating one unique new culture – the English.

THE DOMESDAY BOOK

William the Conqueror's victory over Harold Godwinson at the Battle of Hastings in 1066 is history known to every schoolchild, though it is unlikely that Harold died from an arrow wound to his eye. William brought about an incredible transformation in English society, and also left the country with its foremost literary evidence of the period the *Domesday* book, dating from 1086.

Extract from the Saxon Chronicle:

AD 1085: Then at midwinter was the king at Gloucester with his council, and held there his court five days. And afterwards the Archbishop and clergy had a synod three days... .

After this had the King a large meeting, and very deep consultation with his council, about this land; how it was occupied, and by what sort of men. Then sent he his men over all England into each shire; commissioning them to find out 'how many hundreds (wapentakes) of hides were in the shire, what land the King himself had, and what stock upon the land; or, what dues he ought to have by the year from the shire.' Also he commissioned them to record in writing, 'How much land his Archbishops had, and his diocesan bishops and his Abbots, and his Earls;' and though I may be prolix and tedious, 'what or how much, each man had, who was an occupier in England, either in land or in stock, and how much money it were worth.' So very narrowly indeed did he commission them to trace it out, that there was not one single hide, nor a yard of land, nay, moreover (it is shameful to tell, though he thought it no shame to do it), not even an ox, nor a cow, nor a swine was there left, that was not set down in his writ. And all the recorded particulars were afterwards brought to him.

The country was most likely divided into areas, perhaps eight or nine and a group of William's men would be responsible for each. These areas were then divided into hundreds, or in lands previously subject to the Danelaw, wapentakes.

The word Wapentake is of Scandinavian origin and refers to the voting done at gatherings by the brandishing of weapons. Men from each village were called to their local court to answer the Kings questions. Denby was included in the Staincross wapentake and the following information was recorded:

In (Upper and Lower) Denby, Eadwulf and Godric had 3 carucates of land taxable where 1½ ploughs are possible. Now Alric has (them) from Ilbert. There, woodland pasture, 1 league long and 1 wide. Value before 1066, 10s; now 6s. A cow pasture is there.

The above translation cones from the Phillimore edition of the *Domesday* book, 1986. A slight variation on this comes from Fred Lawton's *Historical Notes on Skelmanthorpe and District*, reprinted in 1986 :

2, manors. In Denebi, Edulf and Godric had three carucates of land to be taxed, where there may be one plough and half. Alric now has of Ilbert. Wood pasture one mile long and one broad. Value in King Edward's time 10s now 6s. There is waste ground.

So what can we learn from this? Lawton mentions the melancholy phrase 'there is waste ground' which refers to the problems William the Conqueror had in subduing his northern subjects. Frequent rebellions and attacks on the city of York finally tried his patience and he rode to what became known as the 'Harrying of the North' in the winter of 1069-70. It took him less than two years to devastate Northumbria, his men killing the people and livestock alike and burning all buildings and tools. The bulk of the population either died or became refugees, hence the reduction of the land values at the time of writing of the *Domesday* book.

Although the statement is used many times in the Phillimore edition, it is conspicuous by its absence from the entry for Denby. Lawton has, conversely, omitted one of the most interesting features – *Ibi est vaccaria* ('there is a cow pasture' or 'there is a cattle house'). This statement was unique to Denby in the whole Yorkshire survey, though there would surely have been others. What was a cattle house? It seems best to suggest that this was a place where cattle were kept and bred, for resale, a little like a nineteenth century American cattle ranch. It is also very interesting to note that the remains of the hill settlement at High Flatts (which would have been more significant at this time) have been linked with the vaccaria. It is possible that the two were one and the same and that the settlement was being re-used to good effect. The *Victoria County History* suggests as much and the thought has not been lost on the *West Yorkshire Archaeology Service*. In effect, we shall never know for sure and to make this assumption without further evidence would be foolish.

Edulf or Eadwulf and Godric are testament to the fact that agricultural activity had been considerable before the conquest. A carucate was the amount of land that could be ploughed by an eight ox plough team and this was composed of bovates, which was the amount of land that could be ploughed by one ox in a year, thus, eight bovates to a carucate. Bovates were also known as Oxgangs. The detail 'where 1 ½ ploughs are possible' refers to the total equipment at the farmer's disposal, which when assembled became a plough, and is an excellent example of how the community would have pulled together during the seasons, each bringing the equipment that he had, be it for ploughing, harvesting or suchlike.

A glance through the *Domesday* book reveals a large amount of manors and villages reportedly belonging to a man named Godric, but was this the same man? It is of course extremely likely that Godric was a popular name, such as today's David, James or John. But with this in mind it could prove illuminating to examine the details of an early Lord of Emley of the same name.

In the first edition of this book I noted that a man named Godric had held lands at Kexborough and had his Hall at Notton, North of Royston, between Wakefield and Barnsley. As to whether the Godric of Denby and the Godric of Emley are one and the same is very unclear.

The Emley man was willing to work alongside the new Norman regime, as we know from the *Domesday* book that he was allowed to keep his lands. The Godric of Denby disappears by 1086 and is supplanted by Ailric, who we shall turn to later.

GODRIC OF EMLEY

Godric was succeeded by his son, Ketelbern (or Ketelbjorn), another common name throughout the locale within the *Domesday* book. His son was a second Godric, this man being the first to make concessions to the monks of Byland Abbey regarding usage of his estates before 1170. He was followed by his son, William Fitz Godric. William was born around 1140 and confirmed the grants made to the monks by his father, he may also be a possible solution to a small enigma concerning ownership of land lying around what is today Papist Hill at Lower Denby. It is also interesting to note that William was the brother of Robert, who became the Lord of Rockley in Worsborough and founded a family that will appear again in our story.

Descent from Godric of Emley

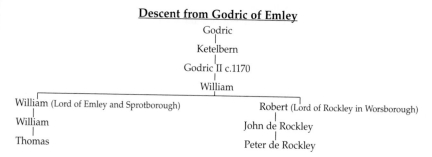

Godric
|
Ketelbern
|
Godric II c.1170
|
William
|
William (Lord of Emley and Sprotborough)   Robert (Lord of Rockley in Worsborough)
| |
William   John de Rockley
| |
Thomas   Peter de Rockley

From an old document relating to High Hoyland Church we learn the following:

> *William Fitz Osbert, Lord of Denby, made a grant to the monks of Byland Abbey, soon after 1177 empowering them to extend their mining operations for their iron industry in the village.* [of Denby]

Although it is not stated, the monks of Byland could also have grazed flocks of sheep here as they did in so many other places, to sustain their huge woollen industry operations. Is it possible that William Fitz Godric and William Fitz Osbert were one and the same? The similarity of names certainly makes this a feasible possibility, scribes were not overly concerned with spelling accuracy. If the above hypothesis was to turn out to be correct then it would also be highly suggestive in arguing the case that Godric of Emley and Godric of Denby were one and the same as William Fitz Godric would be a descendent of a man who owned land in both places, even though his estates at Denby were less important to those at Emley, where he resided. The only other historical record that I have found, which mentions a William Fitz Osbert dates to 1196. This man is certainly alive and active at the right period of time, though not for long!

This man, also known as William 'Longbeard', was found guilty of sedition in 1196 and was reputedly the first person to be executed on the gallows at Tyburn in London. He had his hands tied behind him and was suspended by his feet from the neck of a horse and dragged through the streets of London to the gallows where he was hung until dead.

Although the above story is interesting, it does not explain any possible connection with Denby, though it is feasible that he was a distant landlord, in a similar way to the monks of Byland in other areas. By 1177 – 1196, Denby appears to have been the demesne of the de Denby family, therefore the likelihood of this man being identical to the one mentioned in the High Hoyland record is extremely low.

If we follow the theory that William Fitz Godric and William Fitz Osbert were one and the same, and I must stress this is purely hypothetical, then it would be reasonable to speculate that certainly some of the other manors mentioned in *Domesday* were also held by this obviously wealthy and influential Saxon, more than likely a nobleman, his status being reflected in the significant number of manorships he held. One then has to ponder the question as to why his lands at Denby were passed on to Ailric (or Alric) after the conquest.

The first thing to consider is that he may only have co-held the land at Denby, indeed, Denby may have belonged in the main to his partner mentioned in the *Domesday* book as Eadwulf or Edulf. Perhaps Godric's only interest was in the vaccaria or cattle farm, an obvious money making opportunity. Nothing else is listed within the entry for the village and the likelihood that there were many people living here is slim. As we have already learned, Eadwulf disappears between the years 1066 and 1086, here we are presented by unverifiable possibilities. For instance, was he killed fighting alongside King Harold II either at Stamford Bridge or at Hastings? (Hastings would only be a remote possibility as most of King Harold's army, particularly the levy were replaced en-route south by fresh conscripts). It is also possible that Eadwulf was killed during the 'Harrying of the North', as a dedicated cattle farmer he would have been in grave danger of losing his livelihood. News of the Norman activities must surely have reached him before their arrival, yet he would have felt bound to try and protect his farm and stock, not to say his family and home. His attempts to do this certainly failed if this was the case, it may even be that Godric had not lent his support and as a reward for his compliance the Normans gave him Eadwulf's cattle farm and stock. Of course this is all purely supposition and the less dramatic though just as likely possibility is that Eadwulf was an old man in 1066 and that he died in the intervening years. The reduction in the value of the village from 10s to 6s between 1066 and 1086 would certainly seem to indicate some form of destruction which could only have been the result of Norman oppression, but the debate must go on.

We know little enough of the kings of the period, never mind the nobility and even less the serfs and peasants. It is this very lack of information which limits historians to making informed speculations yet the people and events I have commented on were very real, with very real emotions and human falabilities.

To re-cap: Godric may have been a large landholder not dissimilar to Ailric who was given the manor of Denby after the conquest. Godric would certainly appear to have been the senior partner, particularly if we accept that the lands at Emley and Notton were his. Godric's only interest in Denby may have been the cattle farm which he co-owned with Eadwulf who was in possession of much of the rest of the manor of Denby. Eadwulf died between 1066 and 1086. Either he was killed in battle, during the 'Harrying of the North' or he died of old age. If he was killed and we accept that Godric of Emley was his partner then we can assume that he had not been supported by his partner who may have retained some land at Denby (and, hypothetically, estates at Emley). It could be argued that Eadwulf must have offended the Norman overlords somehow as he is most likely to have had a family and an eldest son who should have inherited but didn't, this giving more support to the 'Harrying of the North' theory, whereby Eadwulf and his whole family were slaughtered.

It is unclear how long the cattle farm continued in use after 1086. It could have been run jointly by Ailric and Godric, or perhaps Godric's interest finished with the death of his partner as his name is omitted from *Domesday*.

Godric of Emley's son, Ketelbern was born between 1080 and 1090 and was still alive in 1135. This would appear to give Godric a birthdate of around 1045-50. He would have been around forty years old at the time of *Domesday* and approximately twenty during the Norman invasion. Forty would have been a good age at this time.

Ketelbern had a son named Godric (Godric II), he was the first to grant the monks of Byland rights on his lands, before 1170.

Godric II had a son named William Fitz Godric around 1140, he still had dealings with the monks of Byland and could possibly be the same man noted in a chronicle from High Hoyland church, William Fitz Osbert, who granted the monks the rights to mine for iron in Lower Denby in 1177, on land that could have been inherited from the original Godric recorded in *Domesday*. Our only evidence for a link between these two men is name similarity, and is tenuous at best. A William Fitz Osbert appears only once in the ancient records, almost from nowhere, yet there is a record that a man of this name was the first person to be executed at London's Tyburn gallows in 1196, this we must accept as purely coincidence.

The line of Ailric took over the manorship of the rest of Denby until its eventual sub-infeudation and take-over by the de Denby and Burdet families.

The Fitz William family are well known to the pages of history, they eventually left Emley and settled at Sprotborough where they made many advantageous alliances, through marriage, and became a very powerful family. Nothing in their lineage remarks upon the village of Denby yet it is just possible that the family founder, Godric, was the same man mentioned in the Denby survey.

BYLAND ABBEY

Byland was, in its day, regarded as one of the three most important monasteries in the north of England, (alongside Fountains and Rievaulx), the earliest of the present day ruins date from the mid-twelfth century. Through clever dealing, manors were acquired and estates were managed, some of these far from the monastery. Some of these estates were run as Manors, others as industrial granges or country houses, such as the one at Bentley Grange, Emley. A grange was originally a branch house of a monastery, the latter one having been in existence since the twelfth century. The monks in charge lived here and also at Kirkby Grange where there was an oratory for services, though they would have returned to Byland for the more important religious festivals, leaving the land to be worked by lay brethren. The Cistercian Abbeys of Yorkshire played a huge role in the economic life of the country, pioneers of their time the monks had interests in foresting, agriculture, sheep farming, and particularly in the case of Emley and Denby, iron working.

Emley was granted a five day fair in early May, much more because of the presence of the Byland monks than the residing Fitzwilliam family in 1253. The iron mined at Denby and any possible wool produce, would almost certainly have been sold at Emley, as carting it along poor quality roads all the way back to Byland would have been pointless as the market for the produce was country wide. All the work would have been administered by the monks at Bentley Grange which was very busy between the twelfth and fourteenth centuries. The mounds of earth extant today are the remains of their ore bell pits and are registered as ancient monuments. The pits were sunk to a depth of around twenty feet and worked outwards from the bottom of the shaft until the roof began to collapse, they then moved on to a site a little further away. They are situated on the Tankersley Iron Ore bed which stretches from the south of Barnsley almost to Brighouse.

Views of the present day ruins of Byland Abbey, North Yorkshire. 1996. *Author's collection.*

Activities began to decrease on the event of the Black Death in 1349 which had far reaching effects upon all the religious houses of England, with more than half the clergy and monks falling victim. Byland suffered just like all the others and by 1381 there were only eleven monks and three lay brothers left. It is inconceivable that any operations at Denby were continued at this time and it may even be that the iron works were never to be re-used in the future. After the plague abated the monks, due to lack of numbers left the iron stone pits at Bentley Grange idle and leased the building and its lands to tenants, in this case the Allot's.

The final end for the monastery came with Henry VIII and the wholesale dissolution of these wealthy religious houses. Today all that remains are the impressive ruins, built by the monks out of profits and loans secured through their estate management and the profits of their labours on many distant manors including their activity at Denby.

AILRIC, SAXON LANDHOLDER OF DENBY

Alric or Ailric was a large landholder in the time of Edward the Confessor, (1042-1066), Birchworth, Hoyland, Silkstone, Cumberworth, Skelmanthorpe, Penistone and Cawthorne (where he is believed to have lived and where there may have already been a church) were all in his possession. The antiquarian, John Leland notes in his itinerary, written during the 1530s and 1540s, that a Richard Aschenald was the father of Aelric (Alric) and that his grandson was Swane.

Leland may not be totally correct in this assertion. Geoffrey Ashe, who excavated South Cadbury Hillfort during the 1960s and 70s was mistaken in the belief that it was the site of the historical Camelot, the fabled court of King Arthur. Later investigation revealed that Leland falsified place, road and field names to perpetuate his wish that Camelot should be found here and misdirected Ashe. In fact South Cadbury was not the historical Camelot (which incidentally could either be in South Wales or was the Roman town of Viroconium (Wroxeter) in Powys), but it did show real evidence that it was re-occupied during the dark age period. At the time this was an exceptional discovery, but over the last few decades many, many more similar re-fortified iron age hill-forts have been discovered, which indicate a large scale phase of re-building after the withdrawal of the Roman's around 406/410 at the beginning of the Dark Ages.

Richard Aschenald is not a typical rendering of an eleventh century name. Whereas we have Eadwulf and Godric, strong and sturdy Saxon names, Richard Aschenald just does not seem to fit the bill. Firstly it sounds too modern, secondly it comprises a forename and a surname, again, unusual in a period when surnames had not widely come into use. Leland may be correct, I do not know his source, but perhaps it would be well to remember his romancing concerning the legends of Camelot and take his evidence as at best only a strong possibility.

Alric's son, Swane (after whom Hoylandswaine derives its name) made various donations to Pontefract Priory and also received an extensive Lordship in Cumberland from King Henry I (1101-1135) and his sons, Adam and Henry also held lands in Cumberland and Lancashire.

Adam Fitz Swane had two daughters, Amabil, from whom the Burgh and Neville families descend and Matilda, from whom the Longvilleirs and Neville families descend. As Adam had no son, these two daughters became his co-heirs and inherited upon his death in 1159. Adam also founded Monk Bretton Priory in about 1154 for the Cluniac monks who observed the rule of St. Benedict and therefore were Benedictines of the priory of St. John at Pontefract. Adam was granted the right to choose the first prior, after whose death the monks were to choose their own. As a result over confusion derived from Adam's two charters regarding the right of presentment of the prior, major disputes blew up between the monks of Pontefract and Bretton which were not ended until the Archbishop of York gained jurisdiction in 1281.

Before the conquest, Aschenald held lands at Pontefract, which subsequently passed to Ilbert De Lacy who when granted his lands by William the Conqueror was obliged to parcel them out to tenants, evidently Alric had caused little trouble to the Normans and so received grants of land, many of which he had held previously – Cawthorne, Silkstone, Hoyland, Clayton, Penistone and now DENBY.

THE DE LACY FAMILY

Ilbert De Lacy arrived in the Conquerors vanguard, and after helping to subdue the English was given 164 manors in the counties of York, Nottingham and Lincoln. These lands were confirmed to him in the tenth year of William's reign, 1076.

He was probably a vassal of Odo of Bayeux from whom he held moderate fees in Lincolnshire and the south midlands. He and his brother, Walter, who was an important Lord in the Welsh marches, were in the second rank of Norman Lords, owing their rank to their military skill. Ilbert's position was further advanced when he was granted the Honour of Pontefract, where he founded the Collegiate Chapel of St. Clement within Pontefract castle.

He was succeeded by his son, Robert (circa 1095), and he in turn by his son, Ilbert. The family continued to add to its possessions and were the forbears of the Earls of Lincoln.

The De Lacys

Ilbert de Lacy d. 1087

Robert de Lacy 1066 - d. by 1130 = Matilda

Albreda 1113 -? = Robert de Lissours	Ilbert 1114-? = Alice	Henry 1117-1187 = Albreda de Vesci	Walter 1119-1138
	(Ilbert disappears after		(Killed at the
	Battle of Lincoln in 1140)		Battle of Standard)
	Alice re-married to		
	Roger de Mowbray	Robert 1166-1193/4	

The De Lacy lineage, according to Fred Lawton, continued thus:

Albreda Lissours	–	half sister to above Robert, married Richard Lord of Halton. Their son, John, assumed the name, De Lacy.
John De Lacy	–	see above.
Roger De Lacy	–	son of John.
John De Lacy	–	son of Roger, Earl of Lincoln, died 1240.
Edmund De Lacy	–	son of John.
HENRY DE LACY	–	son of Edmund, see below.
Alice De Lacy	–	only daughter and sole heiress.

It is a remarkable coincidence that Denby in Yorkshire is connected with Denbigh in Clwyd, North Wales, the link being the second Henry De Lacy, mentioned above. Henry was the campaign commander of King Edward I armies in Wales. He also owned Pontefract Castle, founded by his illustrious forbear, the first Ilbert. During the latter part of October 1282, the King and De Lacy were at Denbigh, planning new fortifications. De Lacy was left in charge of these after the King's departure. The site chosen was an impressive outcrop of rock in the Vale of Clwyd, the name Denbigh actually incorporating the Welsh word 'Dinas', meaning a rocky fortress. Today the castle is all too frequently overshadowed by its neighbours at Conwy, Caernarvon, Harlech and Beaumaris, but its remains still stand as a testament to its builders over 700 years ago.

Henry De Lacy's elder son, Edmund is said to have fallen to his death in the well at Denbigh castle in 1308. His younger son, John, died when he fell from the battlements at Pontefract castle whilst chasing a ball. This meant that it was his only daughter, Alice who inherited from Henry. Alice married Thomas, Earl of Lancaster, the rebel who fought against King Edward II at Boroughbridge in 1322 and was beheaded after his defeat. It is also interesting to note that one of the followers of the Earl was a Robert Hood of Wakefield. Although not the originator of the legend he certainly contributed significantly to the tales about Robin Hood, but we must now return to the development of Denby.

Arriving with the Conqueror, along with the Lacy's were the families of Bosville and Burdet, although initially neither had connections with Denby both were to play a major role in the formation and development of the village which we will examine in the next chapter.

DENBY'S MEDIEVAL POT

In 1937, two young children were playing on a plot of land just above where today's village green stands. Whilst digging around, John White and Harry Heath came across one of the few archaeological artefacts in Denby. Two feet below the surface of the ground, covered by a stone slab they came across

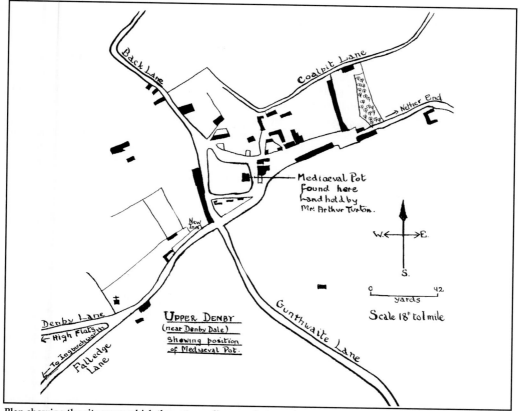

Plan showing the site upon which the pot was discovered. *Courtesy of the Tolson Museum, Huddersfield.*

a pot, which lay in a cavity of rock. On further examination, a layer of burnt earth was discovered just above it. The pot was in poor condition and had no bottom but was certainly placed here rather than accidentally buried approximately 500 years before.

It was presented to the Tolson Museum, Huddersfield by Mr L. Taylor of Upper Denby in September 1937 where it remains today, albeit not on display anymore. It is made of local clay and has a rough finish to it. It was certainly not an artefact once likely to be found on a Lord's table, and is in extremely poor condition, the broken pieces having been glued back together.

In the first edition of this book I adopted a date for the pot of c.1350-1450, which was advised to me at the museum. A chance meeting with an archaeological site team leader has now opened up new possibilities.

Firstly, she identified the pot as being

Medieval pot, discovered at Denby in 1937.
Courtesy of the Tolson Museum, Huddersfield.

Holgate-ware (grit-ware) and dated it to between 1150 and 1250. This takes us back a further two hundred years and predates the coming of the Burdet dynasty. This type of pottery was created by monks, and of course, in Denby we have connections with both Byland Abbey, their activities being around the present day site of Papist Hall, and Monk Bretton Priory, the monks there being given land at Denby called Ebriches by John de Denby and his wife Christian. The monks of Roche Abbey also had free rights of passage through Denby. The pot would have cost around one groat to buy and would have been affordable to even the lowest class citizens.

There have now been a number of theories as to what it was used for, but all must remain pure speculation, despite the missing lid and the fact that no part of the site can now be re-examined, it would seem certain that its days as a useful piece of cooking ware had ended before it was buried. A pot such as this would not have been disposed of unless it had been broken.

Some of the more interesting ideas are:

i) That it was buried during the turbulent years of Stephen and Matilda's civil war,
perhaps around 1140, and was used to hold a fire in which politically sensitive documents were burnt.

ii) That it was used as a sunken fire in a house.

iii) That it was used as an incinerator during one of the many plagues to have swept Britain.

iv) That it was used as a steam or combustion oven.

v) That it was used as a kind of sump, under a fire which heated a cauldron, this
might explain the burnt earth, and the absence of a lid which would have been unnecessary as the pot was already covered by the stone slab.

Perhaps the most important piece of evidence that the pot gives us, is that of probable occupation on the site in the late twelfth or early thirteenth centuries. What form any buildings on the site might have taken is impossible to say, they may have been farm buildings, or perhaps they could have been the lodgings of a labourer and formed part of the original site of the village of Denby. We also now have evidence of the presence of monks in the locale and trading activity between them and the inhabitants of Denby, unless, that is, the monks, being the main source of aid for the poor, had given it to some needy individual.

One can only wonder at what else may lay buried under today's buildings, roads and fields, which if discovered might point the way to a clearer understanding of the as yet hidden past of Denby.

Chapter Two
Medieval Manorial Lords

T he story of Denby and its subsequent growth is closely intertwined with the Lords of the Manor; the landholders on whose property all others dwelt, be they serf, labourer or yeoman.

The Lords of the Manor wielded absolute authority over the lives of the peasants who farmed their lands. The lowest class of peasants were the serfs, who were not even paid for their work and were only able to keep their homes by paying rent to their lord with a large portion of their yearly produce. The next class up were the labourers and small tradesmen, unlike the serfs who lived on the farmland, these people lived in villages and paid both rents to their lord and tax to the crown. Villages consisted of small houses built of timber and mudbrick, with shutters to cover the windows. Food was basic and meat a luxury item. In these villages, some homes were larger and more permanently built, these belonged to the emerging middle class, the yeoman, who were generally more highly paid employees of the estate.

Upon this background, we will now examine the lords of Denby, the original instigators of today's modern village.

The lords of Denby were initially the tenants of the family of Ailric and held Denby as of the manor of Brierley. To re-cap, Ailric's son, Swein had a son, Adam who had two daughters. Amabil, from whom the Burgh's of Cawthorne are descended and Matilda from whom the Neville and Harrington families descend. The latter's tenancy in the honour of Pontefract was estimated at two knights fees, and the families seat of residence was at Brierley. A knight's fee was a landholding from which the service of one knight was due to either the King or his Lord, in this case, two knight's were required by the de Lacy's of Pontefract. An inquisition in 1425 (Henry VI) found that Sir William Harrington of Brierley held the following fees, formerly belonging to Sir Robert Neville:

Brierley, Oxspring, Kexborough, Thurgoland, DENBY, Hunshelf, Worsborough, Silkstone, Penistone, West Bretton, Gunthwaite, Heindley, Skelmanthorpe, Cudworth, Royston, Cawthorne, Clayton, Ardsley, Shafton, Kellington, Chevet.

It was the Heralds of Elizabeth I who were first responsible for creating a pedigree, (by which they were able to authenticate the Coat of Arms of the family of Burdet), for the early lords of Denby.

Heralds originally began life as announcers and organisers of tournaments, they were also used as diplomats, but during the sixteenth century, they gained formal jurisdiction over the granting and definition of coats of arms. They made frequent visitations to investigate and authenticate the lineage and right to bear arms of families such as the Burdet's, and left a detailed pedigree, which has survived to this day.

To enable us to understand the details contained in the pedigree, and to allow us to add more information we will take it in simple stages, the pedigree at the end of the book shows the full descent.

Of the Helperthorpe family I have little more information than contained below, it would seem that Walter and Stephen were alive during the mid-twelfth century and that they were contemporaries of Adam of Hoyland.

The de Hoyland and de Denby families

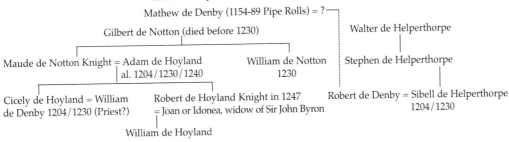

Mathew de Denby (1154-89 Pipe Rolls) = ?

Gilbert de Notton (died before 1230) Walter de Helperthorpe

Maude de Notton Knight = Adam de Hoyland William de Notton Stephen de Helperthorpe
al. 1204/1230/1240 1230

Cicely de Hoyland = William Robert de Hoyland Knight in 1247 Robert de Denby = Sibell de Helperthorpe
de Denby 1204/1230 (Priest?) = Joan or Idonea, widow of Sir John Byron 1204/1230

William de Hoyland

Of Adam de (High) Hoyland, we know far more. He was living in 1204 and seems to have survived until at least the mid-thirteenth century, his name still appearing in deeds and grants during the 1230s and 1240s. The herald's record that he married Maude de Notton, the daughter of Gilbert de Notton and that she bore him at least two children, Cicely or Cecilia and Robert de Hoyland, and that he was a knight. A further document would seem to imply that Maude died well before her husband and that Adam remarried:

Adam de Hoyland – Matilda of Skelmertorp – his widow, granted by Paul de Scel ( ) thorpe, of land, witnessed by William de Deneby and his son Robert.

Of his activities during his lifetime, we have the following details:

Grant – Robert de Wheatley to Adam de Holanda (son in law of Gilbert de Notton) lands held by: Robert son of Giliana, Alan de Dentun & his wife Aliz, Norman the smith, John de Weledun... (amongst others). Witnesses: Gilbert de Notton, his son William, William de Denebi

Grant – Robert de Wheatley to Adam de Holande for homage & service, regarding land known as Stonesforde to Eilrikebirge...
Witness : Robert de Deneby

Eilrikebirge or Ailricbridge was probably named after Alric who we have already met in the previous chapter. There is some evidence that Ailricbridge has become today's Highbridge in Scissett, after some corruption of the language during the fourteenth century, when it may have been called Eibrigg.

Warranty – by Robert de Shelflay to Adam de Holand for homage and service for nine bovates of land in Clayton.
Witnesses: William de Deneby, Master Simon, Parson of Holand

Grant – Robert de Wheatley to Adam de Holanda who paid five marks of silver and had to render a pound of cumin yearly at Christmas.
Witness : Robert de Deneby.

The seeds of the cummin plant were used for flavouring and also as a remedy for flatulence!

The above documents all relate to land in Clayton, Robert de Wheatley would have lived in the vicinity of Wheatley Hill, a mile south west of Clayton. The first document above must be dated before 1230, as Adam's father in law, Gilbert de Notton died in that year, and the others are of similar age.

Adam's name can also be found as a witness to numerous other deeds, many involving his relations the de Deneby family, who also held significant areas of land in Clayton. Indeed, from the wealth of material available it is easy to understand how the manor of Clayton became so inextricably linked with that of Hoyland due to the efforts of Adam and his son Robert.

Robert was recorded by the heralds as being a knight in 1247, and that he married the widow of Sir John Byron, whose name was either Joan or Idonea. By this time, he had probably inherited his father's wealth, though the two were active together:

> Grant – by Simon le Vilur to Robert son of Adam de Holand, land at Clayton... etc.
> Witnesses: Adam de Holand, William son of Robert de Deneby.

> Grant & quitclaim – by John de Byrweyt (Birthwaite ?) to Robert son of Adam de Holanda, of the service of Roger the chaplain of all the land which he held of John in Clayton for 15d pa. Payable in two instalments and also the homage of the chaplain.
> Witnesses: John and Simon, Parsons of Holand, William de Denebi.

> Grant – by John son of Roger the chaplain of Clayton to Adam de Holand of land abutting land belonging to Osbert de Claiton. Adam gave him 18s.

It would seem that father and son managed between them to obtain a chaplain for Clayton, by the name of Roger, the witnesses to the above are interesting, not only do we have the parsons of High Hoyland but also a possible early vicar of Cumberworth, and a member of the de Denby family to boot.

From *Hunter's South Yorkshire*, Volume II:

> ...reciting that the above named parties held certain messuages in Denby, which were given by William de Denby who before the making of the statute quia emptores (before the manor was sold to the Burdet's) was mesne lord of the manor of Denby, to one John the son of Adam de Denby and one Adam the son of William (de Denby) the priest of Cumberworth.

William de Denby the priest of Cumberworth could be the same person as William de Denby who had married the daughter of Adam de (High) Hoyland. It is unlikely that there were many William de Denbys alive at this time, but other evidence we have will help to confirm this theory. We know of two lords of Denby, who must have been contemporaries, above we have noted William, but a Robert de Denby would also seem to have been the lord here. As contemporaries, we could surmise that they were brothers, though there is unfortunately no evidence for this. For them both to be recorded as lords of the manor at the same time would certainly seem to indicate that they were closely related but that is as far as we may go. We are also in the dark as to the identity of the father or fathers of these two, the only de Denby known from existing records was Mathew who is mentioned in pipe rolls dating to the time of Henry II, 1154-1189. Pipe rolls were the annual accounts of Crown revenues, which were sent by Sheriffs to the exchequer where they were rolled around rods (pipes) for storage.

Mathew must have been a fairly important individual, the fact that his name has survived indicates this. If we surmise that he may have been the first lord of Denby, then the question arises as to how he became so entitled.

We have seen that the Manor of Denby passed via Alric, the Saxon who was given the land here by Ilbert de Lacy, to his son Swaine. Swaine was succeeded by his son Adam Fitz Swaine. Adam died in 1159, by approximately 1189 Robert de Denby was Lord of the Manor of Denby, a gap of only thirty years. It is just possible that Mathew was his father though the absence of dates makes life very difficult. The heralds make Robert the first lord, but they do not mention Mathew, but as their job was to create an authentic pedigree to legitimise the Burdet family's right to bear a coat of arms Mathew may have been ignored. Adam Fitz Swaine or his heirs, as of the manor of Brierley, may have sub-infeuded the manor to either Mathew or the first Robert during this time, though it is perhaps more likely that the de Denby's came in to possession soon after Adam's death, during the early 1160's. This theory would help to explain the importance of Mathew who is first recorded at exactly this time.

As to whether he was Robert de Denby's father we will leave it, though we now face another dilemma. Robert de Denby the first, had a son and heir, also called Robert, we must now try to disentangle the story so as to allow us to make an informed guess as to which Robert was the contemporary of William de Denby, the possible priest of Cumberworth.

The pedigree left by the heralds tells us that Robert I was alive during the reign of Richard the Lionheart, 1189-1199, and goes on to tell us that his son, Robert II was alive during the reign of King John, 1199-1216. The only other detail that they left may be very significant, the second Robert had become 'Sir Robert de Denby'. As William never bore such an epithet any claim he may have had to be lord of Denby must now be diminished to that of inferior partner. It is possible that as a priest he was unable to be a lord in the true sense of the word, though this would indicate that he was a younger brother and not eligible anyway. The following documents have survived which contain details of these early de Denby's:

> Grant: by Robert de Wheatley to Robert son of Robert de Denby for his homage and service, of six acres of arable land... called Norman Rode, which extended from Wheatley Brook towards the cast to the ditches... and then reached... Lady Margery's land towards the south. For this Robert de Denby gave him a silver penny and he also received one mark of silver in recognition.
> Witnesses: Adam de Holand, Robert son of William de Deneby.

A further grant made by the above named Lady Margery, daughter of Robert de Seleflei (Shelley or Shepley?) was made after the death of her husband Robert. This gave Robert, son of Robert de Denby, her lands which abutted those in the previous document in Clayton. For this Robert gave her nineteen silver shillings, the document was witnessed by amongst others Adam de Hoyland.

> Sale and Confirmation: by Jordan, son of Simon de Deneby to William son of Robert de Deneby of all right in the land, lying under Thorntelay and stretching from Thorntelay to Laisingkerode and from Laisingkerode to the boundaries of Holand to Robert de Wheatley's asart.
> Witnesses: Adam de Holand, William de Gunnelthaut, William son of Robert de Deneby.

> Grant: by Parnell (Petronilla) formerly daughter of Adam de Clayton in her widowhood to Sir Robert de Denby (this must be to the second Robert) of all meadow lying in breadth between Gosserode and part of the meadow of William de Lysurs and in length reaching one end to the wood of William son of Robert de Hoyland.

This document would seem to be of a slightly later date, the second Robert de Denby was the first to bear the title Sir, and Robert de Hoyland's son William is also on the scene. The following document in the series also mentions a John de Deneby as a witness, the documents do seem to follow a chronological order, and so John must have also been around at this time.

> Release: by Thomas de Dronefeld to Robert de Denebi (not Sir ?) of a service of a pair of white gloves a year, that is wardships, reliefs...
> Witnesses: Jordan son of John de Denebi.

So what do we have? Of the local lords, we know that Adam de Hoyland was the neighbour of Richard de Wheatley of Clayton, though Adam was continually acquiring lands here to increase his original demesne of Hoyland. Adam's neighbours were the de Denby family, the earliest of which, Robert de Denby was his contemporary. Robert also increased his possessions by acquiring land in Clayton and inter family marriage between the Hoylands and Denbys contributed to the families influence and power. It was due to these early lords that subsequent lords of the manor were able to include the villages and lands at Denby, High Hoyland and Clayton West in their demesnes.

Both Adam and Robert were succeeded by sons, both knights, indeed Robert de Denby II seemingly became Sir Robert during the early thirteenth century.

We now leave the family of Adam de Hoyland to concentrate on the de Denby's.

As we have seen from the documents above, there were numerous members of the de Denby family alive and active during the twelfth and thirteenth centuries. We have noted William de Denby and Sir Robert de Denby (II) and it is through these that we will follow the descent.

WILLIAM DE DENBY

William as we have noted may have been a priest at Cumberworth; he married Cicely, the daughter of Adam de Hoyland and is recorded by the heralds as having a child, named Agnes de Denby. She was certainly not the only child and though exact proof for some of the following table is lacking, I believe that the family grew as follows:

Descent of William de Denby

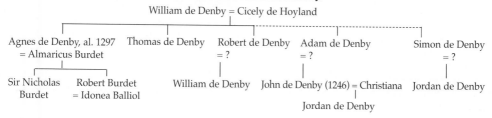

We know that William was active in 1204 and probably again in 1230 (though there could be some confusion with his grandson, William), it is likely that his family were being born between these two dates.

Confusion could also have been caused by the possibility that there were two William de Denby's living at the same time. Joseph Hunter discovered a William de Denby in the rolls of the lords of Midhope, who married Sarah the daughter of Alexander Venavre, who had an elder son who was Lord of Denby and Okynthorpe. Hunter noted that the author of the rolls believed that this Lord of Barnby was of the same stock as the de Denby family.

BARNBY

Barnby and its hall was only a mile or so east of the Manor of Denby. It would appear that William de Denby, its lord, was a member of the family that gave the present day estate of Cannon Hall its name.

The Lords of Barnby

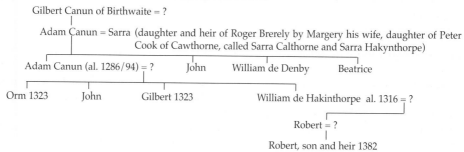

The era of the first Gilbert was early thirteenth century. How this William earned his surname is unknown, though one cannot see further than him having had some important connection with the area, he must have been alive during the mid-thirteenth century. His wife Sarra (daughter of Alexander Venavre or Hunter) bore him at least six sons.

Descent of William de Denby of Barnby

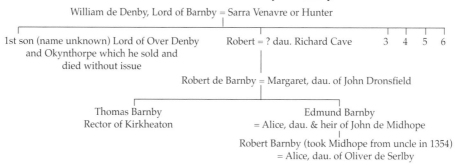

William de Denby, Lord of Barnby = Sarra Venavre or Hunter

1st son (name unknown) Lord of Over Denby and Okynthorpe which he sold and died without issue

Robert = ? dau. Richard Cave   3   4   5   6

Robert de Barnby = Margaret, dau. of John Dronsfield

Thomas Barnby
Rector of Kirkheaton

Edmund Barnby
= Alice, dau. & heir of John de Midhope

Robert Barnby (took Midhope from uncle in 1354)
= Alice, dau. of Oliver de Serlby

We can be reasonably certain that the two Williams were not the same person as a record exists which appears to show them both witnessing the same document regarding land at Cawthorne, this at least leaves us with the knowledge that they were contemporaries. The Barnby line ran out in the seventeenth century.

Perhaps the key phrase used to describe his son is that he was 'Lord of Over Denby', the exact site of which we will examine later. This may have been a separate manor at this time, and his surname may have resulted from his ownership there, alongside a more established de Denby family. This might also explain why both the Robert de Denby and William de Denby that we have been examining were noted as being lords of Denby. One of them held land which abutted Hoyland and the other, probably William held land abutting that of his (brother?) further to the south around what is today's Upper Denby.

With the second William out of the way we can now concentrate on our William de Denby's children, about whom we have the following details:

Grant: Almaricus Burdet to Thomas de Denby, all land and services which William de Denby, father of Thomas de Denby once gave to Agnes his daughter, which Adam de Hoyland gave in marriage with Cecilia his daughter to William de Denby in the town of Skelnerethorp for a certain sum which Thomas gave into his hands, and which land the aforesaid Almaricus had after the death of Agnes, daughter of William de Denby who was his wife 'per libertatem anglie', at a yearly rent of one abol.

Feoffment: Nicholas Burdet of Rande, knight, to Robert Burdet his brother all his lands and rents in Skelmerthorp. That is those which William de Deneby his uncle gave to Agnes his mother to be held of the chief lord of the fee.
Witness: John Burdet

Unfortunately the above documents are undated but we can be sure that they come from the period 1217-1265.

Joseph Hunter also noted the following, that John de Denby, (son of Adam de Denby), and his wife Christian gave the monks of Bretton, three acres of land in Denby at a place called Ebriches, by deed, with free common right through the whole township.

Dr. David Hey has also noted that Agnes de Denby was recorded in the Wakefield Court Rolls of 1297 as paying 6d for a licence to take three acres of land in the west field at Upperthong.

It was Agnes de Denby's marriage to Almaricus Burdet that was to set the scene for much of the rest of the story of the manor of Denby.

ORIGIN OF BURDET

The ancestral home of the Burdets was in Normandy and the name in its earliest form was written Burdet, Bordet or Bowdett, although other variations were possible as we have seen i.e. Burdeth. Its origin is uncertain. In 1862 the 'Societe De Archaeologie of France' erected a plate in the church of Dives not far from Deauville in Normandy to commemorate the companions of the conqueror some 450 in number. Among these names are Hugo Bourdet and Robert Burdet, two brothers who were lords of Cuilly. In return for his services to the conquest Hugo Burdet (who took the anglicised version of his surname, Burdet) was given lands in Leicestershire, the greater part of his property being at Lowesby and it was here that the family established itself, Hugo becoming Lord of Lowesby. Robert chose de Cuilly as a surname and his line developed other spellings of this surname, a line which the Burdick Ancestry Library in Florida would have us believe led to the Duke of Wellington, though I have no proof of this. Later the Burdets acquired more and more property, particularly around the area where Leicestershire, Derbyshire and Warwickshire join, east of Tamworth.

The meaning of the surname is unclear, of which there are many variations, Bordet, Bourdet, Burdette, Burdit, Burditt, Burdick etc. There are two explanations as to its meaning,
1. That it derives from the Old French word, 'Borde' which meant a small farm or cottage, or
2. That the original spelling was 'Bourdet' and meant dweller on the border or dweller on rented land, or little shield.

Alternatively some researchers connect the name with the same derivation as Burden which brings with it more interpretations:
1. That the name is formed from the Latin 'burdo' meaning a mule,
2. That it comes from the old French word 'bourdon', meaning a pilgrim's staff. Evidently there is some confusion and subsequently no definitive answer.

NB: *In its earlier form Burdet was spelt with only one T, later records from around the late seventeenth century began using a second T leaving us with the spelling we have today, Burdett. It should be remembered that it was up to the individual scribe as to how to spell the name they had just been told on official records and so for the purposes of this book I have tried, as far as possible to use whichever form was originally recorded.*

In 1159 William Burdet, great grandson of Hugo founded Ancote Priory in Warwickshire, to expiate the rash killing of his wife whom a false steward had accused of infidelity during Burdet's absence in the Holy land during a crusade.

Almaricus Burdet descended from a branch of the family that had made Rande, a stones throw from Fulnetby, a few miles north east of Lincoln its home. The village of Rand dates from Saxon times and was first populated by the Burdet family in approximately 1155. The line of descent from Hugo in Leicestershire has not yet been proven, although research work has suggested that it was from the fourth son of the latter William Burdet, Nicholas from whom the Burdet's of Rand descend. Sir William Burdet and presumably his male offspring were involved at the siege of Lincoln in February, 1141 in support of the Earl of Leicester. This was a key battle during the civil strife between Stephen and Matilda for the throne of England. Stephen had laid siege to Lincoln Castle but was defeated by relieving troops led by the Earls, Robert of Gloucester and Ranulf of Chester. He was taken prisoner, only being released when Robert of Gloucester was also captured in a later battle when the two were traded. This battle also saw the disappearance of the second Ilbert de Lacy. Burdet's appearance here does not prove anything beyond his allegiance to the Earl, Robert de Beaumont (1104-1168) who was a follower of King Stephen. Indeed, de Beaumont had used the anarchy at this period to persecute his hereditary enemy, Roger de Tosny, whom he captured with the aid of his brother Waleran de Beaumont. After Stephen's defeat at Lincoln the brothers made a truce with the Angevin party in Normandy and in 1143 had been restored to their lands by the future Henry II. Robert continued to rise in royal favour from here on, even working to try to reconcile the King with Archbishop Thomas Becket during their famous dispute.

The reason for this branch of the Burdet family's move from Leicestershire into Lincolnshire is a little unclear but seems to be linked to the marriage of William Trussebutte to Aubreye de Harcourt in the early 1150s. The Burdets were tenants on land which Aubreye brought to the marriage as her dower. The Harcourts had been brought into Leicestershire from France by the Earl of Leicester to support him in his control of the area. William and Aubreye Trussebutt had two sons and three daughters. Geoffrey, born 1154/5 died 1187/90 without issue, and Robert who died in 1193, again without issue, subsequently the three daughters inherited. These daughters each made advantageous marriages and it is through the wills of these eminent lords that we find the names of the knights holding their lands, which include the Burdets who had served the Trussebutte family for nearly two centuries.

During Robert Trussebutte's control he granted to Stephen Burdet half a knight's fee at Rand and to John Burdet (presumably Stephen's brother) a quarter of a knight's fee at Fulnetby, only a mile or so from Rand. This appears to have been the foundation of the two lines in the area. Records of knights fees in the area record that in 1187, Rand is held by Stephen Burdet, though there is evidence of an earlier Stephen, signing a charter in 1164. The probable line is therefore:

Descent of Almaricus Burdet of Rande

Stephen Burdet at Rand 1155
|
Stephen Burdet al. circa 1175/1190
|
William Burdet 1194
|
Nicholas Burdet b. circa 1200, al. 1250
|
Almaricus Burdet b. circa 1230, al. 1304

Nicholas Burdet c. 1270-1320   Robert Burdet c. 1272 al. 1304
| Denby, West Yorkshire
Nicholas Burdet 1346

There would seem to be little doubt that the Burdets were responsible for re-founding the ancient Saxon church at Rand and that they built the moated manor house. This would have been in the years immediately following the anarchy of Stephen and Matilda when it was forbidden to build any fortification other than a gatehouse and moat and when it was difficult to obtain a license to crenellate, or build battlements.

The line of Burdets at Rand died out by 1340 and at Fulnetby by 1360, the record of knight's fees in 1380 shows that the Burdet family had totally left the area by this time.
Nothing remains today of the deserted medieval village of Rande except a few earthworks, surrounded by what was once a moat. The church has been re-built, but one can still sit in the centre of what was once the manor house and look down the well worn path that led to the church and feel a sense of atmosphere as one imagines the footsteps of these medieval Lords.

Almaricus or Aylmer, was the son of Nicholas Burdet knighted in approximately 1250 when a great deal of effort was being spent on the number of knights who could be mustered to fight for the King (Henry III). The county Sheriffs of that time were instructed by the King to prepare a list of those landowners who qualified by the number of knight's fees of hides they held for knighthood whether they wanted it or not.

How Almaricus Burdet ever met Agnes de Denby will always remain a mystery, though the de Denby's were influential they were certainly not as powerful as the Burdet's. It could be argued that the Burdets as a Norman family were more likely to be in this position, though it does not necessarily follow that the de Denbys were a Saxon family, it is just as likely that they were a group of Norman immigrants who came to England in the years after the conquest, ended up at Denby and so chose the place name for their own surname. I believe that their close associations with Adam de Hoyland and their possible purchase of the Manor of Denby from Adam Fitz Swain, and their relatively humble demesne, coupled with their subsequent take-over by a Norman family argues strongly for a family descended from Angle/Danish Viking stock, but the lack of evidence renders this an argument for speculation only.

We do know that Almaricus was alive in 1271 and Agnes in 1297. Almaricus outlived Agnes and indeed passed land on to her brother, Thomas de Denby that had fallen to him after her death. We speculated that Agnes may have been born during the mid-thirteenth century, therefore she must have died soon after being granted her licence to take land in Upperthong, perhaps around 1300. As fifty would have been a good age at this time we might also speculate that Almaricus died shortly afterwards (though we know he was alive in 1304) as it is unlikely that he would have married a woman older than himself at this time.

Their union produced two children, Sir Nicholas Burdet of Rande, knight, alive 1304 and Robert Burdet, also noted to be alive in the same year.

We have details of Robert Burdet which survive from the year 1297. Robert represented his family in London at the Court of the Arches, noted in the Curia Regis (the King's church matters). His presence here was caused by a dispute regarding the right of the presentation of the chaplain at Rand church. As the family had built the edifice and were the foremost persons in the locale it is hard to believe that someone was 'trying it on', but the matter was evidently very serious as it had ended up in the King's court. In the event, Robert Burdet was vindicated, perhaps, largely, because of the fact that the other party, causing the problem did not turn up to plead his case. The document also mentions Nicholas Burdet, Robert's brother and Margerie Burdet, who is currently unknown. What the document does tell us is that Robert was at least twenty-one years old at this time.

It was Robert who was to re-unite the family of William de Denby with that of Sir Robert de Denby, and so we must now return to their lineage and history.

Before we do, I should make it clear that there is some confusion about the place Skelmerthorp mentioned in some of the records I have included. On the pedigree drawn up by the heralds, they note Almaricus Burdet as holding lands at a place called Skelmarthorpe, Co. Lincolnshire as of his wife Agnes. Her eldest son Sir Nicholas inherited these lands. Only a couple of miles to the north of Denby in West Yorkshire is the village of Skelmanthorpe, a place name of very similar derivation. The document related above involving Almaricus and Thomas de Denby regarding land at Skelnerethorp would, at first seem to relate to the West Yorkshire village as the land was Cecilia de Hoyland's dowry given to her by her father Adam on the occasion of her marriage to William de Denby. It would seem improbable that these Yorkshiremen would have had interest in lands in Lincolnshire, how they could have been involved here will probably never be known. Of course, Agnes de Denby and Almaricus Burdet did have to meet for the first time, therefore, somehow there must have been a connection, be it property, land or rents, between Yorkshire and Lincolnshire. It is also unknown as to where the family of Almaricus and Agnes lived. Almaricus would probably have wished to stay close to his estates at Rand(e), though we find Agnes involved with land at Upperthong, in Yorkshire, in 1297. Certainly his eldest son, Sir Nicholas inherited these Lincolnshire lands and titles from him on the occasion of his death, whilst his second son, Robert was the first of the family to settle at Denby, and indeed become lord of the manor of Denby.

An undated document, probably from sometime around 1300 gives us the following details:

Feoffment. Nicholas Burdet of Rande, knight, to Robert Burdet his brother, all his lands and rents in Skelmerthorp. That is those, which William de Denby his Uncle gave to Agnes his mother to be held of the chief lord of the fee.

Here we have Sir Nicholas transferring his inherited possessions from his father, to his brother who was Lord of the Manor of Denby, the ancestral home of their mother Agnes. It is interesting to note that the document was witnessed by a John Burdet, a certain relation, and possibly lord of Fulnetby near Rand(e). The lordship of Denby was earned by marriage with the daughter of a direct lineal relation of the Kings of Scotland, and it is to this descent that we will now turn.

Descent of Sir Robert de Denby

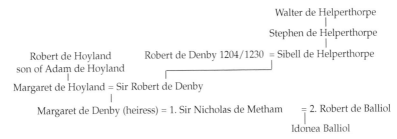

Sir Robert was the son of Robert de Denby and seems to have been alive during at least the first half of the thirteenth century. Other than the details we have already examined concerning the first Robert de Denby we also know that he gave the monks of Roche Abbey and their men free passage through his lands at Ingbirchworth towards the grange of Eniker, or elsewhere. Founded in 1147, the Cistercian monks of Roche held numerous estates in Yorkshire as well as other adjoining counties, though exactly what their interests in our area were is unknown at present.

As to how or why the second Robert de Denby became a Sir, we are at present ignorant, though as we have seen, King Henry III was recruiting knights on a large scale at this time, and this seems to be the most likely scenario. We do know that he married into the family of Adam de Hoyland. I speculated earlier that the first Robert de Denby and the first William de Denby could have been brothers, and possibly the sons of Mathew de Denby. This would mean that Sir Robert was making a diplomatic family marriage when he married Margaret de Hoyland, the daughter of Sir Robert de Hoyland and Joan or Idonea Byron.

The following detail has survived concerning Margaret:

Confirmation of grant: Margaret de Denby in her widowhood to Adam son of Matilda de Krageliston. A bovate of land in the town and territories of the same for 8 shillings a year.

We know that Margaret was a widow around 1250, which at least gives us a general date for the death of Sir Robert de Denby, perhaps around the 1240s and as we know he was alive during the reign of King John he would have been, most likely around forty or fifty years old. This means that their daughter, also called Margaret was born around this time at the latest. The heralds are quite explicit when they state on the ancient pedigrees that Margaret was Sir Robert's only heir. If we accept her date of birth as occurring in the 1240s it would have been around 1308/9 when she married her second husband, Sir Nicholas de Metham (Meltham ?), knight. No details of the termination of this marriage have been found as yet, violent death or disease cut life very short during the thirteenth century. Their union produced two children, Alice and Elizabeth. This information has come from the Heralds of

Elizabeth I and does not seem to correlate with dates acquired from other sources. According to my estimates, Margaret would have been far too old to bear two children from a second marriage in 1308, and I would suggest that the Heralds , in this instance have got it wrong, and that her union with Nicholas de Metham was her first marriage. Margaret's second husband is a different proposition.

SIR ROBERT BALLIOL

The pedigree drawn up by the heralds during the reign of Elizabeth I in 1584/5, makes no doubt that Robert Balliol was descended from the family of that name who were Lords of Barnard Castle, County Durham.

This estate was granted to Guy de Balliol in 1095, a knight of Picardy who was probably recruited by King William II (Rufus) whilst campaigning in the area two years before. Guy was responsible for the foundation of the first castle and appears to have survived for around thirty years (approximately 1125) when his nephew, Bernard de Balliol (c.1125-1155), succeeded him. Bernard fought at the Battle of the Standard in 1138 against King David I of Scotland where the Scots were soundly beaten by the prowess of the English archers near Northallerton. He also sparred frequently with the Bishops of Durham regarding the Lordship of Barnard Castle.

Bernard was succeeded by his son, Guy de Balliol II who held the lordship for a short period of time having died before 1162. His brother, Bernard de Balliol II, (who along with the first Bernard was responsible for much of the impressive ruins of the castle extant today, and also for the first part of the town's name), succeeded and held the estates until 1199. Without a male heir, he was succeeded by some procedure unknown to us, by Eustace de Heliscourt, a member of a local family who were tenants of the Balliol's. Eustace changed his name to Balliol on succession but the relationship with Bernard II is unclear.

At the beginning of the thirteenth century the Balliols appear to have been in financial trouble, Hugh, the son of Eustace who inherited in 1205, was in debt to the Bishops of Durham, who for a while received feudal homage from the Balliols. It was perhaps this allegiance to the Church rather than to the Crown, which angered King John so much as to bring him to deprive Hugh of his castle and lands. However, by 1213 he had regained them and had also become one of the King's closest Northern allies. Hugh's influence on the Crown declined after the coronation of Henry III in 1216 and he died in 1228.

Hugh was succeeded by his son, John de Balliol and it was now that the lordship reached its greatest extent. John's fame and influence spread over a wide area. His marriage to Dorvoguilla de Galloway allowed him to possess ancestral lands in England and Piccardy, the lordship of Galloway and the honour of Huntingdon. From a struggling baronial family background, John was now one of the wealthiest men in Britain. An unflinching supporter of Henry III he fought at the Battle of Lewes in 1264, only to see Simon de Montfort capture the King and his son, the future Edward I. John died in 1269 and was survived by his wife until 1290, his successors were, Hugh de Balliol (1269-1271), Alexander de Balliol (1271-1278) and John (1278-1296).

With the death at sea of Margaret, the Maid of Norway in 1290, the only heir of Scottish King Alexander II, it fell to King Edward I of England to convene a council to decide who should succeed as King of Scotland. The two strongest candidates were Robert Bruce, Lord of Annandale and Hart, and John Balliol (c.1250-1313) who had inherited Galloway and all the other possessions of his forbears, and who had a strong power base at Barnard Castle. Balliol was chosen and became King of the Scots in 1292.

Subjected to the English King's overbearing treatment John was left with little option other than to rebel. He was defeated at the Battle of Dunbar by the English forces, King Edward I had already declared the Scottish throne null and void and it was in July, 1296 that John was finally captured and sent to the Tower of London. In 1299 he was released into Papal custody and was later handed over to the French to be used as a political pawn. He spent his last days on his ancestral lands in Piccardy, all that remained of his family's possessions.

The question of Scottish independence did not fail with him. Thanks to the film, *Braveheart* many of us will be aware of the exploits of William Wallace, a guerrilla leader who rose to prominence due to his military abilities. He was initially a strong supporter of John Balliol, though his defeat in battle at Falkirk by Edward I in 1298 signalled a downward spiral in his career, until his eventual capture and execution at Smithfield in 1305.

Robert Bruce, John Balliol's rival for the throne of Scotland now came to prominence. Edward I of England's death in 1307 left his weak and ineffectual son, Edward II as King of England. Bruce took his chance well and crushed the English forces at the Battle of Bannockburn in 1314; he then signed a truce with the demoralised King and took over sole rule of Scotland. He died of leprosy in 1329 leaving his five-year-old son as King. Internal strife ensued, and after victory at the Battle of Duplin Moor in 1332, John Balliol's son, Edward Balliol, was crowned at Scone, but his hold on the Crown was unsteady and heavily dependent on English arms which caused him to pay homage to Edward III of England in 1333. Only three years later he was forced to retire to the English court and in 1356 he surrendered his claim to the Scottish crown to the English King.

This is, in brief outline, the history of the rise and fall of the Balliol family and their links to the throne of Scotland, but where does our man, Robert Balliol fit in and what do we know of him?

Pedigree of Balliol of Barnard Castle, Kings of Scotland

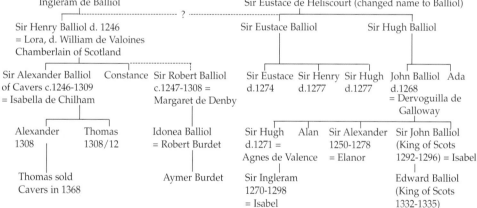

The genealogical table is a little confused and as yet lacks definitive proof; it would at present seem to appear that Robert was not a particularly close relation of the Scottish King. His father may have been Sir Henry Balliol who married Lora, daughter of William de Valoines, the Chamberlain of Scotland. Henry, who was definitely a grandson of Bernard Balliol II of Barnard Castle, was invited by King John to take his side prior to the signing of Magna Carta in 1215, though he appears to have refused. If this was the case then his brother would have been Sir Alexander of Cavers, who was born around 1246. Alexander would certainly seem to be a contemporary of Robert but there is great confusion over the Balliol family ancestry. Alexander served for Edward I in his Welsh wars and married Isabella de Chilham. It seems likely that he fell from grace during the turbulence which occurred during his kinsman's rule of Scotland, he may even have served time in prison with John Balliol.

Barnard Castle, County Durham, ancestral home of the Balliol family. 1998. *Author's collection.*

One can see from the above table, that if correct, how proud the Burdet's must have been, particularly Almaricus, whose son, Robert married Idonea, and therefore into Scottish nobility. According to the historian, Hunter, there were plasterwork coats of arms inside the old Birthwaite Hall (discussed later), these coats of arms depicted the families, which had married into the Burdet lineage over the years. He also noted that the orle (the border around the coat of arms) of the Balliol's was a favourite and appeared upon the seal of the first Sir Francis of Birthwaite. Hunter also noted that the orle might be seen carved on the tower of the church at Darton, another indication of the pride in which the Burdet family held their connections.

Of Robert Balliol himself, we can learn much from a roll, which details the knights in the service of Edward I during the thirteenth century.

1267	23 October. The King owed him 19/- arrears of wages.
1278	18 May. He was to appear before the King charged with forest trespass.
1280	11 February. He was to pay his fine of 100 marks at 20 marks per annum (1 mark was worth 13 shillings and 4 pence, so this was a huge amount).
1280	16 September. He was minister of the King's forests North of the Trent.
1282	2 August. He served as a knight under the Bishop of Durham against the Welsh during King Edward's conquest of the country.
1284	8 February. It was reported that he did good service in Wales.
1297 & 1301	He was a knight of the shire of Yorkshire.
1308	He was a witness at the proving of age of one Rob. Bertram of Bothal. Robert Balliol said that on 23 April 1287 he was attacked by robbers on his way from Corbridge and reached Morpeth on foot, his horse being killed, and that Rob Bertram was born at about that time.

From this, we know that Robert fought for King Edward I during his conquest of Wales as part of the army lead by the Bishop of Durham, possibly even alongside his brother, Alexander of Cavers. The Welsh revolt of 1282 followed an earlier uprising, which had been quelled by the English King. The Welsh Prince Llywelyn, was now faced with an even more concerted assault by the English troops, which ended when the Welsh ruler was killed near Builth.

To consolidate his conquest Edward I began the construction of the castles such as Caernarfon, Conwy and Harlech in 1277 and it is very likely that Robert Balliol would have witnessed the building activity and possibly even stayed under one of their roofs.

His military career was certainly in motion by 1267, only two years after the Battle of Evesham, where the followers of the King had soundly beaten Simon de Montfort and his army in the Baron's war, in Worcester. It is very possible that Robert may have fought for the King (Henry III), though the battles absence from the above document would appear to indicate that his military career began around 1267, the record following his progress chronologically. The King did owe him 19/- in arrears of wages though, and this could point to an earlier start for the young Robert.

His interests in his families lands around Barnard Castle were still strong as proved by his statement, dated 1308, where he recounts a trip from Corbridge (initially a Roman fort just to the south of Hadrians Wall), to Morpeth, approximately fourteen miles to the north-east, in Northumberland, a neighbour to his home county of Durham.

As minister for the King's forests North of the Trent, Robert would have been responsible (alongside others) for the implementation of forest laws, which were generally hunting rules and regulations.

The term forest does not necessarily imply a large wooded area, it was a more general legal term for an area which was subject to forest law, these areas could contain land which was let for grazing, and even cottages or villages. The king was usually the owner of these estates and would have had sole hunting rights to such game as deer or wild boar, and the use of the timber for building houses and ships.

The penalties for breaking forest laws were severe, offences included cutting down saplings or trees, and it was also forbidden to make a hedge. It was forbidden to carry arms in the forests or to keep greyhounds, indeed if a wild animal were found dead an inquest would be held.

Until 1217 the cutting of firewood in a Royal forest incurred only a fine, but shooting a deer would lead to death or severe mutilation, King Henry II reduced this punishment to banishment, though this was still a terrible price to pay.

We also have the following deed relating to his activities at Denby:

> *Easter term, in the reign of Edward I in 1304.*
> *Fine, between Robert de Balliol and Margaret his wife, querents, and Nicholas de Wortley, deforciant of the Manors of Denby and High Hoyland. Robert and Margaret recognised the manors to be the right of Nicholas as of their gift. He in turn granted the manors to Robert and Margaret for their lives, remainder to Robert Burdet and Idonia his wife, in special tail, remainder for default of issue of Robert Burdet to the right heirs of Margaret.*

A second grant survives, dated between 1304 and 1309 made out by Robert Burdet. It states that he and Nicholas de Wortley had granted the manors of Denby and High Hoyland to Robert de Balliol and Margaret his wife in the Kings court by a fine levied between them. The grant continues:

> *Robert Burdet grants that by reason of the cost of repairing or ruin of the houses, gardens, woods, tenantry or anything else made by Robert de Balliol or Margaret within the said manors the grant will not oppress them by writ or waste or any other plea, wishing and granting for himself and his heirs that Robert de Balliol and Margaret may approve as much in wastes, marl pits (manure), turbaries (a place where peat is dug) and mines as exel.*

These two documents show that Robert and Margaret held the Manor of Denby for their lifetimes after which they were to pass to their daughter, Idonea and her husband Robert Burdet, with a further clause stating that should this be impossible then the heirs of Margaret should inherit.

We have also seen the first mention of the Lords of Wortley, although here the picture becomes rather complicated. The exact origin for the Wortley family to be involved in dealings with Denby is unknown to me. The Nicholas Wortley mentioned above would seem to be the fifth of the family to have born the name. A family which considerably enriched their landed possessions throughout the eleventh, twelfth and thirteenth centuries as well as endowing their village of residence from which they took their name. A particularly interesting charter was noted by Joseph Hunter which details their connections to the manors of Horbury and Shitlington, it lists the names of many of the most prominent people from the area between Wortley and Thornhill, including that of Sir Robert Balliol. Hunter does not give a date but as with the latter two documents it appears to date from the late thirteenth or early fourteenth century.

From the above we can speculate that certainly Robert Balliol, if not his wife, was probably absent from Denby for most of the time, and that he may have placed the keeping of his manor in the hands of a stable and trusted local lord, but to forestall any future difficulty he assured his daughters legal inheritance by deed.

A knight in the king's service would be duty bound to follow the instructions of his Lord, though what Robert made of the wars surrounding his relatives accession to the throne of Scotland we do not know. We do know that he was recorded as a knight of the shire of Yorkshire in 1297 and again in 1301, precisely the time from which our documentary evidence for his deeds at Denby survives. Perhaps he settled here at this time, maybe in retirement hence the surviving references which appear to be tidying up his affairs.

One of the documents also states that the heirs of Margaret should inherit if Robert Burdet and Idonea do not produce a son, Margaret's first marriage, to Nicholas de Metham produced two daughters. Alice, who married William de la Sancery and Elizabeth who married John Fekelton.

Margaret as we have already noted must have been born around 1240/50, therefore if we take a mean time of twenty years before her first marriage we arrive at 1260/70, it cannot have lasted for very long, therefore I would speculate that her marriage to Balliol must have occurred around the mid 1270s, this would fit with the evidence we have for her still being young enough to conceive what appears to have been their only child, certainly the only one which grew to adulthood. If the marriage had been consummated shortly after the wedding then Idonea would have been around twenty-five years old when she first appears in documentary records.

How Margaret de Denby and Robert de Balliol met will, unfortunately never be known, one would consider that Balliol was the older of the pair, alive and active in 1267, one would expect him to have been at least fifteen or twenty years old at this time which would take his date of birth back to 1242/47. He must have died sometime around 1308/9 as his name is absent from records after this date, so even if we take the earlier date for his birth he would have only been in his mid 60s, though at that time in history it was a very good age.

Idonea, and via her, Robert Burdet, appear to have come in to the possession of the manors of Denby and High Hoyland during the latter years of Edward I. As King Edward died in 1307 and the grant relating to Balliol's successor was dated to 1304, it would seem reasonable to assume that as an old man the document was produced to safeguard his daughters inheritance. There were plenty of the old De Denby families still around and as large landowners themselves they would certainly have had a case to contest the lordship. The 1304 document also gives us one more vital piece of evidence, it makes no mention of Aymer Burdet, son of Idonea, it only mentions any future heirs, therefore he had not yet been born.

What do we have of Robert Balliol? He was a fighting man, a knight, serving alongside his King during his wars of conquest. He was a local landowner, concerned about his properties and his revenue. He was a man of such close proximity to the Scottish throne that after the downfall of John Balliol he must have been uncertain about his own future. He was a man who cared so much for his daughter that he took care of her inheritance before he died, leaving the responsibility in the hands of a trusted friend, Nicholas de Wortley. In short he was a man of his time, strong, skilled in battle, probably a great one for sports and pastimes, such as hunting and falconry, he was a survivor as can be seen by his escape, aged somewhere around forty years old, from the robbers near Corbridge even though he lost his horse, he still managed to make it to safety. Robert Balliol was the man who paved the way for the Burdet family to dominate the next few centuries of Denby's history. We may not be totally certain of Robert's lineage but the evidence I have examined and my conclusions I believe, are as close as it is possible to get to the truth with the evidence available at this time.

We have moved from the disjointed and fragmentary members of the de Denby family dating to the mid-twelfth century through to the take-over of the Norman French family of Burdet. We have seen how the respective lines of William de Denby and Sir Robert de Denby separate and were then reunited by marriage. We have been focusing on the upper echelons of medieval society, mainly because little enough evidence survives to flesh out their lives let alone the poorer tenantry and slaves. Before we continue the descent of Burdet, via Idonea Balliol and Robert Burdet we will examine some of the other people who were living upon the manor of Denby at this time:

> *Agreement: between William de Netherdeneby and Adam son of Godfrey of the same; namely, that William demised to Adam a bovate of land, which William Broune formerly held in the vill of Deneby, for a term of twenty years; Adam to take of the wood for burning and building on the said land, (waste or sale excepted); and to grind at the lessor's mill all his malt, made and used in his house, without multure; paying 5s of silver yearly at three terms, 20d at Whitsuntide, 20d at the feast of St. Oswald the King, and 20d at Martinmas, for all service. Adam gave William 20s of silver.*
> *Witness: William de Overdeneby.*
> *Dated November 11th 1261.*

Nether Denby as we shall see later on, was central to the manors of Denby and High Hoyland and here we have details regarding land ownership between a family known as Netherdenby. The name died out before the Poll Tax of 1379 and it would seem likely that the family were dispossessed by the Burdets. The surname Overdenby would appear to have gone the same way.

The de Denby family continued to flourish in the village, we find many references to them in the next few centuries, not least Richard Denby, Radulphus de Denby and a John de Denby, a smith, in 1379, but by the time of the Hearth Tax of 1672, they were gone. I have tried, as far as is possible to add to the heralds ancient genealogical table. It is at best an honest attempt to give substance to the family, all of whom must have been related. I do not intend trying to include the de Denbys of the fourteenth and fifteenth centuries as without more hard evidence even a hypothetical scenario is impossible.

We can learn a little more about the later de Denbys from the Wakefield Court Rolls:

> 1331-1333 - *Holme: William son of John de Denby sues Richard son of Stephen de Cumberworth in a plea of debt; pledge for the prosecution, Thomas de Longelay. Richard attached by 10s in the hand of William Spink, does not come therefore destraint is to be kept and more taken and the matter adjourned until the next court at Wakefield.*

> Wakefield: *William son of John de Denby plaintiff offers himself against Richard son of Stephen de Cumberworth in a plea of debt, and Richard attached by 10s in the hand of William Spink does not come,*

therefore order is given that destraint be kept and more taken.

Holme: William son of John de Denby, plaintiff does not prosecute his suit for debt against Richard, son of Stephen de Cumberworth, therefore he and the pledges for the prosecution are amerced 2d.

William may have been the son of John de Denby who had married Christian, if so his brother could have been Jordan de Denby. Whatever his lineage he does not seem to have been very successful in pursuing his claims against his near neighbour from Cumberworth!

13 May 1349 - *Tourn held at Kirkburton, Wednesday 13th May 1349*
John de Denby and Richard del Morhous senior do not come to the tourn, (fined) 2d each.

A tourn, as from the word 'tournament', implied a local court, where two parties would be heard in a legal battle rather then a physical one.

1349 - *Kirkburton: Alice de Denby, once at 2d, brewed at a penny.*

Here we have evidence of Alice de Denby brewing substandard ale and trying to undercut her rivals by selling at half price, if only we could get present day landlords to do the same thing, though being fair, ale was at this time a staple part of the diet in England.

1350-1352 - *Held, Monday 3rd January (24 Edward III)*
1351 - *An enquiry held on oath ...also Margery de Denby 6d, drew blood against the peace from William, son of Robert de Birton. And the said William 12d drew blood from the said Margery.*

Who can say why these two came to blows? Evidently, it was thought unreasonable that a man should strike a woman as William de Birton was fined twice as much as Margery. They were perhaps lucky to be fined; stocks and pillory, the whipping post, and branding or maiming were common punishments at this time. Men and women could have their ears torn off, their noses split down each side or their tongues cut off for even minor indiscretions, maybe the above was just a spat which was over as soon as it had begun.

For more minor offences the stocks could be employed, wood stealers, women of ill repute, gamblers, Sunday drinkers and even those who refused to help bring in the harvest could all look forward to this fate and although humiliation was the objective, some missiles could be more dangerous, hurled along with taunts and jibes. Though many village stocks still survive (i.e. those at Cumberworth) the last recorded instance of their being used in England occurred in 1872.

What of the Denby stocks? Aside from the group of buildings at Lower Denby, called Stocks Hall little can be speculated as to the location of this important village fixture. It is reputed that the pair of stones forming the gate to the former Wesleyan Chapel in Upper Denby, just above the present day village green, were once the supports of the Denby stocks. To my mind, the stones are neither long enough nor wide enough, but of course they could have been cut to size in order to function properly for their new purpose. It is unlikely that these were the only stocks on the manor owned by the Burdets, there would certainly have been some at High Hoyland and Clayton.

The pillory was another similar form of punishment for more minor offences, dating back to at least 1269. It consisted of a wooden frame, supported by an upright post with holes through which the offender's head and hands were placed, the offender was left upright though entirely unable to defend himself, or indeed herself, from any attack. This contraption was finally abolished in 1837.

Medieval times also saw the use of the Scold's bridle, to gag nagging, sharp-tongued women and in some cases, men. The Cucking Stool, sometimes wrongly referred to as another name for the Ducking Stool, which saw common brawlers, fraudsters and scolding women have to sit on a chair or commode outside their own home and endure all manner of derision. Whipping either tied to the back of a cart, against a village whipping post or even through the town was always a threat to sheep stealers and their like, as was being branded with hot irons so as to be instantly recognised for what you were. All this, at a time when the death penalty could vary from beheading, for nobles, to hanging, drawing and quartering for traitors, it certainly paid to behave oneself.

The court rolls preserve only moments in time, but they do allow us to see a very human side to these people who were, contrary to widespread opinion, just as intelligent as we are, another falsehood is that they were much shorter in stature than people of the twentieth century. Because in most cases all that remains of their lives are odd dates and property details it is very easy to dismiss them, but do that at your peril, if you were to meet one of them today you would certainly have met your match!

We now leave the de Denbys and return to Robert Burdet and Idonea Balliol and the birth of their son, Aymer who was to found a ruling dynasty that lasted for nearly 350 years.

THE EARLY BURDET LORDS OF DENBY

We know that Robert Burdet was the Lord of the Manor of Denby at around the turn of the fourteenth century, he probably became the sole owner after the death of Robert Balliol. Robert may have dwelt in Denby although it is likely that he still made frequent visits back to Rand(e). We have already seen that his brother, Nicholas, lord of Rand(e), granted him the lands and rents in Skelmerthorp, Co. Lincolnshire, which had descended to him via their mother, Agnes de Denby.

Of his wife, Idonea, we have already examined her parentage in some depth; it is likely that she remained in Denby for most of her life. As for her death, one would imagine that it took place some time around the 1320s or 1330s at the latest. I was informed that her tomb might be found in Beverley Minster, though, it would appear that this has proved to be an erroneous piece of information. Although the name is uncommon, the Idonea at Beverley is buried in the Percy family vault and was the wife of a gentleman of that family. Further research would be required to ascertain whether Robert Burdet died prematurely and if Idonea remarried. It is a possibility as the Percy lineage does include a number of different Balliol's, but the Idonea at Beverley appears to have been living too late to correspond with the lady of Denby.

Robert and Idonea had a son and heir, Aymer Burdet. Probably born in the first decade of the fourteenth century we have the following details of Aymer:

Sunday after St. Mathew the Apostle (Sept. 25th), 1344
Grant: by Robert, son and heir of Adam de Denby to Adomar son of Robert Burdet, of a plot of land containing 15 acres called le Stubbing, in the territory of Deneby, one end of which abutted on the high road leading to the vill of Deneby, paying the chief lords 12d yearly.
Witnesses: John de Gunnildthwayt, John de Deneby

Wakefield Court Rolls: 1348-1350
3 March 1349 - Baliff: Order is given to distrain (to seize goods for debts) *Edmund Burdet (Eymer) to answer for what services he holds 2 bovates of the lords fee.*

17 March 1349 - Eymer Burdet to answer by what services he holds 2 bovates of the Lords fee in Crigglestone.

7 April 1349 - Order is given... to distrain Eymer Burdet to answer the Lord by what services he holds 2 bovates of the Lords fee in Crigglestone.

And so it goes on, the distrain of Aymer was discussed on the 5 May, 23 June, 14 July and 20 October. One presumes that the matter was somehow sorted out soon after this date as no further entries are listed in the court rolls. Evidently, Aymer did not wish to make his answer known, probably because he knew that he did not really have a case. It could be that the lands are connected with the grant made

Margaret de Denby, widow of Sir Robert de Denby, who granted Adam de Crigglestone a bovate of land here during the thirteenth century. Here, at least, we have evidence of the family holding land here.

We know that Aymer was alive and active in 1333 and from the latter documents we know that he lived until at least 1359. We are also made aware by the heralds that he married Isabel Langton, the daughter of a Baron of Newton and Lord of Walton. They had at least two children, Nicholas, first son and heir and Richard. Aymer's name crops up as a witness to documents in 1333, 1341 and 1344. His name also appears as a witness to the deed granting John de Gonildthwaite lands and the water mill at Gunthwaite dated 20 October, 1359. Aymer must have died soon after this, as we know that his wife, Isabel re-married to a man called Ralph Hyde.

It is interesting that the dispute recorded in the Wakefield court rolls (above) regarding Aymer's claim on land and rights at Crigglestone is dated 1349. This was a year of immense instability and a time when even the countryside offered little protection against a vengeful and regardless killer.

THE BLACK DEATH
The main effects of the Black Death were felt in Britain during the years 1348/49. More than a third of the country's population died as a result of the epidemic. Vacant church incumbencies numbered 40-45% and the number of tenants on manorships throughout the country diminished to such an extent that afterwards they were able to resist the old feudal system and its obligations.

The plague spread from Asia, carried by rat fleas to the ports of the Black Sea, it comprised two forms. Bubonic plague caused swellings that inflated the lymph nodes at the neck, armpit or groin, whilst pneumonic plague affected the lungs and caused its victims to choke on their own blood.

Responses varied, some blamed the Jews, others, poisoned wells, whilst some barricaded themselves into their homes in the hope that their isolation might protect them. Many fled to the countryside, whilst some resorted to riotous living. Villages, towns and cities were in many cases barricaded, but all these measures failed.

With the spread of the plague law and order broke down, victims died alone, many abandoned by their own families, corpses lay unburned in the streets. Agriculture was at a standstill and livestock roamed freely and unattended.

Blind to rank, status, class or privilege it was only during 1349 that it abated, although there were further epidemics during 1360-1362 and 1369, indeed plague continued to abide in Britain until the latter part of the seventeenth century.

It is also interesting to note that plague also occurred at Kirkburton. Henry Moorhouse noted that,

It's first appearance was in 1558 and was confined for the most part to Burton, High Burton and adjacent townships extending to Woodsome Mill in the adjoining parish of Almondbury...the plague began in June and continued till the following October during which time 120 persons fell, a sacrifice to it's malignity.

As an aside, the Derbyshire village of Eyam, known as the 'plague village' was visited by the epidemic during 1665/1666 and it is now a very popular tourist destination. Perhaps something similar ought to be in operation at Kirkburton today, although Eyam has the advantage of one hundred years, and many of its original houses still stand, and of course it was concurrent with the Great Plague of London, also dated 1665.

The effects of the plague must have visited Denby, High Hoyland and Clayton though I have no details to hand, certainly Aymer, Isabel, their sons and all the villagers would have been well aware of the consequences of catching the disease, and subsequently fear must have gripped the locality.

Before we continue with the descent of the Burdets we must briefly examine the origins of their near neighbours who were to outlast the Burdets as Lords of their own manor.

THE GUNTHWAITES and BOSVILLES

A family called de Byrton from Kirkburton originally held the Manor of Gunthwaite before they passed through an heiress to the Darcy family. In 1281 John de Rodes de Gunnildthwayt made a quitclaim (a deed of release) to his Lord Henry de Byrton, regarding all waste land from the Gunthwaite estate, this deed was interestingly enough witnessed by John, son of Alan de Denby, amongst others. It is possible that this was an error on the part of the scribe, and that he was referring to Adam de Denby, if not, then we have yet another de Denby who we cannot fit into the genealogical table.

A charter drawn up during the time of King Edward III (1327-1377) has Henry Darcy of London granting John Gonnildthwaite lands in Gunthwaite and also the water mill thereby elevating the Gunthwaite family to a land-owning position instead of being tenants of the de Byrtons and Darcys.

This grant gave John and his wife Christiana the manors for their lifetime, but on their deaths, they were to pass to Thomas Bosville of Newhall and Ardsley (East of Barnsley) and his heirs. The document was dated Sunday 20 October 1359 and was witnessed by, as we have seen, Aymer Burdet of Denby, along with John de Dronsfield and John de Stainton, possibly the father of Elizabeth de Stainton. She became the prioress of Kirklees, and could have been the relative of Robert (Robin) Hood of Wakefield, who is said to have bled the outlaw to death.

The de Gunthwaite family had been prominent for more than a century, the earliest I have a record of is William de Gunthwaite who was living during the reign of Henry III (1216-72). He was succeeded by John de Gunthwaite, Laurence de Gunthwaite and Henry de Gunthwaite who all appear to have lived during the latter half of the thirteenth century and early fourteenth. Whether their relationship to each other was father to son is now impossible to tell. A Roger de Gunthwaite can be found in 1310 and 1321, he was most likely the father of John who married Christiana. The document dated 1310 related to corn milling rights at a rent of 4s 8d per annum. There would appear to have been a corn mill and dam at their current sites in Gunthwaite for many centuries. Indeed, the water wheel was used for grinding corn right up until the period between the two world wars when it finally ceased productivity. My own Grandfather, Ernest Heath, a carpenter, was one of the last people employed on the wheel itself when he replaced some of the buckets which had rotted.

By 1374, John de Gunthwaite was dead and his wife released the manor to Thomas Bosville. It seems that the reason for the Bosville inheritance was that John and Christiana's daughter, Alice, was the wife of Thomas of Ardsley, though there is no documentary proof of this. Thus, the Bosvilles took over at Gunthwaite.

The Bosvilles were, like the Burdets, part of the Conqueror's vanguard. They originated from the place in Normandy, Bosville, 'Bos' meaning 'ox' and 'ville' meaning 'town'. Sir Martin Bosville was treasurer for William the Conqueror's army and later for William Rufus. He died in 1092 having had three sons, William, John and Ellias. It was from John that Thomas Bosville of Ardsley was descended.

NICHOLAS BURDET and the POLL TAX OF 1379

The records are silent after 1359, and so one presumes that Aymer Burdet died sometime during the 1360s, he would, after all, be at least in his mid fifties. We know from the poll tax roll that his eldest son, Nicholas had inherited by 1379 and it is to this record that we will now turn.

This is the first record of the names of the ordinary villagers of Denby, and was levied in the reign of King Richard II (1367-1400), in 1379, it was, as now, unpopular with the public. A Kent man, we know only as Wat Tyler (almost certainly a pseudonym) organised a revolt only two years later in 1381, leading peasants against landowners airing grievances about the poll tax and the feudal system in general. He led his followers into London where he presented a petition to a young King Richard. As Tyler and the King drew nearer, the Mayor of London, in the belief that Tyler was about to do the King harm, slew him with his sword. To appease the angry crowd the King offered to take Tyler's place and lead the rebels, he then pardoned them all. With Tyler dead and the crowd disbursed, it took the government only a few days to revoke these pardons.

Denby appears in the Staincross section of the returns as can be seen from the printed version, dated 1882. Everyone over the age of sixteen was to pay 4d, though a graduated rate was applied to the more affluent, taking in to account rank and occupation. Widows had to pay the same rates that their husbands would have paid and married men had to pay 4d for themselves and for their wives.

It should be noted that the Lord of the Manor, Nicholas Burdet, appears with his brother, William and his maidservant, Diot. The de Denby families are also still very prominent and the Robinson and Marshall families make their first appearance. John Marshall and John de Denby were both smiths and are the only two where a trade is marked after their names.

The total amount to be collected from Denby was 11s 8d, the following villages make an interesting comparison:

Clayton	3s 8d	Penistone	5s 2d
Ingbirchworth	3s 2d	Gunthwaite	4s 6d
Cumberworth	5s 6d	High Hoyland	3s 6d
Hoylandswaine	6s 8d	Kexborough	6s 2d

The highest local amount came from Cawthorne with 47s 2d, followed by Barnsley with 33s 8d.

The following is my rough translation of the record:

THE DENBY POLL TAX ROLL – 1379			
Villata De Denby		**Village of Denby**	
Nicolaus Burdet, ffrankeleyn	xl.d	Nicholas Burdet, freeholder	40d
Willelmus, frater, ejus	iiii.d	William Burdet, brother	4d
Diot, famula, ejus	iiii.d	Diot, maidservant of above	4d
Willelmus Elkoc	iiii.d	William Elcock	4d
Thomas Dey, Alicia vx-ejus	iiii.d	Thomas Day & Alice his wife	4d
Robertus Bromelex	iiii.d	Robert Bromley & his wife	4d
Johanna Horn	iiii.d	Johanna Horn	4d
Johannes Marschall, Alicia vx smyth	vi.d	John Marshall & Alicia, wife, smith	6d
Johannes, fillius, ejus	iiii.d	John, son of above	4d
Alicia, famula, ejus	iiii.d	Alice, maidservant of above	4d
Johannes Skalter & vx ejus	iiii.d	John Skalter & his wife	4d
Johannes Buring & vx ejus	iiii.d	John Buring & his wife	4d
Ricardus de Denby & vx	iiii.d	Richard de Denby & his wife	4d
Johannes Robynson & vx	iiii.d	John Robinson & his wife	4d
Thomas Pek & vx ejus	iiii.d	Thomas Peck & his wife	4d
Johannes Dicson & vx	iiii.d	John Dixon	4d
Johannes de Denby & vx, smyth	vi.d	John de Denby & his wife, smith	6d
Ricardus de Denby	iiii.d	Richard de Denby	4d
Simon Horn	iiii.d	Simon Horn	4d
Elena, filia ejus	iiii.d	Eleanor, daughter of above	4d
Johannes Dicson minor & vx	iiii.d	John Dixon, minor & wife	4d
Johannes filius Johannis	iiii.d	John son of above	4d
Ricardus de Haytfield vx	iiii.d	Richard of Hatfield & wife	4d
Radulphus de Denby vx	iiii.d	Randolph (?) de Denby & wife	4d
Robertus Elkoc & vx ejus	iiii.d	Robert Elcock & his wife	4d
Summa xjs	viii.d	Total	11s 8d

Take note from the above that the two smiths, presumably blacksmiths in the village both paid an extra 2d over everybody else except Nicholas Burdet the Lord of the Manor. Indeed John Marshall was wealthy enough to employ a maidservant.

We also have a record concerning Nicholas Burdet, dating to the year 1395. It concerns a complaint made by the Lord of Emley, Sir William Fitzwilliam who had inherited his estates on the death of his father in 1385. Three years before his death in 1398, the following was recorded 'That Nicholas Burdet and others broke into his park at Emley and hunted without licence'. We can be sure that it was the Nicholas Burdet mentioned on the poll tax roll as we know that he was still alive in 1402.

During medieval times the feudal system had caused the land to be split into manors, these were held by either the Crown, Church or Knights. These knights and churchmen were the beneficiaries of the 'Game Laws' which protected their right to hunt, not only for pleasure but for skins and food. Therefore early medieval Kings and Nobles enclosed areas of land, parks to keep game in. These could be distinguished by banks and ditches, surmounted by fences, hedges or walls.

The favoured animals kept included fallow deer, roe deer, red deer and wild boar (hunted to extinction in England by 1750). Parks, the preserves of private landowners, though not subject to forest laws, still gave the owners exclusive rights to hunt within them but by the eighteenth and nineteenth centuries hunting as we know it today had developed signalling the demise of the park system.

Hunting was not the only recreation of these times, tournaments and jousting were very popular with landowners up until the sixteenth century, as was tilting, which was of a similar nature though far less bloody! Archery was not only a sport (subsequently replaced by shooting) but a compulsory activity during the fourteenth and fifteenth centuries when the English bowmen were the scourge of the world. Falconry was also a popular activity amongst the elite. The poorer classes had to be content with being spectators for much of the time, though they did celebrate Holy days and Saint's days until the reformation.

It is likely that Nicholas Burdet participated in most of these pursuits and indeed his forefathers and the generations yet to come. We do not know whether the complaint made against him by the Lord of Emley was upheld. If he broke into the park to hunt without licence on purpose, then he was either a very confident man or a very foolish one. He obviously had little respect for his neighbour, perhaps there was trouble between the two, perhaps the raid was alcohol induced or perhaps Nicholas was the scourge of the local people, a 'black knight' maybe. Or it could be that he was in the midst of a thrilling chase after a boar or hart of such size that he would not abandon the chase even when it meant trespassing to continue the pursuit. We can speculate for ever, in truth we will never know, but this does illustrate the importance of hunting in medieval times.

Nicholas's lineage was as follows:

Descent of Nicholas Burdet II

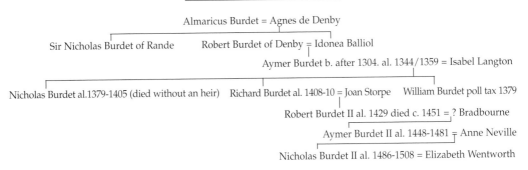

We know that Nicholas Burdet never married, and consequently had no male heir to leave his lands and titles to. We find him acting as a witness to a transfer of ownership of Gunthwaite Hall in 1402, and again as a witness to a Bosville land grant in 1405/6, but he seems to have been dead by 1408, when we find his younger brother, Richard Burdet, who became his beneficiary, involved in the following:

December 1st, (10 Henry IV) 1408.
Receipt from Richard Bunny, feodary of the honour of Pontefract, to Richard Burdet, for 31s 3d relief for two carucates of land in Clayton.

Also in 1408, a land grant was drawn up by Richard Burdet, to William Scott the Vicar of Dewsbury, John de Manyngham of Ardeslawe, William de Maltby and John Walker a chaplain of Mirfield. This document gave to the above, apparently unconnected parties, all of Richard Burdet's lands in Denby and High Hoyland and all his land in Yorkshire, the document was dated the 6 December.

It was witnessed by amongst others: Robert Rockley, John de Wortley, Richard de Keresforth, William de Dodworth and John Marshall of Denby.

This was followed only a year and a half later by a quitclaim (a deed of release) made by William Scott and John de Manyngham to William de Maltby and John Walker as to their rights on the above document. This left the remaining two parties to pass the land and rights back to Richard Burdet and his wife Joan later in the year, with a proviso that if Richard should die without an heir the properties should pass to the Lords of Wortley.

To participate in the above so soon after inheriting his brother's titles and rights would seem to suggest that Richard either took over a financial nightmare, perhaps caused by his brother's tenure as Lord of the Manor. On the other hand, in order to inherit, perhaps he had to go through some curious legal investure at the hands of the four parties named in the document above. He certainly did get his rights and titles back, and here we see the connection between Denby and the Wortley family, who again seem to be the beneficiaries should the Burdet line fail.

Richard and his wife, Joan Storpe, the daughter of a family in Worcestershire, did produce a son and heir, Robert Burdet and things seem to have returned almost back to normal by 1410, when Richard witnessed the following deed:

5th September 1410
Demise: John Bosville of Erdeslay to William de Staveley and wife Joan for her life :- the manor of Gunnylthwayt with 1 messuage, 70 acres of land... etcetera.

Richard's father, Nicholas Burdet appears to have inherited the manor between 1359 and 1379, he was probably born sometime around the 1340s and would have been around forty years old at the time of the poll tax which would make him around sixty-eight years old when he died. As we know his brother Richard died in 1437 from his will, it would seem that Richard was much younger than his elder brother. He does not appear on the poll tax list but another brother, William does. Evidently William died before Nicholas, and Richard may have been the youngest brother of the family, hence his much later date of death. His absence from the poll tax list would indicate that he was a minor at the time and not due to any payment, this would suggest that he was born sometime during the late 1360s or early 1370s, and that he was around sixty-five to seventy-five years old when he died.

We have very few details of his son, Robert Burdet, even the heralds did not know the first name of his wife who was the daughter of Humphrey Bradbourne of County Derby. He certainly was a witness to a deed in 1429 and he appears again in 1449 and could possibly be the Robert Burdet, referred to by Hunter as being buried at Penistone church in 1451, unfortunately the early records of the church have not survived to prove this.

His son, the second Aymer Burdet was certainly alive in 1456 when he was a witness to a deed. This activity would seem to corroborate a date of 1451 for the death of his father. We also find him acting as a witness to the following deed:

Barnsley: 10th July 1460
Feoffment: Thomas Anne, Thomas Beaumont and John Gysburne chaplain to Richard Bosville and his wife Joan, all property at Keresforth which they had in the gift of William Mirfield and Percival Greenacre esqs.
: To R. & J.B. and heirs of their body and then to Isabel Langton.
Witnesses: Aymer Burdhed, Robert Wortlay.

Aymer married Ann Neville, the daughter of Sir Thomas Neville of Liversedge in 1448 and had a son and heir, Nicholas II. The Nevilles of Liversedge were ancestors of the Nevilles who had inherited the manor of Denby as of the right of Brierley from the Saxon family of Ailric. Their lineage continues thus:

Genealogical Table of Nevile Family of Liversedge

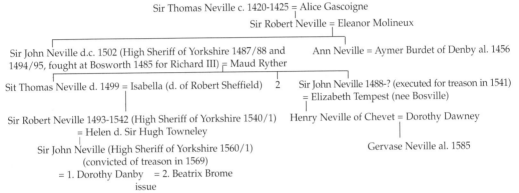

This Liversedge branch of what became an important and hugely influential family were almost certainly relatives of the Nevilles of Warwick, of whom Richard Neville is the most famous. Known almost as well by his nickname of 'Warwick the Kingmaker' this family was central to activities during the Wars of the Roses, although the exact genealogical context to connect Liversedge and Warwick is at present uncertain. What is certain is that Aymer Burdet had a brother-in-law who fought for King Richard III at Bosworth, and so must have taken a deep interest in political matters at this time. The Battle of Wakefield took place in December 1460 only a matter of miles from Denby and news of its conclusion must have spread to the village very quickly. It is also interesting to note that the Bosville family of Chevet, another branch of the Gunthwaite family, were also related by marriage to the Liversedge Nevilles.

At some point during his tenure as Lord of the Manor, Aymer granted away the possession of his lands:

Feoffment. Robert Normanville esq. Son and heir of Ralph Normanville esq. Deceased to Richard Burdet esq. Son and heir of Nicholas Burdet esq. (Aymer's son and grandson). Deceased, the manors of Denby and Holande with their messuages rights and appurtenances in Denby, Holande, Netherbretton, Barnesley, Mapilwelle, Clayton, Dyrt asse Derton, Kexburgh, Keresforth, which Ralph (Normanville) had by grant of AYMER BURDET esq. Richard Burdet (together with) John Neville, knight, Thomas Neville his son, Robert Froste, rector of Thornhyll, William Neville esq. Richard Burdet and William Burdet, now deceased, making (?) Woddcokke and Richard (Swifte) his attorneys.
Dated 12th May 1522

Why Aymer was reduced to doing this is unknown, perhaps he was financially unstable and granted the lands on a similar principle to pawnbrokers shops of today, with a guarantee that once his fortunes had improved he would be entitled to claim back the lands legally.

The Normanville family were Lords of Billingley, but their connection with Denby is unknown, they appear to come from a wealthy background, and also seem to have adopted a somewhat expansionist policy during the fifteenth century. As the document stated above, the lands and rights were legally referred back to Richard Burdet in 1522, though Nicholas was still holding court at High Hoyland in 1500. Evidently, the family powers were not depleted, but without further evidence this period of the families history is somewhat shadowy and uncertain. The fact that the Neville in-laws of Aymer were heavily involved would indicate that the agreement related to the manor of Brierley of which Denby was a part but the particulars of the reasons involved are currently unknown. Documents dated 1479 and 1481 prove Aymer's existence up until this time, though it is likely that he died soon after.

We have concentrated, up to this point, solely on the Lords of the Manor and their heirs in the Burdet family. It would be wise to remember that there were many more siblings throughout these generations who have been forgotten, through no fault of their own, mainly because they were not the eldest sons of the family. These people were still prominent members of society and achieved ,in many cases, positions of respect and authority, such as John Burdet, who became vicar of the church at Cumberworth in 1365 after being presented by John de Dronsfield. Unfortunately, he does not appear in the poll tax returns of 1379 for the village, either he had moved on or he had died. Either way he must have been a contemporary of the first Aymer Burdet or his son Nicholas and was very likely brother to one of the two. His incumbency may have lasted to only 1372 when we find the Archbishop of York making a new presentment.

The first record we have of Nicholas is dated to 1486, though he surely inherited the manors earlier, probably in the reign of King Edward IV (1461-1483). Alive during the Wars of the Roses, he was a distant witness to the turbulence caused by 'bad' King Richard III's accession to the throne of England, and his subsequent overthrow by Henry Tudor at the Battle of Bosworth in 1485.

In 1486, he granted his son, Richard all his manors and rents throughout all the land that he owned, making provision for his son's succession. The grant would seem to have been premature as we know that Nicholas was still alive in 1500. This piece of information would seem to be at odds with the records relating to the Normanville family, the situation is very confused and I do not propose to speculate without further evidence.

During the reign of Henry VII, Nicholas can be found giving two messuages and all lands in Mapplewell, with certain free rents there to Richard Woodruffe, Ralph Snital and the chaplain, Edward Haigh, the document is dated 1495.

December 1st, (16 Henry VII) 1500
High Holand, Court of Nicholas Burdet, esq. Held there. Richard Oxle took a piece of land in Clayton, lying at le Whyte crosse and another piece lying at Clerkpyttes below le bank, both pieces in his tenure, for a term of twelve years from Martinmas last, paying 14d yearly at Whitsuntide and Martinmas by equal portions.

Nicholas married Elizabeth or Isabel Wentworth of West Bretton. She was the daughter of Richard Wentworth and his wife Cecilia. Richard Wentworth's will is dated to 1447, and his eldest son's (also named Richard Wentworth) will is dated to 1488. The Wentworths were a large and powerful land-owning family, one of their number, Sir Thomas Wentworth becoming the Earl of Strafford who was reluctantly beheaded by the King on the order of parliament in 1641. With lineage in Wentworth Woodhouse, Stainborough and Bretton amongst others, this families history is too expansive to be included here. Suffice to say, that throughout the generations many matches were made between the family and most of the other prominent local dynasties, including the Savilles and Burdets.

The couple must have had more offspring than we are aware of, though Richard, as the eldest son is the only name to survive today. As he must have been born around 1470, we may speculate that Nicholas must have been around twenty to twenty-five years old, which would make his, date of birth sometime around 1445.

In 1508, Nicholas made a quitclaim (a deed of release) to Richard Beaumont of Whitley with regard to land rights at Shepley, this was twenty-two years after he made his son legally possessed of all his manors. This is the last record we have of Nicholas, he died between 1508 and 1522 when we find his son acting alone. In 1508, Nicholas would have been around sixty-three years old, so his death probably occurred within the next decade.

Throughout these medieval centuries we have been able to see how many advantageous marriages were made by the Burdet family. For the purposes of this book I have tried to disentangle the Burdets from these as much as possible. The story would not only become too complicated but would also increase in size, so much so, as to become too large to publish. The fact is that, they were very involved with so many important local and in many cases, national, families who held large spheres of influence upon Yorkshire and England. To take them out of context leaves them relatively isolated which is why we cannot always understand the grants of land and rents of which only fragmentary documents survive. The Burdets still held some of their manors as of Brierley, though they had picked up other lands and rents over the years from other families, perhaps as dowries from the various marriages or agreements between neighbours. In the reign of Henry VI(1422-61 & 1470-71). William Harrington, Lord of Brierley, held knight's fees in Denby, Gunthwaite, Clayton, Penistone and other places, but the Burdets were known to be Lords of the Manor of Denby as of the right of Brierley. Right through until the time of the enclosure of the open fields the Gentry held parcels of land in many places besides their own manors. This can lead to great confusion when trying to chronologically tell the story of a village, as the reasons or documents for many changes of land ownership have been lost and the historian is faced with blanks which can only be filled with speculation. As with all landholding families, the Burdets would have been keen to increase their wealth and property at every opportunity, not to mention their social standing and political and economical influence.

King Henry VII's accession to the throne of England, not only signalled the end of the Wars of the Roses, but also gave rise to a new era of British history, the first Tudor King now sat on the throne of England and it is to this period that we will now turn.

Chapter Three
The Tudor and Stuart Burdets

RICHARD BURDET (II)

Richard was the eldest son of Nicholas and Elizabeth Burdet, he appears in a record of 1485 though his exact date of birth is at present unknown. As he died in 1546, he was at least sixty-one years old when he died, a very good age at this time, I would therefore speculate that his birth must have occurred somewhere around 1470 at the latest.

Descent of Richard Burdet who split the Manors of Denby and Hoyland

Richard Burdet c1470-1546 = Elizabeth Rockley

| Aymer = Maud Saville | Thomas = Isabel Wentworth | Roger | Phillip | Alice = George Woodruffe | Grace = George Farley (of Filey) | Isabel = ? Elland | Dorothy = ? Birkenhead (of Cheshire) | Elizabeth = ? Clayton (of Clayton) |

Henry = Elizabeth Jackson   Richard   Nicholas   John

A grant dated 6 February, 1486 has the following to say:

> *Grant with warrant, by Nicholas Burdett, esq., to Richard Burdett his son and heir apparent and hence to the legitimate heirs male of the said Richard of all his manors, tenements, rents, reversions, services etc. in the places named.*
> *Denby, Ingbirchworth, Smallshane, Bilcliffe, Barnby, Kerisforth, Barnsley, Mapplewell, Darton, Kexborough, Hoyland, Little Bretton, Clayton, Skelmanthorpe, Cumberworth, Bagden,*
> *The grantor appoints John and Arthur Burdett his attorneys.*
> **NB:** *It would seem likely that John and Arthur were Nicholas's brothers.*

Richard married Elizabeth Rockley sometime just before 1497, when the couple had their first child, Aymer (the third of the dynasty to be so christened), eight further children followed, three more sons and five daughters.

Elizabeth Rockley was the daughter of John Rockley of Worsborough and his wife, Elizabeth Meveral, the Rockley family having been the Lords of the Manor of Worsborough from at least the fourteenth century. They also held the Manor of Birthwaite, which appears to have been the dowry Elizabeth brought to her union with Richard. Her elder brother Thomas (1476-1517) was knighted in 1514 and her Aunt Jane had married William Bosville of Wortley, surely a member of the prosperous family that held the ownership of Gunthwaite.

As already mentioned, land was also regained via a document dated 12 May 1522 which has Robert Normanville, son of Ralph, granting the lands leased to them by Richard's Grandfather, Aymer II back to Richard, 'with all their, messages, rights and appurtenances'.

By this time, Richard had inherited his father's Lordship as set out in the earlier grant. Nicholas held a court at High Hoyland in 1500. (The document could even be suggestive in arguing that the original residence of these Lords of the Manor of Denby was actually at High Hoyland, though it could also be that Nicholas had retired to live there and left the Hall at Denby for his eldest son and his family, and we should not forget that courts were itinerant and could be held anywhere. We have already noted him as being alive in 1508 in the last chapter which is his last appearance in the records that I have seen to date which would seem to imply that he died shortly afterwards.

Thirteen years after the Normanvilles handed back their lands to Richard, who at this time would have been living in relative luxury and security, his eldest son was to be involved in a riot at Birthwaite. In the first edition of this book, I speculated as to the cause of this riot. It was the time of Henry VIII, who had, via a feud with Papal authority over his marriage to Anne Boleyn placed himself at the head of the Church of England and because of this had alienated many of his subjects. His increased power enabled him to bring about the dissolution of all the monasteries, thereby increasing his own wealth and causing further hardship and suffering to his subjects, as the monasteries were in many cases the only source of refuge for these people from famine or disease. He executed Sir Thomas More in 1535 and left Catholics fearing for their lives.

Although these were important considerations at this time, details have survived in the Yorkshire Star Chamber Proceedings, which explain the real events of 1535, and interestingly the testimony of Aymer himself still exists.

The Star Chamber, involved the Kings Council, sitting in a court of law in a room at Westminster, whose ceiling was decorated with stars, hence the name. Developed greatly by Cardinal Wolsey, by the mid-sixteenth century it consisted of the Privy Council and Chief Justices and dealt mainly with public disorder. Contrary to widespread belief, the use of torture was not applied.

To the King, our Sovereign Lord.
In full humble wise showeth and complyeth unto your Highness your faithful subject, Thomas Hungate, Gent. That whereon Rauffe Ellerker, Thomas Goyre esqs., Rauffe Hungate, Frances Frobisher, Wilfred Pigbourne and Alexander Castycforthe were seased of and in a messuage called Birthwaite Hall, and of (other) land, including pasture, meadow, and wood, with the appurtenances in Kyxforthe and Barton, in the County of York.

The lands were held by rent, from Roger Rockley of Worsborough and his heirs and had been since an indenture of 31 January 1534 had legally endowed Thomas Hungate with them. The term of the lease was ten years. The rent was paid twice yearly, at the feast of St. Michael the Archangel and at the feast of the Annunciation of Our Lady.
For an unknown reason, on the 27 April 1535:

*James Frankyshe, Gent., Robert Chaumber, John Coo, **AMORE BURDHED**, Thomas Ganaunt (Gaunt?), William Hurst, Thomas Denby, Wilfrid Smith, John Brown, Nicholas Denton, John Gledhill, clerk, William Pode, William Ellis and Richard Turton, with diverse other riotus persons to the number of 60, to your said oratore unknown, with force and armies, that is to say with bylees, bowes, arrows and staves, themselves assembled in riotus manor at Birthwaite Hall aforesaid, and then and there expelled out of the premises the tenant of your said subject, whereby his wife and children for great fear were put in jeopardy of their lives, and also the said riotus persons not herewith contented but of further malice hath put in beasts into the premises and destroyed the corn and grass of your said subject, to the most perilous example that hath been seen in that county, only condoning punishment with expidition may be had in that behalf. In consideration thereof it may therefore please your Highness the premises considered to grant your most gracious wyttes, of sub pena to be directed unto the said James Frankyshe, Robert Chaumber, and the other said misdemeaned persons, commanding them and every one of them by the same personally to appear before your Highness and your most honourable council in your Star Chamber at Westminster at a certain day and under a certain pain by your Highness to be limited.*
[signed : John Sutwell]

So, what do we have? Evidently Roger Rockley had granted the lands he believed were his at Birthwaite to Thomas Hungate, Rauffe Hungate and the others, interestingly there already appears to be a Hall here, some time before the present day construction was undertaken by Thomas Burdet (of which more later). The document takes great pains to explain in detail their rights on the land, and their payments for it. Had the document listed Aymer Burdet as the leader of the rioters one could have conjectured that the Rockleys and the Burdets were having a feud as to who owned the land and the rents to be gained from it, but as his name appears only third on the list, and only once, it renders this possibility open to error. It could be that James Frankyshe and Robert Chaumber had been evicted from their lands here, (initially granted to them by Richard Burdet) by Roger Rockley and that Richard had sent his eldest son and some of his tenants over to Birthwaite to put the matter right. If he did it certainly proves his confidence over his ownership and gives an idea of the strength and power he held over his manor, in as much that he could command at least sixty men. That the rioters sent such as cattle, sheep, and pigs into the Hall and destroyed all the corn and grass around the premises would seem to be construed as a rebuke for Roger Rockley and a message informing him that no money would be forthcoming to him from these tenants and properties.

Aymer Burdet's answer to the charge was as follows:

The said Aymer Burdet for answer saith that as to any force, riot, unlawful assembly or any other misbehaviour supposed by the said bill to be done by the said defendant against the King's peace that he thereof is not guilty nor of any part thereof and as to the residue of the contents of the said bill he saith that they are matters determinate at the Common Law and not at this honourable court, whereunto he praith that he may be remitted all such matters the said defendant is ready to verify and prove as this honourable court shall decide, and praith that he may be dismissed with costs and charges wrongfully sustained in this behalf.

Although Aymer has denied taking any part in the riot, he does not deny that there is a problem, presumably that of ownership of the land, but in his opinion it is a matter for the local court to decide. At thirty-eight years old, heir to his father's vast lands and estate, Aymer was a man in a position of power. Surely, he would have been well known to Thomas Hungate. Whether Aymer was involved in the riot, we shall probably never know for sure. He was bound to deny so serious a charge, but my own opinion is that he was there and took a very active roll in the devastation caused, I have no proof for this, just a gut feeling, particularly when his next act is considered.

It is possible that Richard Burdet, by 1535, had already lost his wife. His sons had reached manhood and his daughters a marriageable age. At some point during the period 1535-1536, for an unknown reason, his son and heir, Aymer accused him of treason.

Having already had a brush with the King's authority, and not just any King but Henry VIII, Aymer was back at the forefront of events.

I believe we must be back to my original hypothesis of religious division as regards this accusation. Richard, before the King's elevation to the head of the Church of England and his hatred of all things pertaining to the Papacy and Rome, was probably a Catholic. He may have been dismayed to hear of the King's high handed actions in flouting the authority of the Pope and horrified that not only had a break with Rome occurred but that the King was now supreme head of the English church. As a Catholic he would have had little chance to complain and little reason to as Catholics all over the country were being persecuted for their non-compliance in following their King, many to the point of death. The 'Pilgrimage of Grace', which protested against the latter, took place in 1536, led by Robert Aske. Trouble spread north from Lincolnshire and outright battle was only prevented by Royal pardons and promises of concessions.

In private, his thoughts were his own, but at some point, he must have committed an indiscretion, overheard by Aymer. Up to this point, Richard may have trusted Aymer and utilised him as a strong right arm, preparing him for the estates and titles that would come his way when he inherited, but from this point on, a persistent hatred must have befallen the two.

Aymer did not leave matters here; after accusing his father he made a public declaration of his accusation, which can only have widened the gulf appearing between father and son. It may have been that Aymer was an ambitious man, eager to inherit what would one day be rightfully his, and that he had designs to speed up the process. Was his accusation true? Did his father actually do more than utter treasonable words? Perhaps we should let the pardon he received from the King speak for itself - *'Pardon. Henry VIII to Richard Burdet of Denby Esq., alias Richard Burdet of Howlande Esq., for all offences and rebellions, insurrections, misprisons, etc'.* Richard Burdet promised himself and his dependants in the King's service at need in Lord Darcy's command. The document is dated 1 October 1536.

Records from the John Goodchild collection in Wakefield also connect Richard to a man called George Throckmorton. The document states that Throckmorton was interrogated for knowledge of treasonable conversations, and that during the questioning he mentioned his brother-in-law, Richard Burdet. There appears to have been some confusion in this document regarding which Burdet, Throckmorton was referring to.

The Throckmorton family lived at Coughton Court, Warwickshire. Sir George, who died in 1553 had seven sisters one of whom married into the Burdet family.

Thomas Burdet of Bramcote and Seckington, Co. Warwicks Esq., d.1540, married Mary, daughter of Sir Robert Throgmorton of Coughton, Warwick. This branch of the Burdet family eventually leads to the more famous Sir Francis Burdet of Ramsbury (a theme we will return to later). Sir George was a squire to King Henry VIII and was knighted around 1526, he later became a knight in the King's household at £10 per annum. Unfortunately, there is no connection with the family at Denby and when Sir George mentions his brother-in-law, he was in fact referring to Thomas Burdet and not Richard of Denby.

Not all the inhabitants of Denby were involved in such weighty matters, for instance, a detail has survived concerning a yeoman of Denby, William Marshall, dated to the time of Richard Burdet's lordship. Marshall received a payment of rent from William Blackburn of Huddersfield to the value of 5 shillings. He granted it to Richard and others who decided that it should be used for the Priest of the Chantry Chapel of St. John the Baptist in Penistone who would receive 4s 11d, leaving the one remaining penny to be paid to William Marshall and his heirs.

As Richard's life drew to a close his hatred of his son had not abated. Aymer was still in disgrace in his father's eyes and it was this hatred that caused Richard to split his manors of Denby and High Hoyland. Inherited by the eldest son for more than two hundred years a division in the family was about to be made. Richard decided that his second son, Thomas should inherit Denby and that Aymer would only receive High Hoyland.

Richard died in 1546, a year before the King, his administration was carried out a year later. He left: seventeen messuages (homes with outbuildings attached), 1200 acres of land, 550 of meadow, 4000 pasture, 1200 of wood, a water mill, two fulling mills and £9 10s rent.

AYMER and THOMAS BURDET and the LORDSHIP OF DENBY

A series of documents from diverse collections will enable us to make a little sense of the confusion that followed Richard's death and the conditions of his will.

13 October 1546 - Gift. *Thomas Burdhed of Denby Hall to Amery Burdhed of Birthwaite, Gents: - his manor of and all property and mills in Denby (reserving suit of the mills): and all his property in Penyston and Claiton, Skelmondthorp and Cawthorn, sometime hereditaments of Nicholas Burdhed, dec'd, Grandfather of Thomas and Amery Burdhed. Reserving to Thomas Burdet a meadow in Denby called Deffurth (or Desfurth), Fott, a tenement in Pennyston called Redwood and a tenement in Claiton. Power of attorney to Nicholas Saville, Gent. And William Turton to deliver seisin.*

NB: Deffurth means a 'deep ford' and the Deffurth referred to in the document is probably land near today's Deffer Wood).

1547 - Bond in £1000 by Thomas Burdhede of Denby Hall, Denby in respect of an undertaking by him to submit to the arbitration of Thomas Wentworth of West Bretton, Arthur Kay of Wodsom and Thomas Saville of Athersley Esqs., in a dispute of title between the aforesaid Thomas and Aymer Burdhede of Birthwaite over the estate of Richard Burdhede, Esq., late of Denby Hall, deceased.

16 August 1547 - Award by the a/m Thomas Wentworth, Arthur Kay and Thomas Saville concerning the differences between the two brothers, Thomas and Amer Burdhede over the estate of Richard Burdhede, Esq., late of Denby Hall, deceased, inherited by the said Richard from his father Nicholas Burdhede, deceased.

1550 - Indenture of a fine between Amer Burdhed, Esq., querent, and Thomas Burdhede, Gent. Deforc., concerning the manor of Denby and lands etc. in the places named: Denby, Clayton, Ingbirchworth, Cawthorne, Skelmanthorpe, Langsett, Carlecotes.
Consideration – 200 marks of silver.

It would seem that the two brothers were at odds over their father's will. A bond dated 12 August 1546 informs us that just after Richard Burdet's death, Aymer was living at Birthwaite and Thomas at Denby Hall. This, although in compliance to their father's wishes was a situation neither was happy with. Thomas much preferred Birthwaite and can be found here in 1541 (five years before the death of his father), he was probably responsible for the foundation of a new Hall.

To redeem the situation both brothers invoked the aid of both their fathers-in-law, Thomas had married Isabel Wentworth, daughter of Thomas Wentworth of West Bretton, and Aymer had married Maud, the daughter of Thomas Saville of Exley. They along with Arthur Kay decided that in order for Aymer to return to Denby he would have to pay his brother a thousand pounds, and Aymer was required to agree to this proposal before the next feast of St. Bartholomew. He agreed, though this may have caused further enmity between the two brothers, but by this award Aymer could now style himself, Lord of the Manor of Denby.

Aymer's domestic life by now included four children. He had been involved, (possibly) in ugly scenes at Birthwaite, which had invoked legal proceedings, he had accused his father of treason and so split the honourable family into two distinct branches. As a hard, confident and ruthless Lord of the Manor, his pedigree speaks for itself. By comparison, the rest of his life was almost incident free.

His religion, one would imagine, would probably have been Protestant. If we accept that his father was an unhappy Catholic during Henry VIII's reign and that the accusation of treason made against him by Aymer was religiously oriented, then Aymer must have supported the King. Of course, if this scenario is true then Aymer would have been in danger of being pursued on charges of heresy, the punishment for which was either a public burning or beheading, particularly during the reign of 'Bloody' Queen Mary (1553-1558). Alternatively, considering his relatively rural isolation and his desire to succeed, Aymer, probably diplomatically followed whichever religion circumstances dictated, depending on who he was talking to. The families survival under Queen Elizabeth I surely indicates their future religious persuasion, particularly when one considers their stance during the Civil War (considered later).

The following details have survived concerning his later fortunes:

Bosville Collection , Penistone, 2 May 1557 - Final concord of £40 : Godfrey Bosville, plaintiff and Amery Burdett, deforceant Esqs. : 60 ac. Pasture in Penyston.

As any wealthy local Lord, Aymer spent a reasonable amount of time in arguing about the ownership of local lands, here it would appear that he paid Godfrey Bosville £40 for certain lands at Penistone.

This must have been a fascinating case as the two parties involved were both strong men who would have been seen by the peasantry that farmed their lands as almost godlike.

> Wakefield Court Rolls 1550-1552 - *Holme: Ralph Handby by Thomas Calles, tenant and sworn, surrendered into the Lords hands three parts of one messuage called Chopperdes and three parts of all the lands and tenements pertaining to the same messuage with appurtenances to the use of Amery Burdhed and his heirs for ever. Agreed, entry fine 3s.*

> Wakefield Court Rolls, Wakefield 3 July 1551 - *Holme: Amery Burdhed, Gent., Present personally in this court, surrendered to the Lords hands a third part of one messuage called Chopperdes and a third part of all lands and tenements pertaining to the same messuage to the use of Nicholas Burdehed, son of the said Amery and his heirs for ever. Agreed, entry fine 6d.*

Within only a short period, Aymer had passed on the rights to this land, as can be seen from the above two entries in the Court Rolls to his third son, Nicholas. A further grant dated 20 January 1574 stated that Nicholas was also to receive rent to the amount of 46s issuing out of lands at Bagden under the tenement of Gilbert Wood, and that Henry Burdet (Aymer's son and heir) was to suffer this and not interfere.

His fourth son, John also purchased land from him in Denby in 1556/1557, a document from 1573 has also survived. Dated to only a year before Aymer's death, it appears he was trying to assure the security of his youngest son. An annual rent of 46s 8d was to be paid to John issuing from lands at Denby, Clayton, Ingbirchworth, Skelmanthorpe, Langsett, Penistone, Thurlstone and Barnby. The first payment of this annuity was not to be made until after the death of Aymer. From the evidence above, one would presume that Aymer endeavoured to make provision for his other son, Richard, as well. Henry, being his eldest son, was already heir to the manor, and perhaps, if he was anything like his father, Aymer was trying to ensure that before his own death, all of his sons would be financially secure, legally, before Henry could do anything about it.

The dates on these documents would seem to imply that Aymer had some idea about his imminent death. At the age of seventy-seven he was certainly no spring chicken, but if these documents were drawn up whilst he was well and active then it was certainly a coincidence that he died shortly afterwards. I would conjecture that he was at the time they were drawn up quite ill and was preparing for the end.

Aymer died in 1574, his administration is dated 19 March 1573. i.e.: 1574 in the modern calendar, his inquisition post mortem did not occur until 18 November 1575 to 17 November 1576. His departure made way for Henry Burdet to become Lord of the Manor of Denby.

Before we continue the descent of Henry we must first examine Thomas Burdet and his family who became the Lords of Birthwaite.

BURDET OF BIRTHWAITE

Thomas was born around the turn of the fifteenth century, the second son of Richard Burdet and Elizabeth Rockley. His advantageous marriage to Isabel Wentworth served him well during his dealings with his elder brother Aymer regarding his father's last wishes, due to Thomas Wentworth her father, being one of the triumvirate who sorted out the destination of the manors.

Previously the demesne of the Rockley family of Worsborough, the Manor of Birthwaite had come into the Burdet inheritance via Elizabeth Rockley, Thomas's mother. Probably responsible for the foundation or at least the rebuilding of a new hall, little has survived of Thomas's life. We do know that he and William Hawksworth, a yeoman of Gunthwaite were leased land by the Dean and College of Penistone and Birton in a document dated 17 November 1546. The rent was £53 per annum and the two were to pay the Vicar of Penistone £4 a quarter and maintain the Chapel of St. John the Baptist a little way distant from the town.

Thomas seems to have died around 1571, he outlived his wife by only three years, Isabel's will being dated to 1568. They had at least five children. Francis, first son and heir was born in 1548, and married Elizabeth, daughter of Robert Rockley of Worsborough. Indeed all these children made very advantageous marriages. His sister Frances married twice, first to Francis Wortley of the Wortley Lords, second to Francis Foljambe of Aldwark. Frances Burdet was Francis Wortley's second wife, the union seems to have produced at least two illegitimate children, Ambrose Burdet, alias Wortley, described as being of 'Grays Inn' and Samuel Burdet, alias Wortley of Swinton. At least one other son, George Wortley of Normanton, was legitimate, he went on to marry Mary, the daughter of Richard Bunny of Newland and had a son, Francis Wortley, born in 1614. Beatrix married Thomas Barnby of Barnby, near Cawthorne. Jane married Nicholas Saville and her sister Mary, married his brother Thomas. Already connected to Scottish Royal ancestry via the Balliols, the antiquarian, Joseph Hunter, recorded that inside Birthwaite Hall there were plasterwork coats of arms on the walls celebrating the families rich heritage and powerful dynastic links.

Descent of Burdet of Birthwaite

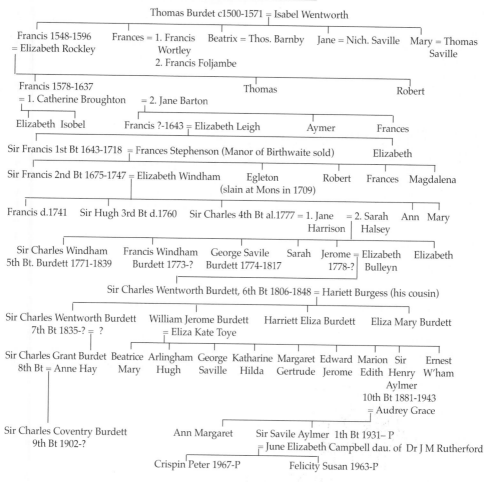

All the heirs to the manor of Birthwaite were named Francis. The first Francis, noted above died in 1596 aged forty-eight, but a gradual decline befell the family from now on. Francis II (died 1637) preceded Francis III (died 1643). This Francis accrued debts of £1775 during his lifetime and also gave his personal estate and the profits of his lands to his Uncle, Robert Rockley. Clearly the Rockleys were keeping a close eye on events at Birthwaite and endeavouring to help this younger branch of their family. Francis IV, not only inherited these debts but also added to them. He was said to have been a 'profligate man' and had borrowed as much as £4000 from his neighbour and kinsman Thomas Wentworth before 1675. His costs were not helped by his social and family life having had a large brood of illegitimate children by a woman called Ann Watkins, whom he may have married after the death of his wife. He sold off his large estates, piece by piece, during the course of his life, Hoyland, with lands at Dykeside and Kexborough went to Sir Mathew Wentworth to help pay back the money he owed to him. In 1665, he was created a Baronet but by the time he died in about 1718 aged eighty, the Burdets of Birthwaite were no more. The Hall was taken over by John Sylvester, who was succeeded by his nephew, Edward. According to Hunter, Sylvester was smith to the Tower of London and is said to have made a long chain across the Thames to prevent the Dutch fleet from sailing up the river. He became a very rich man and he and his nephew built much of the present day fabric of the Hall during the eighteenth century.

The Birthwaite Baronets did not cease to exist just because they had sold their manors. Debrett's *Illustrated Baronage* notes that the eleventh Baronet, Sir Savile Aylmer Burdett was born in 1931 and married June Elizabeth Campbell. The couple had two children, Crispin Peter, born in 1967 and Felicity Susan born in 1963. The Burdetts of Birthwaite, cousins of the Denby Burdetts live on through these people.

HENRY BURDET AND THE DESCENT OF THE MANOR

During his father's final weeks, we know that Henry had been forced to endure the lands, rents and entitlements, due to him as his father's heir, being in part packaged off to his younger brothers, Nicholas, Richard and John. His reaction to this is unknown, but his father had taken care that he was powerless to change these deeds. When his father died, Henry was required to make the same payment as his father for his estates at Denby, to Francis Burdet of Birthwaite. A bond dated 14 April 1575 confirms the payment of £1000. This was a huge sum of money and must have had a crippling effect on the family finances. Henry's date of birth is unknown, he was certainly alive in 1584, when he was listed in a document which names the principal freeholders within the Staincross area, (I have modernised the Latin names):

Principle Freeholders within the Staincross Area 1584
George Woodruffe of Wooley, Gervase Neville of Chevet, Radulphus Wortley of Wortley, Francis Bosville of Gunthwaite, William Rockley of Worsborough, Mathew Wentworth of West Bretton, Thomas Barnby of Barnby, Henry Burdet of Denby, Francis Burdet of Birthwaite, Thomas Savile of Tankersley, Nicholas Bird (Birdet?) of Swawell, John Popelay of Morehouse, Anthony Woodrove of Wooley, Roger Castleford of Worsborough Dale, Roger Arthington of Lanes, John Clayton of Clayton Hall, Thomas Kerresforth of Kerresforth, John Moxon of Hoylandswaine.

This gives us a splendid indication of Henry's eminent contemporaries, some of whom were also relations, some more distant than others.

The list above was recorded just three years prior to the expected Spanish invasion of England in 1587. Believing that the invasion would occur in December a Council of War was held in November where it was decided that all private gentlemen with a certain yearly income must take up arms and armour and do their duty, or find another man to take their place. Also, each township, would, according to its rateable value, pay and equip a number of soldiers. The fear of an invasion was very real and a sense of panic would have been felt in Denby but although an army of 130,000 men answered the call, they were soon able to breathe more easily when it turned out to be a false alarm. Santa Cruz died on the point of sail from Spain and the invasion was delayed for six months. As we all know, his replacement, Medina Sidonia, met with Francis Drake, Frobisher, Effingham and Hawkins who between them engineered the destruction of the armada in 1588, thereby ending the possibility of invasion enabling the volunteers to stand down.

Denby supplied six men for the cause:

Private Men: Thomas Jenkynson (pikeman) and his man Richard Willmson, John Mitchell (pikeman)

Town Soldiers: Raufe Clayton (archer), Richard Owdom (caliver), Laurence Hawksworth (caliver)
  NB: *a caliver was a kind of light musket.*

The muster took place in Barnsley on 4 December 1587 under the command of Richard Wortley and George Woodruff. The muster comprised seventy-one gentlemen and seventy town soldiers.

Why was Henry not involved? Perhaps he bought his way out, he was certainly rich enough, but if one conjectures that Aymer had probably married Maud Saville around 1525 and that Henry had been born reasonably soon afterwards then he was probably too old to be called up, being around fifty-five to sixty years old. We do know that he married Elizabeth Jackson, the daughter of Henry Jackson of London and that he had nine children, the son and heir, Richard, followed by Ralph, Henry and six daughters (see chart overleaf). Using the same hypothesis as above, if Henry was born around 1530, then his marriage and subsequent family must have begun during the 1550s.

Joseph Hunter also attributed a child by the name of Bartholomew as a son of Henry and Elizabeth, but although he got the father right, he made a mistake regarding the mother!

Archbishop Grindel's Visitation 1575

Henry Burdet, Gent., keepeth and harboureth in his house one Dowsabell Casson who being never married, hath had and brought forth a child and now is suspected to be with child again.

Henry's mistress lived with him at Denby Hall, seemingly alongside his legitimate family and more remarkably, his wife! However, on further examination a more plausible excuse can be found.

It would seem that the infant child who gave such offence to the Archbishop was Bartholomew. Henry's legitimate heir, Richard would have been around twenty years old and the other eight children progressively younger, if this was the case, then Bartholomew was born after the youngest of Henry and Elizabeth's children. Surely then, the explanation is simple, Elizabeth was dead and Henry had taken a mistress, who not only shared his bed but helped keep his house and look after the younger children. Perhaps his wife had died giving birth to either the last daughter, Susan or even a tenth unnamed child that died with its mother.

Dowsabell must have been much younger than Henry, perhaps attracted to him by his wealth and power, this is proved in the fact that she bore him a further eight illegitimate children, though why Henry never married her is unknown. He was certainly embarrassed when the Archbishop found out his guilty little secret as the records show that he tried to remove the responsibility onto one John Sydell of Bosom's Inn, London. Henry's connections with London were probably stronger than one would at first think. He must certainly have been here either when he met or when he married Elizabeth, and from this, one would presume that, infrequently or not, journeys south must have ensued for her to keep in touch with her parents. Perhaps Henry became acquainted with Dowsabell in London and Sydell was an old flame. Either way he was probably too far removed from the events at Denby to contradict. It could also be that Henry did not marry Dowsabell because she was of a much lower class than he.

Henry's legitimate family

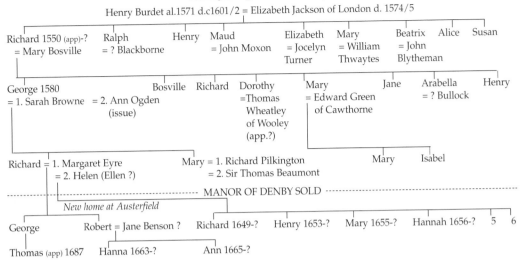

Henry Burdet al.1571 d.c1601/2 = Elizabeth Jackson of London d. 1574/5

Richard 1550 (app)-? = Mary Bosville | Ralph = ? Blackborne | Henry | Maud = John Moxon | Elizabeth = Jocelyn Turner | Mary = William Thwaytes | Beatrix = John Blytheman | Alice | Susan

George 1580 = 1. Sarah Browne = 2. Ann Ogden (issue) | Bosville | Richard | Dorothy = Thomas Wheatley of Wooley (app.?) | Mary = Edward Green of Cawthorne | Jane | Arabella = ? Bullock | Henry

Richard = 1. Margaret Eyre = 2. Helen (Ellen ?) | Mary = 1. Richard Pilkington = 2. Sir Thomas Beaumont | Mary | Isabel

-------- MANOR OF DENBY SOLD --------

New home at Austerfield

George | Robert = Jane Benson ? | Richard 1649-? | Henry 1653-? | Mary 1655-? | Hannah 1656-? | 5 | 6

Thomas (app) 1687 | Hanna 1663-? | Ann 1665-?

Henry's illegitimate family

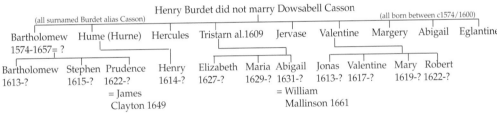

Henry Burdet did not marry Dowsabell Casson

(all surnamed Burdet alias Casson)   (all born between c1574/1600)

Bartholomew 1574-1657= ? | Hume (Hurne) | Hercules | Tristarn al.1609 | Jervase | Valentine | Margery | Abigail | Eglantine

Bartholomew 1613-? | Stephen 1615-? | Prudence 1622-? = James Clayton 1649 | Henry 1614-? | Elizabeth 1627-? | Maria 1629-? | Abigail 1631-? = William Mallinson 1661 | Jonas 1613-? | Valentine 1617-? | Mary 1619-? | Robert 1622-?

As Dowsabell was pregnant again in 1575, presumably with Hume (or Hurne), then allowing for breathing time, most of this base born brood must have been alive by the early 1590s, Henry would have only seen some of these children reach their teens before he died, and he must have been in his mid to late sixties at best when the last was born.

Two documents have survived which give a brief glimpse into the world Henry inhabited and the lands that he held:

1573/4 - Claiton, Co. York. Parcel of the lands and possessions of the Duchy of Lancaster within the honour of Pount'. 2½ carucates of land, late belonging to Nicholas Burdhead and afterwards to Amarius Burdhead, and now to Henry Burdhead, held of the Queen as of her duchy of Lancaster by knight service and a yearly rent of 2s. at Pountfrett Castle.

1 October 1585 - Bond in 200 marks by John Moore of North Leverton, Co. Notts. To Henry Burdett of Denby Hall in the parish of Penniston, Esq., for the performance of covenants contained a pair of indentures dated the same day, being a Bargain and Sale by the said John Moore of his lands and tenements in Ingburchworthe and Thurleston Meare.

A further document, this dated 1592 records that Henry had to pay 57s 4d out of his rents to the vicars of Silkstone for the upkeep and repairs to Silkstone Church. As the above document is dated 1592 it can only have been after this that Henry abandoned Denby and the Hall to his heir, Richard and set up home at Walton, near Wakefield. I would suggest that he waited until his eldest son was old enough and able enough to assume the responsibilities that Henry would pass to him and that when he had reached his mid thirties Henry felt confident enough to take his leave. Presumably, he took his illegitimate family and his mistress with him (all given the surname Burdet alias Casson) as records later show that at least Bartholomew and Tristarn were to remain in this area throughout their lives.

Although Henry could not settle his Lordship on these children, in his will made 19 February 1601/2 he made no mention of his lawful kin but left everything to the seven sons and two daughters born to him by Dowsabell. Perhaps his legal family had seen fit to snub him, for desecrating their mother's memory or for embarrassing them with his illegitimate family, or perhaps they saw Dowsabell as a harlot and a schemer who held their father under her influence. It could also be argued that as Henry's legitimate family were by now fully grown and able to fend for themselves (or sponge off his son Richard's generosity), he felt obliged to make ample provision for Dowsabell and his younger offspring who would probably need every penny they could get.

As for the illegitimate children, I have only brief details. Bartholomew settled at Walton and became so rich, probably due to his father's will, that he had to pay to avoid a knighthood from Charles I in the 1630s, due to the expense that it would have caused him. He had at least three children, Bartholomew, Stephen and Prudence all baptised at Featherstone. Bartholomew died at Walton in 1657 aged eighty-three.

Tristarn Burdet is recorded in the Wakefield Court Rolls on the 29 April 1609. He would have been in his mid thirties when the following entry was made: *'Sandal: The township sworn presented that Tristram Burdet (5s) made affray and drew the blood of Thomas Preston'*.

Tristan also had a family of at least three, Elizabeth, Maria and Abigail, all these were baptised at Saint Peter's, Huddersfield. Hume had a son, Henry, baptised at Thornhill, near Dewsbury in 1614. The family certainly continued to live here, in 1664 we find that a John Burdet had a son, christened Robert. Perhaps this John was the son of Henry and Grandson of Hume. It is also possible that his Grandfather was Valentine, whose sons, Jonas and Robert were baptised at Thornhill in 1613 and 1622 respectively. Evidently Valentine had left the village in between times and lived at Normanton where we can find baptismal records of two more children, Valentine born in 1617 and Mary born in 1619. As for the rest, I am reliably informed that most of them can be traced to good careers in later records.

Henry Burdet himself had died by 22 April 1602 when his will was proved, he was probably buried at Sandal, Wakefield. Although in possession of Denby Hall and the Lordship here and at least some of the other manors subject to it, it was only now that Richard Burdet could at last officially style himself Lord of the Manor of Denby, in the same way that his Grandfather, the renowned Aymer would have done.

RICHARD BURDET (III)

Probably born during the 1550s, Richard must have been around fifty years old when he inherited Denby from his father. Little of his early life is known but we do know that he married Mary Bosville and so united two of the most prominent and influential families in the area.

Up until 1460 the Bosville estates at Gunthwaite had been leased and re-leased to various tenants but around this time the manor settled upon a younger branch of the family. It was John Bosville of Newhall and Ardsley who became Lord of Gunthwaite.

Godfrey I, the great, great grandson of John, was the first member of the family to patronise the Gunthwaite estates, although in his will he styles himself as of Beighton. He was born in 1519 and died in 1580 and in that time raised the stature of Gunthwaite significantly. In 1550 he was involved in a lawsuit regarding his lands in the parish with William Turton, Ottiwel Marsden and John Burdet (probably the youngest brother of Henry Burdet) and as we have already seen he was involved in a dispute over land entitlement with Aymer Burdet in 1557. Indeed, this first Godfrey Bosville not only spent more time than his predecessors at Gunthwaite but also more time in the law courts, disputing rights of way, land boundaries and ownership, for example:

A bill was exhibited in the Court of the Lord President of the North by William Turton, John Claiton and Edward Woodcock of Denby, complaining that Godfrey had used his power to stop a footpath from Denby to Penistone, where their parish church was and also another one which led to Thurlstone. The petitioners alleged that they were only poor men and that he was 'a man of great mastership and friendship' and asked for redress. A document of 1566 details some of the lands and boundaries in dispute - a boundary from Crawhill in Gunthwaite was the dividing line for lands at Denby, held by Richard Marshall at a place called 'Butcroft'. Others mentioned are 'Longgrene' to 'Southcroft' at Denby held by John Jenkynson and lands, which abutted Denby, held by farmers in the employ of Godfrey Bosville such as Thomas Bower and the Hawksworth family. It seems that Godfrey was possessive of his lands, perhaps as a result of the years of neglect by his ancestors, which may have led to local inhabitants utilising his land for their own ends.

He bought the manor of Oxspring and was granted by his brother the rectory, manor and advowson of Penistone Church. He was also responsible for the construction of the present barn at Gunthwaite Hall (though the original Hall has long since gone). The barn, today considered by most to be the finest example of its type in the district was built around the middle of the sixteenth century and it is reputed that a boy served his entire apprenticeship making all the wooden pegs which held the beams together.

The barn is immense, having 7100 square feet of floor space and its distinctive black and white timber and plasterwork above the nine feet high walls still conjures up an imaginary picture of the area 400 years ago. It was claimed that a wagon and six oxen could turn round inside it.

Godfrey may also have been responsible for flagging the old pack horse route which led down from the Hall to the mill dam. The raised causeway would enable animals to use the road in extreme

The sixteenth century timbered barn at Gunthwaite. 1996. *Author's collection.*

Interior and exterior views of Gunthwaite barn in 1950. *Author's collection*

Example of a boundary marker stone between Denby and Gunthwaite still in its original situation. 1996. *Author's collection*

weather conditions even when the sunken road at the side was impassable. He would have needed easy access to the mill throughout the year and the path would appear to date from this time.

Godfrey had also made a very advantageous marriage, to Jane Hardwick, the sister of the famous Bess of Hardwick, Countess of Shrewsbury. The Earl of Shrewsbury had been put in charge of Mary Queen of Scots. But whilst a prisoner in Sheffield Castle suspicions were formed by Elizabeth I and her advisers that the Earl may be a secret sympathiser. Orders were issued for certain papers in the possession of the Shrewsbury family to be seized. A Miss Bosville who was one of Bess of Hardwick's maids managed to convey the documents to her sister, Jane at Gunthwaite, where they were stored for some time. Nothing else was heard of them. It would seem that Queen Mary was writing letters to the Duke of Norfolk. Many years later the fourth Godfrey Bosville (the family historian 1717-84), had amassed a huge collection of documents and on instructions he was later to regret ordered many of them to be destroyed. It seems likely that the papers were included in this clear out.

Godfrey's wife preceded him to the grave and his only son, Francis succeeded on his death in 1580. Francis died when he was only approximately thirty years old (by 1596) without an heir and it was on the son of his Uncle Ralph that the estates became settled. Francis' sister, Mary, along with her other sisters became his co-heir and her marriage to Richard Burdet of Denby sometime around 1580 not only unified the two powerful families but also increased their wide ranging influence on the lands around them. It was the four husbands of the sisters of Francis Bosville who inherited the right of presentation of the vicar at Penistone Church.

The Bosville Family & Burdet Union

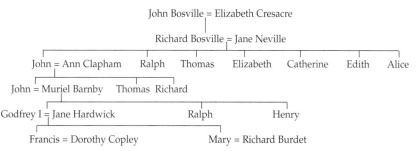

Richard Burdet and Mary Bosville were probably married around the time of the first Godfrey's death. Without the exact date it is impossible to deduce whether he was a barrier to the union of the families. His old adversary, Aymer Burdet had been in his grave for six years, yet the court battles over lands and rights may have led to more than a little friction between the neighbouring Lords. Their family certainly prospered and thrived, a son and heir, George was born in 1580 to be followed by two more boys and four girls.

The two distinct branches of the Burdet family were now multiplying and very prosperous, but they weren't isolated from each other as the following document shows:

7 March 1607 - Gift in fee simple by Francis Burdet of Birthwayt, esq., to Richard Burdet of Denbyie Hall, esq., and George Burdet his son and heir apparent of those several parcels of common known as 'Cliffe' or 'Harcliffe' within the lordships or townships of Cumberworth and Denbie, with all appurtenances and rights etc. (Hartcliffe was on the north, west or Cumberworth side of Denby Dale, its opposite, Munchcliffe was on the South or Denby side, around the area of Toby Wood.)

Richard also took a hand in witnessing an agreement between Francis Bosville of Gunthwaite Hall and John Hawksworth of Broad Oak regarding an exchange of land in Hoylandswaine dated 8 May 1575. Francis was his brother-in-law, the son of the first Godfrey at Gunthwaite. He inherited the manor and hall in 1580, but was dead by 1596.

As Richard did not inherit from his father Henry until 1602, it would seem that he held the manor for only a short time, at least officially. Although his tenure at the Hall may have begun around the late 1580s, he may only have run the manor on behalf of his father. His will made in 1616 would seem to indicate a date of death somewhere around 1616/17, aged approximately in his mid sixties. He left his son George with not only all that he possessed but also new ingredients, such as the right of presentment of the vicar of Penistone gained as a result of his union with a daughter of the Bosvilles of Gunthwaite. We will see more of this later in the chapter concerning Religion and Worship.

We now approach a very confused and complicated period in the history of Denby. Although many documents still exist for the period between 1617 and 1700 a good number have also been lost. Unfortunately, some of those missing are very important indeed.

GEORGE BURDET

Born in 1580 it would seem that at the time of his father's death, and his inheritance of the Manor of Denby, George was around thirty-seven years old. He married Sarah Browne, the daughter of Edward Browne of Creswick sometime just prior to 1610, when his first and seemingly only son and heir Richard, was born. Sarah also bore George a daughter, Mary, who through two very advantageous marriages became a Dame. Her first husband was Richard Pilkington, her second was Sir Thomas Beaumont. Dame Mary Beaumont made a gift of a bell to Denby chapel in 1678 and a silver chalice to Penistone church dated 1673. Both gifts were inscribed and recorded her as the daughter of George Burdet of Denby Hall, she died in 1682 and was buried at Wooley. It would seem highly likely that Sarah died before approximately 1618, as this was when George took his second wife. He was licensed on 26 January 1618/19 to marry Ann Ogden of Worsborough at Penistone or Worsborough. A document, which has survived, dated 1620/21 records George Burdett Esq., transferring lands at Denby to Edmund Ogden, Gent., probably either Ann's father or brother. Ann gave birth to two more daughters, one of which, Elizabeth, married the Revd. Daniel Clarke, the curate of Denby's Chapel of Ease. The other Ann married William Ramsden of Longley but this daughter may actually have sprung from George's first marriage, as her daughter, was christened Browne Ramsden.

George was certainly no stranger to the law courts, particularly when it involved rights of land and territories which he was very sure belonged to him. In the time of King James I (1603-1625), the Burdet claim to their manorial rights at Clayton was disputed. Barten Allott, Richard Clayton, Nicholas Hawksworth and Ralph Clayton opposed George Burdet and were able to air their grievances. In 1618, another suit was made against George, this time by the inhabitants of Denby, comprising:

George Hurst	(Dighton, yeoman)
John West	(Denby, yeoman)
John Blagburn	(Denby, son and heir of Robert dec'd, and John Micklethwaite)
Thomas Clayton	(Clayton, tanner)
Thomas Haugh	(Over Bagden, Denby)
John Shaw	(Bargh, clothier)

The suit concerns property rights claimed at Denby, which were purportedly given to the claimants by William de Denby, via John the son of Adam de Denby and Adam son of William de Denby, the priest of Cumberworth (see earlier). The parties did not agree that George was a Lord of the Manor in the same sense as William de Denby and argued that they were not prepared to do suit at his court.

We have many details concerning further grants of lands and suchlike, all are worth noting though for the purposes of space I shall edit them to just the essential details:

1. *7 April 1612 - Richard Burdet and his son George Burdet of Denby Hall agree to acquit John Hawksworth of Denby, Yeoman, for the sum of £13, of all his arrears of rents and services due to them for land in Denby called 'Netheroodes' alias 'Roods'.*

2. *27 August 1617 - Richard and George Burdet grant for the sum of £6 13s 4d to John Micklethwaite of Ingbirchworth and William Shirt of Cawthorne the wardship and marriage of the son and heir of John Hawksworth, Richard and his brothers, Josias and Jonas until they attain the age of 21.*

3. *27 August 1617 - Richard and George Burdet granted lands at Denby called 'Netheroydes' or the 'Roydes' to Elias Micklethwaite, John Micklethwaite and Richard Hawksworth. These men were to pay suit to the court of the manor of Denby.*

4. *Grant, for a consideration of £36 to George Burdet by Thomas Burdet of an annual rent of 46s 8d payable out of the manor of Denby and other lands at Clayton, Ingbirchworth Skelmanthorpe, Langsett, Thurlstone, Penistone and Barnby, award dated 22 April 1620*

5. *24 September 1620 - Rents recvd. By George Burdet, yearly:*

William Clayton	*9d*	*(land at Bagden in Over Denby)*
Henry Haigh	*1d*	*(land at Nether Denby)*
Robert Smyth	*2d*	*(land in Denby called Springhouse)*
John Mosley	*1d*	*(land at Over Denby)*

6. *29 May 1622 - Robert Rockley, John Kaye, Francis Burdet (of Birthwaite Hall) and Robert Snawsell were arbiters in a dispute between George Burdet of Denby Hall and Godfrey Bosville of Gunthwaite regarding land known as: Long Greene, Ould Field alias Swifte Farm, Boothes Farm, Crowell Hill alias Colman Cliffe, Fearnehill Leiz, Pighells, and Hunger Hill all lying between the two manors.*

7. *1 October 1623 - George Burdet leased for life to Brian Robinson of Denby, husbandman and Joan his Wife a cottage built on Denby Common with waste ground at annual rent of 12d.*

8. *1 March 1625 - George Burdet granted to Thomas Wainewright of Denby Milne in Denby, collier and Elizabeth his wife and their heirs a cottage lately built at great cost by Thomas on Denby Common with a garden and parcel of ground (lately enclosed from the common by consent of the freeholders) at an annual free rent of 5s 2d.*

9. *Lease for 21 years for a consideration of £20 by George Burdet of Denby Hall to John Burdett of Denby, Gent., part of a messuage situated in the East part of 'Trister' Close, with buildings etc. lying within the demesne of Denby Hall, at an annual rent of 28s, dated ,20 January 1627.*

10. *Lease for 41 years of a water mill called Denby milne and a cottage and grounds by George Burdett of Denby Hall to John Suydall of Denby Milne, milner, at an annual rent of 13s 4d, dated 1 February 1627.*

11. *Lease for 21 years by George Burdett to Richard Brooke of Hollinghouse in Clayton, tanner, of the east part of a close called 'trister' in Denby Hall at a rent of 10s, dated 1st June 1627.*

One of the old barns at Denby Hall Farm dating to approximately the sevententh century. *Author's collection*

And so the list goes on, other documents refer to an inquisition held at Barnsley into the death of Thomas Copley late of Emsley who had held lands in Clayton of George, in 1630. An order of the Queen's council also survives whereby George brought an action of trespass against Francis Oglethorpe in 1636 with regard to land rights and an assignment for a consideration of £20 to Joan Marshall of Over Denby, a widow, allowing her the wardship and marriage of her son Richard Marshall and custody of a messuage and lands in Over Denby previously held by her deceased husband Robert in 1636.

It would be interesting to speculate about the whereabouts of the original Denby Hall at this point. Firstly, it must be stated that at present the original Hall's whereabouts are unknown. We have already noted that Nicholas Burdet was holding court at High Hoyland in 1500, though this for reasons already stated may be a blind.

We should firstly establish the various different names given to the local villages throughout the centuries – Upper Denby was known as Overdeneby in 1261, Over Denbe in 1564, Over Denby in 1573 and High Denby in 1822; Lower Denby was known as Netherdeneby in 1261, Neyther Denbye in 1573, Low Denby in 1822. Nether Denby is now actually called Nether End.

From one of the latter documents we find that Bagden is classed as Over Denby which is heading in completely the wrong direction towards Clayton. This must have been an error as a part of Bagden was also known as Over Bagden. Incidentally, Bagden means badger valley. Denby Milne must have been situated on the banks of the Dearne, down in the valley of what is today Denby Dale, the mill which was there needed water for power and so we can surmise that the only possible source was the river in the valley floor. Finally, we come to Denby Common. Today situated in lands between Upper Denby and Ingbirchworth, the boundaries of this area seemed to have changed very little throughout the centuries. Where then does this leave the Hall?

Our first piece of vital evidence pertaining to the location of the Hall is the name of 'Trister Close'.

This piece of land, which evidently contained at least one building is expressly clarified as being a part of Denby Hall. The document above which refers to Richard Brooke of Clayton paying rent for lands in 'Trister' close would suggest that perhaps the Hall stood closer to Clayton and High Hoyland than to the centre of today's Denby, which would argue a good case for the present Denby Hall Farm laying a claim to be built on the site of a much more ancient structure. What seems to be very obvious is that the centre of the manor of Denby was sited not as today, where we have Upper and Lower Denby, but around the Nether Denby, Deffer Wood, Bagden area, central to not only Denby but High Hoyland as well. Estates such as Denby Common and Denby Milne were very much on the edge of the manor.

Standing a little away from the modern road, many of the present buildings at Denby Hall Farm can be dated to the seventeenth century. The large barn is dated 1698 and was originally living accommodation. A George Burdett was seemingly responsible for its construction around 1632 and as George Burdet of Denby Hall would have only been fifty-two at this point he would certainly fit the bill of a man with the finance and drive to achieve this aim. Before we examine this more closely, we must first return to the events of George and his son, Richard's lives.

George's date of death is currently unknown, though we do know that his son and heir, Richard was born in 1610 and that he married Margaret Eyre, the daughter of Gervase Eyre of Rampton. He appears to have had a son, George and maybe another, Robert, whilst living at Denby, one would presume that these two were born around the late 1630s. By 1648, Richard had moved to Austerfield, south east of Doncaster, and had re-married, this time to a widow called Helen (Ellen), who bore him more children. Richard in 1649, Henry in 1653, Mary in 1655, Hanna in 1658 and two others. A Robert Burdet also appears in Austerfield records as having married Jane Benson in 1662, two of their children are also noted, Hanna, born 1663, and Ann in 1665. This may be the man born to Richard and Margaret at Denby, who would have left for Austerfield with his father on the sale of the manor. Richard's will was dated 1661, though it would appear that he lived for another five years before passing away in 1666. Why did he leave Denby? In addition, what happened to George, his father? Purely through a lack of evidence, the correct sequence of events and their causes can at present remain almost totally speculative. What is certain is that in 1643, the manor of Denby was in the hands of the Savile family of Thornhill. Hunter has the following to say:

> *For £1500 and certain lands in the Level near Finningley he (Richard) assigned Denby Hall and all his estate thereabout to the Savile's of Thornhill. The manor of Denby is in the inquisition of Sir William Savile, bart, in 1643.*

William Savile was the third Baronet, born in 1613 he inherited from his brother at the age of fourteen. After his father's death he became the ward of his Uncle, Sir Thomas Wentworth, who became the Earl of Strafford and was beheaded at the bequest of parliament in 1641. Sir William was very much a King's man, and being a nephew of the executed Strafford, he was expelled from parliament in 1642. At the beginning of the first Civil War, he was with the King at Nottingham when the standard was raised. He became Governor of Sheffield and later York, but he died in 1644 aged just thirty-one. This then was the man to whom the manor of Denby was sold, why was it sold, and who sold it?

Hunter believed that it was Richard Burdet, George's son that was responsible. If this is the case then George must have died before around 1642, he was certainly alive in 1636, when he would have been around fifty-six years old. Hunter may have had access to documents not now in existence, but there is no other proof that it was the second Richard. The first Richard Burdet's death in 1616/17 occurs only just prior to his son, George becoming involved in legal activities trying to justify his claims as to being Lord of the Manor. It is possible that Hunter ascribed the sale of the Manor to the wrong Richard, this would explain George's difficulties in trying to play a roll that he was not now entitled to. We have already seen the amount of money that had to be paid to their Birthwaite cousins for the manor of Denby and it may have been that it had become financially impossible to continue with this. The family fortunes had also been seriously weakened when Henry Burdet had bequeathed all his wealth to his illegitimate children. All we can be sure of is that the manor was sold between 1617 and 1643. It would seem unlikely that George ever left Denby as documents attest to his activities here up until the late 1630s. The second Richard, may have moved to Austerfield for reasons of his own, though it must be said that the sale of Denby also included the Burdets acquiring lands at Austerfield. The logical solution as to why Richard moved away would be that he did indeed sell the manor and went to live on his new lands. Perhaps when he inherited from George the family fortunes had reached a very low ebb and he could not afford the payment to Birthwaite. George had spent time in the law courts, as we have seen, the locals fighting against paying suit at his court. George had styled himself an old fashioned Lord of the Manor and wanted to be such. It is not impossible that he squandered the families finances on doing this and it would also appear that he either built or re-built Denby Hall Farm in 1632 which would also have cost a great deal of money. George's relationship with Francis Burdett of Birthwaite would also appear to have been somewhat acrimonious. When Francis was knighted in the early part of the seventeenth century, George refused to attend parliament to act as a witness. There may have been extenuating circumstances

Sir William Savile 3rd Baronet, of Thornhill, the man to whom the Manor of Denby was sold, sometime prior to 1643. *By kind permission of the Savile estate.*

but, considering the latter it is very possible they fell out about payments for the Denby manor. The Denby branch of the family had, from the time of Aymer Burdet, been losing ground to their cousins at Birthwaite. The crippling costs of keeping their manor must surely have been the reason for its ultimate sale.

CIVIL WAR

The death in 1625 of King James I (two years before the construction of the Chapel of Ease in Denby, considered later) brought his son Charles I to the throne. One of the most turbulent periods in English history was less than twenty years away. When at length parliament declared war on the King, the country was thrown into chaos. As we have already seen, William Savile declared for the King. Godfrey Bosville, Lord of Gunthwaite, grandson of Ralph Bosville though he had abandoned Gunthwaite as a residence and was living at Wroxall in Warwick, where he became an MP, declared for parliament. He had married Margaret Greville, which meant that one of his brothers-in-law was Arthur Haselrig. In January, 1642, the King had attempted to arrest five MPs at the Houses of Parliament, namely, John Pym, John Hampden, Denzil Holles (the speaker), William Strode and Arthur Haselrig – Godfrey's brother-in-law. For those of you wondering, Oliver Cromwell was not involved in this action as

Colonel Godfrey Bosville at the time of the Civil Wars. *W H Senior.*

depicted in the film, 'Cromwell' starring Richard Harris. Do not believe everything Hollywood has to say! Although these men fled and escaped , they returned triumphantly once the King had abandoned the capital. Godfrey was named as one of the Deputy Lieutenants for Warwickshire on the 'Roundhead' side.

Being a large landholder, he was reputedly able to raise an army of 1000 strong and the story goes that not one of these men was less than six feet in height; propaganda perhaps! However, they could have been known as the Yorkshire regiment the 'Havercake Lads'. Godfrey took to praying and became chaplain to his men. During the Civil War a regiment of 'Roundhead' soldiers were stationed at Gunthwaite, probably housed in the then newly built barn. Whilst there, many were infected with typhoid fever and died, it is believed that they were buried in a mass grave by the giant oak at Gunthwaite Hall, possibly a true story, the ancient oak still survives to this day, although somewhat the worse for wear, it is distinguishable from its great girth, knarled and knotted appearance and the singular lack of sustainable new growth.

It is difficult to follow the movements of all the individuals active in our area but the following should give a brief insight into movements local to Denby.

The Earl of Newcastle, William Cavendish, came to assist the Royalists of Yorkshire in November 1642, he held principal command until he was joined at York by Prince Rupert, just prior to the Battle of Marston Moor in 1644. In December, after the Battle of Tadcaster, Wakefield submitted to the Earl's Royalists and under his orders, Sir William Savile was to garrison the town. Savile's family had divided loyalties, his Uncle, Sir John Savile of Lupset was a Parliamentary commander under Ferdinando, Lord Fairfax. The Earl of Newcastle also set up a large garrison in Leeds, and many other smaller ones in nearby towns and villages, including one at Barnsley, commanded by Sir Francis Wortley. Sir Francis also garrisoned Penistone Church and fortified his own manor house. It was from Penistone that his men 'robbed and taxed many honest people', unfortunately for him the local area was heavily pro-parliament and a puritan stronghold. He led a kind of 'guerrilla resistance' which naturally made him a great many local enemies, and was eventually captured at Walton House near Wakefield in June 1644, being sent to the Tower of London for several years. Reports suggest that he may have died here, but rumours also abound that he was released, though being heavily in debt he lived in White Friars, Fleet Street in London until his death at an unknown time.

The village of Emley suffered repeated raids in January 1643, first the Old Hall was attacked and ransacked with £1000 of Sir William Savile's goods being taken, this in turn alerted other Roundhead troops. On 4 January 1643, 300 soldiers from Bradfield, Burton and Penistone parishes (including men from Gunthwaite billeted in the barn) raided Emley and took its constable, Michael Greene, prisoner, though he was released within two days. On Saturday, 21 January about 1000 soldiers from Burton and Penistone raided Kirkby Grange, looting and pillaging anything from horses to weapons and money. The rectory and Thornecliffe were also raided.

Eventually an appeal for help got through to Savile at Wakefield, and approximately 300, well equipped men were despatched to Emley. The Roundheads met them and sent them to flight, marching onwards to Wakefield which they took in the absence of the Earl of Newcastle in May. The bulk of the Earl's army had been left in the town, whilst, at the end of April he had marched on and taken, Rotherham and Sheffield with the residue. The news that Fairfax had taken most of his troops prisoner and acquired all his arms and munitions caused him to abandon his intended move into Derbyshire and to return to York.

It wasn't all one way traffic, a letter written by Sir Thomas Fairfax relates that, 'some of Penistone men came also to demand aid', he advised them to seek help from Rotherham and Sheffield, unfortunately, this was only days before the Earl of Newcastle had taken both places.

Sir William Savile had fled Wakefield and linked back up with the Earl, he afterwards became

Governor of Sheffield and later of York, though he died in 1644 aged only thirty-one, whether this was in battle or from illness is currently unknown.

In June 1643 the Earl of Newcastle led his forces to a glorious victory over the Roundheads at Adwalton Moor near Drighlington. Many of the parliamentarians were pursued to the borders of Lancashire. Ferdinando, Lord Fairfax, and his son, Sir Thomas took refuge in Hull to which the Earl now turned his attention. He laid siege to the city until the 11 October at which point he withdrew and returned to York. As the new year dawned, the fortunes of the Royalists turned. In July 1644 the Battle of Marston Moor, ended with a crushing defeat for Prince Rupert and his Cavaliers, effectively losing them the North of England in what was to prove to be the biggest battle of the Civil Wars.

When the 'men of Penistone' are mentioned, we must conclude that these troops comprised men from the surrounding areas, including Denby and Gunthwaite. What of the allegiance of the Burdet's?

The diary of Captain Adam Eyre, who was a Roundhead officer, records that in his leisure moments he went to play bowls at the Burdetts at Denby, in the Civil War period.

Richard Burdet had married Margaret Eyre, presumably she was a member of the same family, not only would this give their parliamentary credentials a greater credence but Captain Eyre might have been paying a visit to his relatives. Presumably had they been Royalists he would have been neither invited nor welcome. If we accept then that the Burdets were Roundhead sympathisers, how is it that the manor they once held had been sold to an ardent Royalist, although the Savile family itself had divided loyalties. If the second Richard had been under pressure to sell due to his lack of support for the King, then surely he could have informed Godfrey Bosville that duress was being used to force him out and enlisted his support. After all, Richard's Grandfather, Richard had married Mary Bosville and united the two families. The Saviles could have been backed up by the Catholic, Blackburn family at Papist Hall, only a stones throw from today's Denby Hall Farm, and sited in today's Lower Denby (of which more later). The walls in the inner court of one of the barns still bear musket holes created at the time for the defence of the property by the Blackburns, who presumably were cautious enough to realise the potential of a surprise attack, possibly from near neighbours. Their allegiance to the King seems a certainty as Catholicism was one of the outstanding disagreements of the Civil War, a lot of hate being directed to Charles I's own wife, Henrietta Maria, herself a practising Catholic. Although Charles I was a Protestant and head of the Church of England, a legacy of his forbear Henry VIII, it was his wavering support for Catholicism and his idea of a divine right to rule that was at the core of the Civil War disagreements.

It would be a very romantic notion to suggest that some kind of pressure, military or otherwise had been used to evict Richard Burdet from his lands. The more obvious suggestion that his father had accrued large debts is an easier possibility to believe. As we have already noted, the manor may have been sold at any time from 1617 onwards. It is probably just coincidence that Hunter records that William Savile held Denby in the same year that King Charles raised the standard at Nottingham Castle to begin the first English Civil War.

Austerfield, where Richard retired to, is south east of Doncaster, and is only a mile or two from Finningley, land that Hunter recorded as having been part of the settlement paid by William Savile. As Richard was born in 1610, he would have been in his thirties at the start of the war, but unfortunately, I have no details to hand as to whether he ever took up arms in anger.

DENBY HALL

As already stated, the early whereabouts of Denby Hall are unknown, we speculated that the site of today's Denby Hall Farm could overlay the site of the original Hall. From a geographical perspective, it seems to be very central to the size of the Burdet manorship. With Denby Common to the West, High Hoyland to the North East, Clayton and Bagden to the North and Nether Denby just below the site of

John Speed's map of 1611. Note 'Denbye Hall', 'Gunthwaite Hall' and 'Over Denbye'.

Jeffries map of 1772. Note the chapel, village green, Stocks Hall and the road linking Denby Hall with Bagden which is very prominent. *Author's collection.*

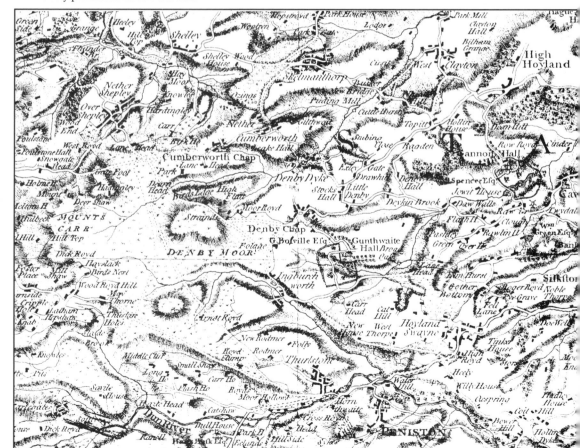

the Hall. John Speed's map, dated 1611, although only small scale may give us other clues. This map clearly shows Over Denby and Denby Hall as being split by Gunthwaite Hall with Hoyland to the North. Over Denby in this instance lying, where one would expect today's village of Upper Denby and the Common to exist. The site of Denby Hall on the map, allowing for a margin of error for exact scale at the time it was drawn, would seem to indicate that Denby Hall in 1611 stood on almost the exact site of today's Denby Hall Farm. As no documents exist to suggest any movement before, or up until, the sale of the manor in between 1617 and 1643, the Burdet family must have lived here. This site would have afforded easy access to their properties, not only in High Hoyland, and Denby, but also Ingbirchworth, Penistone, Clayton, and the others more towards Barnsley, such as Kexborough, Mapplewell, Darton, Keresforth, Staincross and indeed Barnsley itself. The manors of Denby and High Hoyland had been linked since the marriage of Robert de Denby and Margaret de Hoyland in the thirteenth century. Surely it had made sense to dwell in a central position when the early Burdets had considered where to build their new Hall.

The weightiest piece of evidence against this hypothesis lies within the Hearth Tax assessment of 1672. A Mr. Cotton lived in a house with nine hearths, the largest dwelling recorded in the area. From other records we can be sure that this was the old Hall, which would seem to suggest that Denby Hall Farm, which we know was occupied by the Burdet family towards the end of the seventeenth century, was only second in size to its larger neighbour which has led to some speculation that Denby Hall Farm was built on a virgin site. This could be countered by the fact that two of Mr Cotton's hearths were not yet finished, possibly meaning that the residence was a relatively new structure, of course he may have just been making alterations. Either way, it does not mean that Denby Hall and Denby Hall Farm are not one and the same as we shall shortly see.

The other possible contender for the site of an early Hall, are the buildings known as Stocks Hall at Lower Denby. A large, rambling group of buildings, seemingly much added to over the years, these structures date mainly from the eighteenth century, though old maps testify to the site as having existed during at least the seventeenth century. It must certainly have been one of the more affluent residences at the time that the 1672 Hearth Tax was recorded. In one of the upper rooms a stone or plasterwork coat of arms was reputedly filled in and plastered over during the twentieth century. Though eye witnesses remember it, it remains unidentified, perhaps it was the Burdet coat of arms, though this could prove nothing more than a younger branch of the family having made the residence their own.

The final piece in the jigsaw puzzle would appear to be the decisive factor. If one takes a look at the current Ordnance Survey map for the area around Denby Hall (Farm), less than 3/4 of a mile to the north , lying between Bagden Wood and Deffer Wood, lies a hill called 'Trister Hill'. It would appear that the ancient name for a field or area of land has survived from the sixteenth century and has lent itself to a road, which passes either by or through it. Close enough to Denby Hall (Farm) to be a part of its grounds I believe that the area of the old Hall has now been identified, Trister Hill and presumably Trister Close are recorded, as we have already seen as being a part of Denby Hall, they are in exactly the right place to confirm that the old Hall of the Burdet family stood on or close to the site where today's Denby Hall Farm lies. Incidentally, Trister or Trystor actually means, 'hunting station', which could indicate a piece of land long held by the Lords of the Manor and used for that purpose. Perhaps Nicholas Burdet, back in the fourteenth century, began the chase which led him to break in to the park at Emley from this very place? If the present site of Denby Hall Farm is not the original Denby Hall of the Burdet family, then it lies somewhere very close by.

King Charles I eventually lost his war for the Kingdom, as to whether any fighting took place between the prominent families surrounding Denby no records have survived. William Savile, who had died in 1644 did not live to see his home at Thornhill besieged and ultimately destroyed by parliamentarians led by Sir Thomas Fairfax in 1648. Godfrey Bosville was named as one of the High

Court of Justice to sit in judgement of the King at his trial. However, he did not attend, implying that he was not in favour of executing Charles I. Godfrey died in 1658 leaving his son William as his heir. Oliver Cromwell's death, also in 1658 signalled the end of the protectorate and paved the way for the restoration of the monarchy. In 1660, William Bosville made his required declaration of allegiance and apologies to the new King, Charles II for the part he and his father had played in the Civil War. He and his wife retired to Gunthwaite where both died within the following two years.

Shortly after this, two acts of parliament were passed putting the militia on a different level. Every person who had an income of £500 per annum, derived from property, or held a personal estate to the value of £6000 was required to provide, equip and support one horseman. Others of lesser wealth, property income of £50 or personal estate of £600 were to provide a pikeman or musketeer. The services of the standing army were dispensed with, leaving the militia as the country's military strength. A regiment commanded by Sir Michael Wentworth in 1680 included the following men from Denby - Robert Blackburn (musketeer), Thomas Burdet (musketeer), Samuel Clayton (musketeer), John Hawksworth (musketeer), Thomas Hague jnr. (musketeer)

Magistrates had the power to inflict penalties on offenders. Others in the regiment were drawn from various other local villages such as Skelmanthorpe, Clayton West, Cumberworth and High Hoyland.

The end of the Civil War did not mean instant accord between the people of England. Emotions ran high for many years afterwards, take for instance, the following case noted by Brian Elliott in his book *The Making of Barnsley*:

> William Robinson of Denby, giving evidence at Wooley on the 20th of January, 1668, stated that Mathew Crossland of Cawthorne did, on the 12th day of January 'speak these treasonable words viz.' That the King was a Bastard and his Mother a whore and he had more officers under him than was ought.

The outcome of the case is at present unknown.

It would seem highly probable that some contingent of armed forces did pass through the manor of Denby, we have already noted the parliamentarians at Gunthwaite but the following quote from the *Barnsley Chronicle* dated 13 October 1881 is just as compelling:

DISCOVERY OF OLD COINS AT DENBY (DALE)

A second discovery of ancient coins made by a youth in the employment of Mr Jas. Slater, farmer, UPPER DENBY, in his field not far from the parish church, is interesting to many, and we therefore give a list of the various coins found, and examined and compared with authenticated copies of original coins by Mr C. Hargreaves, Denby. (Charles Hargreaves – the Denby National School Headmaster). About 52 coins were found last week, and although some are in a good state of preservation, they are not on the whole in such a perfect state as those found in the same hedge bottom, in a jar, upwards of twelve months ago, doubtless from not having been deposited in an earthen ware jar, as were the former.

Some of the coins are very much worn, especially those of small size, and some are only portions of coins worn very thin, the inscriptions & c., being wholly or partially obliterated. There are several coins which were found in the first set unearthed, such as the silver halfpenny and pennies of Charles I, penny of Elizabeth, and groats of Queen Mary, also two coins which are doubtless Scotch coins of the reign of James I.

There were found – nine groats of the reign of Queen Mary, well worn but able to be identified; one shilling of Elizabeth; ten sixpence's of Elizabeth, various dates, 1565, 1567 and 1575; four shillings, James I; two sixpence's, James I; one shilling, Charles I, one sixpence, Charles I, seven pennies, Charles I, and one halfpenny, Charles I. There are also thirteen small coins which are difficult to identify, but which are probably silver pennies of Charles I. One coin is doubtless a Scotch coin (shilling) of James I., being unlike any English specimens of that monarchs reign, and bears on one side a shield, surmounted by a crown, the shield bearing a lion rampant and 'Jacobus' plainly visible on the superscription, while on the other side is a thistle flower and two leaves, one on each side. Another coin (a sixpence most likely of James I, but not *an English one) has a harp, surmounted by a crown, very well defined.*

Doubtless these last coins found their way into England when James I, of England and VI of Scotland came to reign in England after Elizabeth. As we stated when the first batch of coins was found, it is very likely that the treasure was hidden when Cromwell's Ironsides marched near, and perhaps through Denby and stabled, as it is said, their horses in Cumberworth Church. The owner stowed them in the hedge bottom, and may perhaps have been forced into the army or went out voluntarily and joined either the side of the King or that of the parliament and fell in conflict, for otherwise we should have expected that the coins would have been removed after the supposed danger was past. It is possible other coins may be found still. The police were quickly on qui vive on hearing of the discovery, but we do not anticipate that the authorities will claim the trove, as they returned that previously found to its purchaser.

Maybe more coins and other precious artefacts do actually remain buried under hedgerows or in fields in and around Denby, the survival of the above certainly proves the owner's theory that burying his treasure was the best option. It is also interesting to note, as a little aside, that the references to Queen Elizabeth above do not insert the now traditional I after her name, the article, of course, emanating from a time well before the reign of our present Queen Elizabeth II. The fact that the coins were initially examined by Charles Hargreaves, the Headmaster of Denby National School, would seem to be fairly logical. He probably lived very close to where the coins were uncovered and was probably one of the most learned men in the village, though perhaps the vicar, Job Johnson, may also have been involved. The whereabouts of the cache are now unknown.

The Diary of Adam Eyre

To gain a slightly better insight in to goings-on in and around Denby in the years immediately following the Civil War we will examine, briefly, the remarkable diary of this Parliamentary Captain.

Adam was the son of Thomas Eyre and Ellen Ramscar. The family originally came from Crookhill, near Hathersage in Derbyshire.

Genealogical Table of Adam Eyre

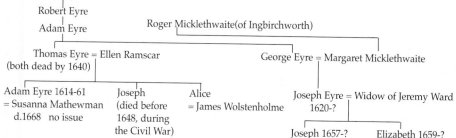

Little is known of Adam's early years other than that he received a good education. He married Susanna Mathewman although their relationship was very poor as can be discerned from the diary. His relations included the Micklethwaites descended from the Lords of Ingbirchworth and the Burdets of Denby, by the marriage of Richard Burdet to Margaret Eyre in approximately 1630. Soon after the Civil War broke out Adam and his brother entered the army on the parliamentary side under Ferdinando Lord Fairfax, then subsequently under Sir Thomas Fairfax. Adam kept a journal of his war which has long since disappeared. His brother almost certainly lost his life during the war as he was dead before 1648. His lieutenant had been Captain Shirt of Cawthorne. It is almost certain that Adam fought at Adwalton Moor, where Sir Thomas Fairfax clashed, and suffered heavy losses against the Earl of Newcastle in 1643.

At the end of the war Adam settled down on his paternal estate at Haslehead which is the period of his life recorded in his diary, taking an active role in the affairs of his parish and socialising with the local gentry and yeomanry.

Adam's diary begins in 1647 and continues until 1648/9 when the last entry records his setting out for London on 26 January so that he would arrive there the night before Charles I was executed. It seems very likely that Adam saw the King of England being beheaded. Up until the day Adam died he was owed a large amount of money by the state which he never received.

The Rich family of Bullhouse, Thurlstone were very great friends of Adam. Aymer Rich had been High Constable for Staincross in 1624, though it was his son, Captain William Rich who was Adam's regular companion. William died in 1649/50, soon after the diary ends, and before his own father, therefore it was his son, Sylvanus, who succeeded Aymer at Bullhouse and built the present mansion. Sylvanus married Mary, daughter of Ralph Wordsworth of WaterHall, an ancestor of William Wordsworth (1770-1850) the romantic poet. Sylvanus died in 1683 aged fifty-six leaving a son, Elkanah who was responsible for erecting the chapel at Bullhouse in 1692. The male line of Rich of Bullhouse became extinct in 1769.

Genealogical Table of Rich of Bullhouse

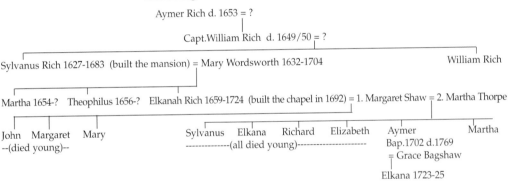

The first entry of note in Adam's diary is dated Sunday, 3 January 1647. It concerns a visit to Kirkburton Church where he went to hear the former Denby chaplain, Daniel Clarke preach. We can only read snippets of information about Clarke, but here we have a man who not only knew him but heard his sermon.

Adam was a man of his time, for instance:

1647, 14 January - *In the presence of Capt. Rich, Edward Hinchliffe, Jo. Micklethwaite, Nich. Greaves, Jo. Cooke, Dan Rich and others, Adam beat and took prisoner Robin Wood, who tried to provoke Adam with words.*

Later he records that he whipped his father-in-law's female servant, Jane Goodyear. Though this seems a harsh way to treat servants, particularly a female one, it was nothing out of the ordinary for the time, indeed, discipline was a route to learning in these puritanical times.

Adam first mentions Denby on 25 January 1647, '*thence to Denby, where we should have been on an arbitration between Ralph Townrow of Swinden and one More of Hoyland, but did nothing*'. And again on the 28 January, '*thence we came to Denby green, where were our two Penistone vicars and some others who called us in to drink*'. This could be evidence of an early alehouse in Denby, though it was also very usual for people to drink in each other's homes. One of Adam's favourite Inns was the *Angel* at Ingbirchworth, the building still exists but is now called Grange Farm. It was built by the local and important Micklethwaite family in 1624, though there is evidence of an even earlier structure. It was a busy coaching house on the Halifax to Sheffield road. An inscription above the door reads 'Let faith enter and fraud depart'. Adam certainly enjoyed his ale, on numerous occasions he records that he drank too much and 'carried himself unsociably'. On the 4 April 1648 he can also be found at a football match in Penistone, though the match was abandoned – due to crowd trouble!

Adam was a frequent visitor to our area, he records on the 6 February 1647.

...to Birchworth moor, to Burdesedge, thence to Denby, to Brice (a villager?), *thence to Birchworth, where I called on John Micklethwaite* (a relation), *who had a daughter sick, thence to Thorp smithy* (his regular smithy in Ingbirchworth), *thence to Thurlstone where Captain Rich, Lieutenant Blackny and Ensign Pasley met me... .*

He also took an interest in local affairs, he records that on 1 March 1647 a Richard Robinson of Denby was married. On the 30 May he wrote a note for Francis Haigh to read out in Penistone Church to bring up the subject of mending the way to Denby bridge. On the 2 March, Adam joined up with Richard Hawksworth of Broad Oak in Gunthwaite and Captain William Rich and rode into 'Denby quarter' where they collected money from the villagers. Those who were unable to pay at the time promised it to Hawksworth before the next Sunday. The group parted at Gunthwaite mill. A document recorded by Adam details the trouble they had to go to, to rid themselves of the vicar of Penistone, Mr Dickinson. A petition was drawn up which gives us the names of many of the important Gentry and Yeoman at the time. Dated 27 February 1646 it was signed by - William Rich (Bullhouse), William Rich (Hornthwaite), Ralph Wordsworth (WaterHall), Adam Eyre (Hazelhead), Francis West (Denby), Richard Hawksworth (Denby), THOMAS BURDET, GEORGE BURDETT, Thomas Haigh, Joseph Hinchliffe, Thomas Wainwright, Joseph Priest, Nathaniel Greaves, William Marsden, Gervas Kay, Ralph Swift and numerous others.

Another petition regarding money to be paid to Penistone Church from a Royalist soldier's estate includes the following names - Godfrey Bosville and his son William Bosville, Aymer Rich, William Rich, Ralph Wordsworth, Richard Hawksworth, Francis West, Robert Blackburn of Denby, John Micklethwaite of Birchworth, Richard Walker and Adam Eyre.

The Francis West of Denby mentioned above belonged to a younger branch of the West family from Hunshelf. As can be seen from the above, he, Adam and the others all belonged to the locally strong Puritan Party. We also find the names of George Burdett and Thomas Burdet. They appear again,

5 May 1647 - *'to Denby green on foot. Thence to Birchworth, where Jo. Micklethwaite gave me in my indenture and after went with me to Denby again, to bowls, where I lost 1s and spent 3d (on drink). There came a man from Mr Copley to offer us a minister and promised to send him tomorrow, and Captain Rich and I promised for our parts to do nothing prejudicial to him, but did conceive that the major part of the election rested with us... and these things passed between us in the parlour at Burdett's in the presence of Jo. Micklethwaite.*

Eyre was certainly no stranger to playing bowls here on a regular basis, and it would appear that a Burdet family lived relatively close by. Which Burdet it was is another question. The list of petitioners given above spells George Burdett (two 'ts') and Thomas Burdet (one 't'). The diary entry spells the individual in question with two 'ts', on this basis can we suppose that it was George? Spelling, particularly with regard to names varied largely in these days when it was out of the ordinary to be able to write at all, subsequently we can never be sure that it was George. It must be said, that George Burdett may have added the extra 't' to his surname to distinguish himself as the pre-eminent member of the clan, and the possibility that Eyre knew of this is not unreasonable.

The subject of Denby green is an important one, Eyre talks of riding up from Gunthwaite to Denby green and then bowling until dark. This would imply that the green was in today's Upper Denby as

Falledge Lane heading towards Denby Church, to the left is Goose Green and the school, circa. 1920. *Courtesy of 'Old Barnsley'.*

Eyre probably used the old pack horse route which went past Gunthwaite Hall. A further note in the diary is also illuminating,

> 22 November 1647 - *... after that I went to Denby and there met William Savile and his wife and spent 2s... spent 1s at Burdet's goose feast today, which is one of the two shillings.*

Goose feasts were usually held on Michaelmas Day, 29 September, indeed, Queen Elizabeth I was said to be eating her Michaelmas goose when news of the defeat of the Spanish Armada was brought to her. In the larger goose fairs, such as the one at Nottingham, all manner of things were sold, sheep, horse, cattle, as well as geese and even wives! Freaks, jugglers and minstrels would combine with pickpockets and petty thieves amidst the noise of the tradesmen and the sound of the animals. Usually the best goose on display would eventually be cooked and eaten. Burdet's feast would have been a much simpler affair, perhaps the result of a late harvest as he was quite late in the year for a goose fair. One would imagine that the bird was roasted on a spit, though in many poorer areas it would have been made into stew, nothing would have been wasted, including the feathers which made excellent quills and mattresses.

The first thing to consider is the siting of this event. We know from Adam Eyre that Denby had a green, sited somewhere in the vicinity of a Burdet household.

Could the bowling green have been used as the site for a goose fair? Possibly – the name Goose Green still exists in Upper Denby. Though not now a green, the triangle of land at the junction between Falledge Lane and Denby common, which heads off towards the relatively modern Greenacre estate is still known as Goose Green. It may once have been large enough for a bowling green and a goose feast, as one would not imagine crowds of people and animals being welcome on a bowling green. I would surmise from the evidence that it was Thomas Burdet (one 't'), who held the feast, and that wherever he lived was only a short horse ride away. In effect we will probably never know exactly where the green was. Maps from the time do not show enough detail but the above theory is at least logical and may provide the reason for the name surviving as it does today.

As an aside, it would appear certain that, when considering the puritan petition, the bowls and the cordiality in the parlour, that the Burdet family were parliamentary supporters and puritans at this time.

Adam Eyre also attended the old chapel at Denby,

Sunday 12 December 1647 - This day I went to Denby Chapel and heard an old fellow preach both forenoon and after.

It is likely that the preacher was the man we know only as Miller. Perhaps Adam attended with other Denby acquaintances such as his former quarter master, John Shaw who we know was living in Denby at this time, or perhaps Francis West.

Livestock also played a large part in the lives of all these local yeoman and gentry, for instance Francis Haigh sent twelve ewes and a tup to be wintered at Eyre's farm on 3 October 1648. The diary of Adam Eyre is the nearest mirror we can get to looking at how the Burdets and other local well to do families would have lived. Try to imagine Adam riding around the area, the area in which you now live, calling at the homes of people long since confined to the pages of history. He knew them personally, laughed with them, drank with them, borrowed money from and lent to them. He knew the faces of the descendants of the Lords of the Manor of Denby, the Burdets and called them friend.

THE RETURN OF GEORGE BURDET

George, the eldest son of Richard Burdet who probably sold the manor of Denby was obviously not happy with his family's move away from Denby as he had returned by 1673.

Born in the 1630s he was his father's heir, though he had seven brothers and sisters. Robert, we have already noted was probably born at Denby along with George before their father's presumed sale of the manor. We also have details concerning another brother, Richard.

Richard was probably only around twenty-four years old when he died, he made his will in 1673 where he describes himself as of London, Gent. Probably buried at Sandal near Wakefield he left £400 to Thomas the son of his brother George, of Denby Hall.

Genealogical Table of George Burdet of Thorne, later Denby

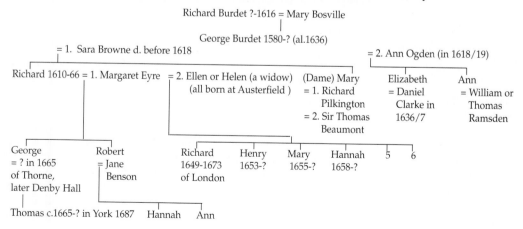

George was married in London in 1665, where he gave his home address as Thorne, north east of Doncaster. Therefore the birth of his son Thomas and his subsequent removal back to Denby must have occurred between 1665 and 1673, he would have been around thirty to thirty five years old. Evidently he had moved away from Austerfield in the years between approximately 1658-1665, more than likely this was his new marital home, away from his father, who was to die only one year later.

As we noted earlier, the Hearth Tax returns, record that a Mr Cotton dwelt in the largest house in Denby, it had nine hearths although two were not yet finished. If Richard Burdet had left Denby in 1642/3?, and his son, George had not returned until 1673, then it seems unlikely that the Hall would remain empty.

WILLIAM COTTON

In a freehold book for the Upper Division of the Wapentake of Staincross the following freeholders appear under Denby, with William Cotton at their head. The record is dated to approximately 1660 (though we know from other sources that Cotton did not come to Denby until 1667):

William Cotton, Gent.	30 li
Thomas Burdet, Gent.	20 li
Emor Burdet	15 li
Joseph Mosley	18 li
Thomas Haigh, de Bagden	15 li
Thomas Haigh, de Denby	20 li
John Clayton	20 li
John Dickenson	6 li

William Cotton was a person of considerable substance and was largely associated with the iron industry, his descendants continuing in this line of business for several generations. The ironworks were based, at different times at, Wortley, Rockley, Barnby, Silkstone and Haigh. At this period ironworks were scattered throughout the district but were relatively primitive. The market was very local due to the state of the roads which made transit difficult. Wood and charcoal were the only fuels used for smelting and as a consequence production was limited. William moved to Hawkhirst, better known as Moor End in the parish of Silkstone when his son, Thomas, was still a young boy. Thomas had been born at Wortley in 1653, and was brought up and educated partly in Silkstone, partly in Denby. William and his family were non-conformists, their residences always offering a ready asylum to the persecuted and ejected clergy of the day. One of those taken in was John Spofford, who lived with the family at Moor End until his death in 1668; he had a heavy influence on William's children. Another great friend of the Cottons was Oliver Heywood, a highly distinguished early non-conformist. His diary records trips to visit the Cotton's at Denby and other places:

2 October 1669 - My son Eliezer and I rode to Mr. Cotton's at Denby, where God mercifully assisted us in the acts of worship, in which we were both engaged.

William Cotton was a gentleman of Cheshire, descended from the Cottons of Cumbermere, and he removed here during the mid-seventeenth century to superintend ironworks carried on in partnership with Lady Middleton, he also being her Ladyship's auditor. He married Eleanor, the daughter of William Fownes of Kendley, County Salop, through whom he acquired Haigh Hall and Moorhouse Ing estates in 1660. Eleanor outlived her husband and was buried at Penistone on 30 November 1699.

On the granting of more liberty to non-conformists by King Charles II by what was called the 'Declaration of Indulgence' in 1672 (the same year as the Hearth Tax was recorded), Mr Cotton had his home at Denby (presumably the Hall), licensed as a preaching house where Christopher Richardson officiated. A document survives which details the whereabouts of William Cotton at various stages throughout his life.

He was at Wortley on 30 September 1656, at Hawkhirst, Moor End on 24 June 1667 but was afterwards styled of Denby. The proof of his residence at Denby Hall comes through the marriage of his daughter, the record states clearly that- 'Rev. James Wright married Eleanor, a daughter of Mr. William Cotton, a gentleman residing at Denby Hall, Nether Denby'.

He died in 1674 and was buried at Penistone Church on 17 March, where there were eight non-conformist ministers at his funeral and 'great lamentations'. In his will he is described as of Nether Denby (the Hall), ironmaster. He left his brother-in-law, George Fownes, minister, £3 yearly.

His eldest son, William lived first at Denby, but removed soon afterwards to Haigh Hall, he continued with his father's interests in ironworking and died in 1703. His daughter, Eleanor's marriage produced a son, Samuel, Eleanor's husband, James Wright died when Samuel was only eleven, Eleanor herself died only one year later and so it was his grandmother, William Cotton's wife, Eleanor of Denby Hall who decided to put him in to boarding school. This means that Eleanor Cotton, nee Fownes was still living at Denby Hall towards the end of her life in 1699. Samuel was born in 1682/3 and would have been eleven in 1693/4 and so lost his mother around 1694/5. With this scenario in place, where was George Burdet and his family?

Pedigree of William Cotton

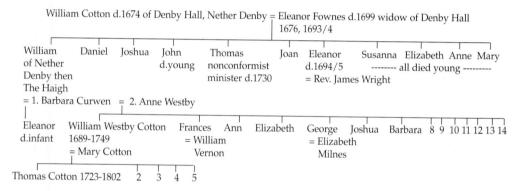

The Hall, in whatever condition at that time, was probably leased to William Cotton by Sir George Savile, the son of William Savile who had bought the manor of Denby. It is also possible that he could have bought the Hall from Lord Savile, he was certainly wealthy enough to do this. That George Burdet was living at Denby in 1673 would not seem to be open to doubt; the record of his son, Thomas, inheriting £400 from his Uncle Richard states this quite clearly. It also states that George lived at Denby Hall, but from the above details concerning the Cotton family, this does not seem to be possible.

As the Cotton family seem to have remained at Denby Hall until the late 1690s, there can be only two possibilities, one, that George lived elsewhere in Denby and christened his residence Denby Hall Farm, leaving off the farm for status reasons, or, two, that he dwelt alongside the Cottons at Denby Hall. Either possibility is likely, George would certainly have been proud to have returned to his ancestors Hall in any way he could. Perhaps it was only after the death of William Cotton in 1674 that this became possible, the dates of his return, 1673 and the date of Cotton's death, 1674 could be more than just coincidence. As we will see, in later years, particularly the nineteenth century, a number of families resided at Denby Hall Farm, therefore the property was big enough, if we accept that the original Denby Hall and Denby Hall Farm were part of the same complex of buildings. That George and his family were back in Denby by 1673 seems certain, but as to whereabouts, we will leave it for the moment.

George had died by 1687, in his late forties, and his son Thomas was at this time apprenticed to Thomas Benson at York. The Bensons were relations by marriage to the Austerfield Burdetts, his Uncle Robert had married Jane Benson, presumably Thomas Benson was either her brother or father. It is unthinkable that Thomas would not have wished to return to Denby Hall (Farm), but as to whether he ever did is unknown as no documents have yet been found to continue the story of the direct linear heirs of the manor of Denby. This though is not the end of the Burdetts in Denby and its environs. Before we return to the brothers of Henry Burdet back in the sixteenth century and consider their descent up until the present day, we must first continue to look at the new Lords of the Manor, the Saviles and their descent.

Before we do this, we should consider some details that have survived concerning the more humble occupants of the village at this time. We have already had the chance to note the lives of:

- The men who made up the militia to face the Spanish invasion threat of 1587, Thomas Jenkyson, John Mitchell, Raufe Clayton, Richard Owdom and Laurence Hawksworth.

- The men fighting for rights of land against Godfrey Bosville in the mid-fifteenth century, William Turton, Ottiwel Marsden, John Burdet, John Claiton, and Edward Woodcock.

The men fighting for land rights against George Burdet in the early seventeenth century, John West, John Blagburn (possibly Blackburn, maybe the father of the Robart Blackburn who built the barn and was alive during the civil war), and Thomas Haugh (Haigh?). The tenants paying rent to George Burdet, again in the early seventeenth century, William Clayton in Bagden, Over Denby, Henry Haigh in Nether Denby, Robert Smyth, Springhouse, Denby (Springhouse farm exists today, it is the first house on the left heading towards Cawthorne after the turn off to Denby Hall), and John Mosley, Over Denby.

Others granted lands by George Burdet in the early seventeenth century, Robert Marshall's widow, Joan at Over Denby, John Suydall and Thomas Wainewright, the millers in the valley floor at Denby Milne, Brian Robinson on Denby Common, and Richard Brooke of Clayton and John Burdet both holding land known as 'Trister Close' within the grounds of Denby Hall. To add to these we have the following:

10 October 1562 - *Bond of £40, John Morton of Denby, husbandman to Godfrey Bosville, Lord of Gunthwaite. Morton to pay an annual rent of 4d and do suit at Gunthwaite manor court.*

18 August 1594 - *Midhope: Lease for 10 years at 4d rent: for £25. Thomas Hatterslaye of Denby to Thomas Barber of Derwen. Co. Derby, husbandman, a messuage and lands in Midhope in the tenure of Thomas Oldham (excepting the dower of the wife of Thomas Oldham).*

18 September 1603 - *Thomas Hatterslaye of Denby par. Penistone, yeoman, bequest to his wife Johane, son and heir, Thomas, daughters, Johane and Marie:- lands in Midhope and elsewhere in Co. York. 'Great Arke' in his home at Midhope, cupboard and canter in house at Denbie. If his wife re-marries tuition of his children to be handled by Houmfray Strit, brother John Hatterslaye and Christopher Marsden.*

Through these documents we can begin to have some idea of the people that were living at Denby and we can also see the ancestry of some of the names which continued to flourish in the manor for many hundreds of years.

There must have been a considerable impact upon their lives when the Burdets sold Denby, and to a prominent Royalist family to boot. Suddenly their Lord did not live among them, but held his court some way distant. It could perhaps be said that initially they may have felt a sense of freedom from the restrictions of a 350 year old regime, but once the dust had cleared and the civil war had ended the situation probably settled down to business as usual.

THE SAVILE LORDS OF DENBY

As we have already noted, Sir William Savile who purchased the manor of Denby was followed by his son, Sir George Savile, 4th Bart. The Rev. Pobjoy, in his history of Emley tells us that this man became the greatest and most famous of all the Saviles. He held the post of Lord Privy Seal under three Kings, Charles II, James II, and William III. He was later made the 1st Marquis of Halifax, alongside this he was still dealing with matters relating to his manor of Denby:

> 10 January 1690 - *Lease for 21 years by the Right Honourable George, Lord Marquis of Halifax to Robert Oldham of Skelmanthorpe, yeoman, of a coal mine in Denby Common, at an annual rent of 20s.*

He died in 1695 and was buried in Westminster Abbey. He was succeeded by his son, from his second marriage, William. Sir William Savile, 5th Bart, 2nd Marquis of Halifax, who was born in 1665 and died in 1700. He had no male heir and so now, the descent begins to spread out to cousins that are more distant. Sir John Savile the 6th Bart. succeeded but died in 1704, unmarried, to be followed by Sir George Savile, 7th Bart. A document has survived detailing leases for a period of twenty-one years by Sir George who is described as of Rufford, Co. Notts., Bart. It concerns lands in Denby that were a parcel of Denby Hall.

> 1. *To Walter Poole of Lower Denby, husbandman, a messuage and lands amounting to 13 acres and 6 perches at an annual rent of £5 10s.*
> 2. *To Simeon Firth of Lower Denby, a messuage and lands amounting to 5 acres, 2 roods, and 2 perches at an annual rent of £20 6s.*
> 3. *To Thomas Burdett of Lower Denby, a messuage and lands amounting to 27 acres, 3 roods, 14 perches at annual rent of £13 3s.*
> 4. *To Elizabeth Sykes of Lower Denby, widow, a messuage and land amounting to 23 acres, 1 rood, 38 perches, at Poppit in Denby at an annual rent of £9.*

The document is dated 20 December 1715. The first thing to note is that the name, Lower Denby has by this time come into use. The second is that all the above resided in Lower Denby, close enough to Denby Hall/Denby Hall Farm to increase our confidence that this area incorporated the ancient residence of the old lords of the manor.

Descent of the Savile Lords of Denby

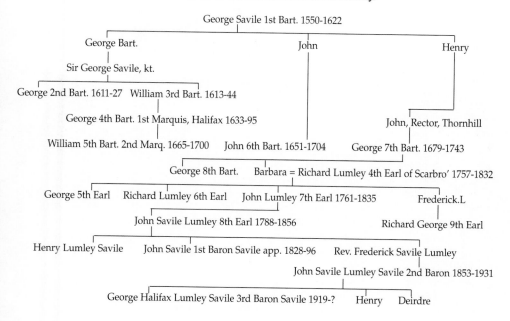

Sir George died in 1743 and was succeeded by another Sir George, the 8th Bart. Born in 1726 he also died unmarried in 1784, which led to the Earls of Scarborough taking control of the Savile lands at Denby. George's sister Barbara had married Richard Lumley, the 4th Earl of Scarborough and it was to her second and third sons, Richard and John Lumley that George left his estates. Richard Lumley became the 6th Earl of Scarborough and inherited his uncle's estates in 1784 and his earldom from his brother in 1807. He was followed in 1832 by John Lumley, 7th Earl of Scarborough who died only three years later. His son, John was born in 1788 who took the name Savile and so became John Savile Lumley the 8th Earl of Scarborough. Here we have proof that the nineteenth century trade directories were correct in their assertion that the Earls of Scarborough were Lords of the Manor of Denby. The family continued as shown on the previous page.

From the time of the Black Death in 1348/9 when the tenantry had first been able to begin to resist, its feudal obligations, the power of the Lords of the Manor, had begun to diminish. The Enclosure Award for Denby of 1802 brought the process of the change of land ownership almost to a close. Although the names of Bosville and Savile were still evident, the common people they now sat alongside were much more important holding their own houses, barns and fields. This course of action has continued to the present day with the result that the distinction of being Lord of the Manor, is little more than just a title. The Lordship of Denby was sold by the Savile estate in 1984, at present I am unaware of the name of the current owner.

With the battle for the Lordship of Denby out of the way, we can now return to the sons of Aymer Burdet. We have already met Henry and his eighteen children (nine of them illegitimate), but there were three others, and from these the name of Burdet continued to thrive and flourish within the manor of Denby and it is upon these lines that we will continue the story of their descent.

The present day dwelling at Denby Hall, re-built in 1923. *Author's collection.*

Chapter Four

The Fortunes of the Later Burdet's

RICHARD, NICHOLAS & JOHN, BROTHERS OF HENRY BURDET
As we have already seen, these sons of Aymer Burdet had been well provided for before his death in 1574. Probably all born during the early to mid 1530s, details about their lives are at best sketchy. We do know that Richard went to live at Royston and later moved to Silkstone, Nicholas was described as living in Darton, possibly on Francis Burdet's land near Birthwaite Hall. John moved to Purston Jaglin, east of Wakefield in the Featherstone district. In later years, he would not have been far from his elder brother, Henry, after Henry removed from Denby to live at Walton. Their families grew up and expanded throughout the years that their cousins were lords of the manor of Denby. To enable us to see their development we will follow the descents of each brother.

Descent of Richard Burdet

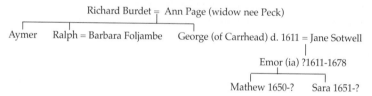

George Burdet, son of Richard, who died 1586/7, married Jane Sotwell of Catling Hall, Hoylandswaine and the couple had a son known variously as Emor, Emoria or Amor. This son was baptised on the 12 of December 1611, the day his own father was buried after which his mother re-married to William Field of Thurnscoe. Emor was assessed in the lay subsidy of Cawthorne at 1/- in 1663 and is mentioned in the Hearth Tax of 1672 as having a home which possessed three fire places, not a small structure, and he seems to have held land in several places. It seems he was also married as I have records which notes the baptisms of a Sara, daughter of an Emoria Burdet in 1651 and also Mathew in 1650, though I do not know the name of his wife. Emor died aged around sixty-seven in 1678.

Descent of John Burdet

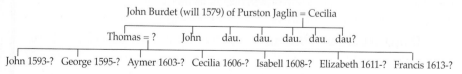

We know that John bought land from his father in Denby in 1556/7 and that his activities here continued throughout the 1570s, though he was certainly at Featherstone by 1567. He died at Purston Jaglin, his will dated 25 January 1575, proved 14 August 1578. His wife outlived him for some years, Cecilia's will is dated 10 August 1588. Their eldest son, Thomas had left Featherstone by 1613, but had returned to Denby by 1630, where he is recorded as acting as executor to his unmarried brother, John, of Armley, Leeds. It is unlikely that he was still alive at the time of the Hearth Tax. There were two Thomas's recorded but we shall return to this subject later.

Descent of Nicholas Burdet

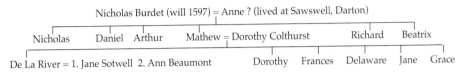

Nicholas Burdet (will 1597) = Anne ? (lived at Sawswell, Darton)

Nicholas   Daniel   Arthur   Mathew = Dorothy Colthurst   Richard   Beatrix

De La River = 1. Jane Sotwell 2. Ann Beaumont   Dorothy   Frances   Delaware   Jane   Grace

Nicholas died in 1598, it is interesting to note that all Henry's younger brothers preceded him to the grave. Possibly living his life on his cousin's land he was probably buried at Darton. In his will he made a bequest to Mr George Brooke and names his master as Sir John Neville. His marriage produced five boys and one girl, though he did have another son, William Goodart, alias Burdett, by an unknown mother who was bequeathed 20s in his father's will. His will also mentions that his fifth son Richard was to receive a hundred marks and that Mathew his fourth son was to receive a black filly. His eldest son, Nicholas moved to Silkstone during his life, though it is through Mathew that we will follow the descent and also sort out a mystery.

Mathew was born circa 1575 and would have been around twenty years old when his father died. He is also very likely to be the Mathew Burdet recorded as being involved in a disagreement over paying tithe of any kind to the agents of Lord Wortley. Mathew, Lionel Rolleston, George Blount and ninety-one others from the parish of Penistone agreed to mutually support each other in this against Edward Rich, Francis West, Thomas Fanshaw and Francis Greaves. It is interesting to note the names of Rich, West and Greaves appearing here during the reign of James I (1603-25) in these pre-civil years, all of whom were later to be recorded in Adam Eyre's diary. It was Mathew's marriage to Dorothy Colthurst which must have taken place around 1600, that was to lead to a strange yet easily remembered name being used by successive generations to christen their sons.

DE LA RIVIERE

Dorothy was born in 1572, the daughter of Edmund Colthurst of Hinton Priory (1527-1611+) and Eleanor De La Riviere. Eleanor was one of four illegitimate daughters born to Thomas De La Riviere of Brandsby, near Castle Howard. When Thomas died in 1577, he left his estates to these four daughters. To preserve her family name on her marriage to Mathew, Dorothy christened their first-born son De la River (as it later became shortened to). One would presume that the name De La Riviere was of French, Norman origin, its literal meaning being 'of the river' though whether the De La Riviere family arrived with the Conqueror is unknown. Therefore, De La River

Descent of Mathew Burdet and reason for christian name of De La River

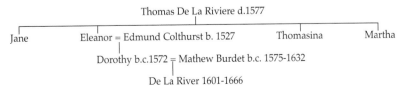

Thomas De La Riviere d.1577

Jane   Eleanor = Edmund Colthurst b. 1527   Thomasina   Martha

Dorothy b.c.1572 = Mathew Burdet b.c. 1575-1632

De La River 1601-1666

Burdet was named after his grandmother, Eleanor.

The name was of great importance to Dorothy, who would only have been around 5 years old when her Grandfather died and it was probably down to her mother's influence that the family name should not be forgotten. Not only did she and Mathew have De La River, but they also had a further son, Delaware (1607-1657) who married Sarah Clayton in York in 1637, though his early death aged fifty allowed Sarah to re-marry Brian Foster. Mathew died in 1632, his will referring to him as of Denby, Gent, leaving De La River as his heir.

De La River, was born in 1601, his name the only way of keeping his mother's family surname alive. It is at present unknown as to whether he ever had a son by this name, though as we know only of Tobias and Mathew there is a high possibility. De La River married Jane Sotwell of Catling Hall, Hoylandswaine, a niece of the Jane who had married George Burdet of Carrhead, son of Richard Burdet of Royston, sometime before 1611. Carrhead is only a stones throw from Cat Hill at Hoylandswaine, both lying close to the village between Cawthorne and Penistone. Cat Hill Farm/Hall was designed by Dr. Catlin in 1584 and was a half way house for travellers between Manchester and Wakefield. The Stanhopes owned the property at a later period.

Descent of Sotwell of Catlin Hall

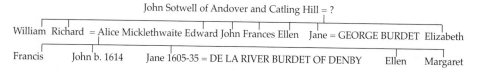

John Sotwell of Andover and Catling Hill = ?

William Richard = Alice Micklethwaite Edward John Frances Ellen Jane = GEORGE BURDET Elizabeth

Francis John b. 1614 Jane 1605-35 = DE LA RIVER BURDET OF DENBY Ellen Margaret

I am assuming that Catling Hill, and Cat Hill are one and the same and that the family must have inhabited Cat Hill Hall, as there is no mention on a present day map of the word Catling. De La River and Jane must have married around 1625, the name Burdett at this time probably still having enormous pull through its links with the then still Lords of the Manor of Denby, though the marriage was not destined to last as Jane appears to have died at an early age. No children have been found recorded from the union, which seems to be unusual, perhaps she died giving birth to their first child.

De La River, undeterred, re-married in 1632 to Ann Beaumont at Kirkheaton who did bear him at least two children, and probably more. De La River's connections with Hoylandswaine may have been severed after his first wife's death, though his death in 1666 means we have no way of finding out whether he returned to live at Denby as the Hearth Tax is dated to 1672. His second marriage lasted for twenty-six years, until Ann died in 1658. As his only son to survive to maturity Tobias, was born in 1636, it would be very unlikely that there were not other siblings, but it is fortunate that via Tobias we can trace the rest of this family through to the present day. De La River would have lived through the period when the sale of Denby Hall and manor became necessitous and unlike myself, would probably have known the real reason behind the sale. At his death in 1666, his son Tobias was already married with at least four children and almost certainly living at Denby, perhaps this is the most compelling evidence for De La River's residence in the village of his ancestors, left without his wife for eight years perhaps he lodged with his son for the remainder of his life. If he had, then he could have been buried in the village as gravestones do survive from this early period when Denby had nothing more than a chapel of ease, but it is more likely that he was buried at Penistone.

Tobias married Mary Dowegill in 1659 and had at least three children, Samuel the eldest being born soon after the marriage in 1660. It is unknown where the family lived, the Hearth Tax notes that he had a house with four fire places, not a small home, perhaps it could even have been Stock's Hall. His death in 1677, occurred only shortly after the return of George Burdet and his son Thomas to Denby, perhaps to the Hall/Farm, noted earlier, though their arrival was just too late to be recorded in the Hearth Tax.

Descent of De La River Burdett of Denby

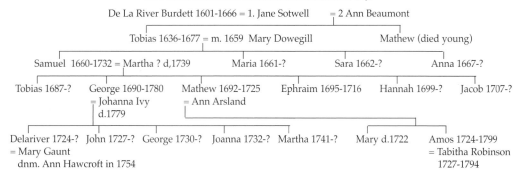

HEARTH TAX 1672

The Hearth Tax was first levied during the reign of King Charles II, who had amassed large debts whilst he was in exile from England. To help recoup some of this money he introduced this tax, along with other measures in 1662. Anyone with two hearths or over was forced to pay although the poor were not taxed at all. The rate was two shillings per hearth, per annum, paid in two instalments, one at the feast of St. Michael the Archangel the other on the feast of the Annunciation of the Blessed Virgin St. Mary, i.e.: 29 September and 25 March respectively. Collection was difficult and only a fraction of the estimated amount was raised, collectors proved unreliable though things improved towards the latter years of the tax's life, before it was abolished in 1689. From it, we are able to determine the size of a person's house by the number of hearths it contained. The more hearths in a house the more affluent the occupant and so subsequently a social order can be obtained, a sort of status index. It should also be remembered that the place known as Denby at this time encompassed a much wider area than the present day villages of Upper and Lower Denby.

There are at least two surviving copies of the tax roll, one in the Public Record Office in London and the other in Wakefield. They differ slightly, the list printed on the next page is my transcription from the copy in London. The Wakefield copy also contains the name of William Hamshire who had one hearth, but who was exempt from charges because his hearth was damaged.

We have already noted in the previous chapter that Mr. (William) Cotton seems to have been living at Denby Hall, recorded as having nine hearths, though two were not yet finished. In the London copy, he is recorded as having only seven, a note at the end of the Wakefield copy instructs the final copy to be adjusted. Whether the work being carried out at the Hall was his idea or the Savile families from whom he may have leased it is unknown, he was certainly able to afford such expense, being the great ironmaster that he was. Although in Denby in 1672, he died here in 1674 though his wife and family continue to abide in the Hall until the late 1690s.

Six Burdet families are listed, including two Thomas Burdets and a George. A Thomas Burdet was recorded as living at Denby Hall during the 1690s, this may have been the son of George who had returned here with his father. It is possible that Thomas and George had moved back to Denby from Austerfield via Thorne prior to William Cotton's removal, if this were so then they would have been in the right place at the right time to negotiate with the Saviles to possibly take up the tenancy of Denby Hall.

It is also interesting to note that the names of Joseph Hinchcliffe and Thomas Shillitoe appear, two years before their families became embroiled in allegations of witchcraft (considered later).

We should also be aware that properties such as Rock House, built 1684, and Manor Farm cottage, built 1677, both in Upper Denby, were not a part of the township at this time.

The Hearth Tax (115 hearths)

1. Mr. Barnby	5		19. John Maister	1		37. Joseph Shaw	1
2. Thomas Clayton	6		20. Emor Burdett	3		38. Ralph Swift	2
3. Widow Burdet	1		21. Thomas Jessop	1		39. Abraham Mosley	3
4. Tobias Burdett	4		22. Thomas Crowther	1		40. Richard Micklethwaite	2
5. John Clayton	3		23. Godfrey Charlesworth	1		41. Francis West	1
6. Mr. Cotton	7		24. John Gawber	1		42. Ralph Horn	2
7. John Lyneley	1		25. Widow Robinson	3		43. Richard Hanwell	2
8. Thomas Burdett	5		26. Elihu Ward	3		44. Thomas Haigh	4
9. Richard Hawkesworth	5		27. Joseph Mosley	3		45. Timothy Booth	1
10. John Rowbucke	3		28. Thomas Marshall jnr.	3		46. Lawrence Hicke	1
11. Thomas Burdett	1		29. Richard Priest	1		47. Jennitt Hatfield	1
12. George Burdett	2		30. John Shaw	1		48. William Gaunt	1
13. Thomas Hage	5		31. John Dawson	1		49. Joseph Pollard	1
14. Joseph Hinchcliff	1		32. Richard Marshall Snr.	2		50. Samuel Gawber	1
15. Thomas Shillitoe	1		33. John Wood	1		51. Rodger Roades	1
16. Widow Moorhouse	1		34. John Thomson	5		52. Thomas Gaunt	2
17. William Moore	1		35. Joseph Bayley	2			
18. Walter Poe	1		36. Edward Goodall	2			

Robert Moorhouse and Mathew Burdet who were either witnesses or inspectors signed the Hearth Tax documents.

We have now brought the important lines of Burdet family descent up to around the same time. Though a number of individuals still had ample finance, they had not now any influence or ownership on the manors appertaining to Denby. They all lived under the lordship of the Savile family, though it should not be thought for one minute that they were not very highly regarded members of the community and that they still possessed contacts with people whose power was greater than their own, for instance their kinsman at Birthwaite, Sir Francis.

FRANCIS BURDETT and THE BLACKBURN FAMILY

One immediate branch of the family has not yet been discussed, the reason for this is the lack of surviving evidence to be able to fit them into any genealogical context. My interest in this branch was roused when I read that Francis Burdett of Denby had left money in his will to the value of £200 to found a charity school in Lower Denby. This was a great deal of money in those days, therefore the branch had to be fairly affluent and of important lineage.

Francis was the third child of Thomas and Elizabeth, he was the executor and main beneficiary in his father's will, and was certainly in business as a Drysalter/Tanner. His own death on 14 August 1731 is recorded in the diary of John Hobson.

Descent of Francis Burdet of Denby

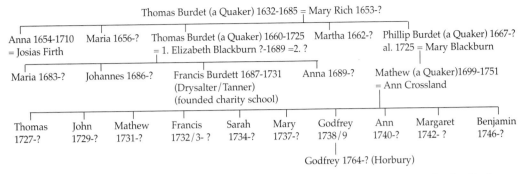

Thomas Burdet (a Quaker) 1632-1685 = Mary Rich 1653-?

Anna 1654-1710 | Maria 1656-? | Thomas Burdet (a Quaker) 1660-1725 | Martha 1662-? | Phillip Burdet (a Quaker) 1667-?
= Josias Firth | | = 1. Elizabeth Blackburn ?-1689 =2. ? | | al. 1725 = Mary Blackburn

Maria 1683-? | Johannes 1686-? | Francis Burdett 1687-1731 (Drysalter/Tanner) (founded charity school) | Anna 1689-? | Mathew (a Quaker)1699-1751 = Ann Crossland

Thomas 1727-? | John 1729-? | Mathew 1731-? | Francis 1732/3- ? | Sarah 1734-? | Mary 1737-? | Godfrey 1738/9 | Ann 1740-? | Margaret 1742- ? | Benjamin 1746-?

Godfrey 1764-? (Horbury)

Francis Burdett died yesternight about 12 o'clock at Halifax. Buried 17th August in the Quaker burial place at Hoylandswaine in the same grave with his Grandfather. He never professed himself absolutely to be a Quaker as his father did, who was buried there 1st May 1726. The said cousin Francis Burdett's inventory comes to £1500. He had £500 in money or bonds, 600 hides. His bend leather hides are valued at £1.6.0 a piece and his upper leather hides at 12/6d a piece.

He seems to have died unmarried, and so in his will dated the day before he died, where he styles himself of Lower Denby he had money enough to leave some for a charity school. It was not until 1769 that the £200 was invested in a cottage, barn and ten acres of land at Hoylandswaine. The site was then let for 12s 6d per annum, half of which was paid to the schoolmaster the other half providing six free places for local scholars.

Francis's grandfather, Thomas, born 1632, married Mary Rich, a possible relative of the Bullhouse family, in 1653. The couple had at least five children, including Thomas and Phillip, and had evidently converted to the Quaker faith (see Religion & Worship). Thomas was described as 'a gentleman'. His eldest daughter, Ann(a) was born in 1654, married Josias Firth and died in 1710. She was buried, according to her gravestone, 'at the feet of her natural father' in the Quaker burial ground at Hoylandswaine. The gravestone now resides in Cawthorne village museum. His son Thomas, born in 1660, the first male, was married to Elizabeth Blackburn in 1682/3 at Penistone and is described as of Denby Hall in 1690.

The Blackburn family, noted in the last chapter, resided at Papist Hall in Lower Denby. According to Hunter the family were Catholics, one of them acting as agent for the Duke of Norfolk in the management of his estates.

Robart Blackburn built the long barn in 1633, though it was rebuilt in 1845 as can be seen from the date stone in the wall, by William Smith. Three small windows in this long barn, inner court side, are reputed to be musket holes dating from the time of the Civil War. It would have been during this time that the building was given its name of 'vulgar reproach' (according to Hunter), Papist Hall. The barn itself is stone flagged and has an archaic wooden rafter roof. The survival of the musket holes would seem to suggest that the barn was only renovated by William Smith and not wholly rebuilt.

Robart Blackburn appears to have been succeeded by his son, Robert, who along with Thomas Burdet were both named as musketeers in the militia of 1680. The two appear to have got along very well, any differences over allegiance during the Civil War that might have existed, now forgotten, so much so that Thomas married either his daughter or sister only a couple of years later.

The long barn at Papist Hall built in 1633 by Robart Blackburn and renovated in 1845 by William Smith. *Author's collection.*

A land lease exists dated 1706 which was made between Thomas Burdet, Phillip Burdet and Robert Blackburn of Denby, again illustrating the co-operation between the brother's-in-law. Robert Blackburn died in 1716, nine years before Thomas Burdet, and left all his lands and estate at Denby to his brother Benjamin.

In 1724, one of the family, another Robert Blackburn from Papist Hall, was made responsible for the management of the Bosville and Gunthwaite estates. He, along with a Mr. Hodgson, who was the Steward to the Earl of Cardigan and a Mr. Mathewman were instructed by William Bosville who died in 1724 aged only forty-two, to see to the affairs of his son and heir Godfrey who was only

The monument to Robart Blackburn and William Smith built into the inner court wall at Papist Hall. *Author's collection.*

seven years old when his father died. The three would have continued until Godfrey came of age in around 1738. The current residential building at Papist Hall was built in 1832, presumably again by William Smith. It is reputed that an underground passage leading from an old cellar comes out in Gunthwaite, a staunch 'Roundhead' stronghold. To the present owner's knowledge no such tunnel exists, but the romantic story probably emanates from the time of the Civil War when refuge and flight were sometimes necessary contingents. It does though seem a little strange that a Catholic family might want to flee into what would presumably be enemy territory.

According to 'Hunter' in the mid-nineteenth century the 'Miss Walkers of Leeds' held the Hall and were representatives of the Blackburn family, their relationship to William Smith is at present a mystery. Ann, Eleanor, Betty and Mary Walker are prominent around the area of Papist Hill on the enclosure map of 1802 but they had other lands, notably between Pinfold and Denroyd farm. Hunter also recorded that,

> *Over the gate is carved a passage from the book of proverbs: Wisdom cryeth at the gates at the entry of the city, at the coming in of the door.*

When Thomas Burdet died in 1725/6 his brother Phillip acted as joint executor with Francis and given that the rest of the family were all of the Quaker persuasion it is likely that he was also. The diary of John Hobson records the following:

> 1726, *At the funeral of Thomas Burdet, of Denby. He married Mary, the daughter of ...Gill, relict of Edward Hobson. He was a Protestant of the Church of England in his youth; afterwards turned Quaker and was buried at their burying-place at Hoyland Swain.*

This would seem to clearly imply that Thomas took a second wife after Elizabeth's death in 1689. Mary Hobson was a relative of the author of the above diary, which is why he makes reference to his 'cousins' the Burdets. John Hobson would seem to record Mary's death on 10 August 1728, when he attends the funeral of Aunt Burdet, again at Hoylandswaine. We now come to the question of the first Thomas Burdet's parentage.

Thomas Burdet, was born in 1632 into a prosperous family of country gentry. Unfortunately, the obligatory baptismal record for him has not survived. There would at present seem to be only two possibilities.

1. That he was the brother of the second George Burdet, born c.1630, son of the second Richard, who may have sold the manor of Denby. If he was then no records have survived to prove it, though a birth date of 1632 makes the possibility very interesting
2. That he was the elder brother of Tobias Burdet, born in 1636, son of Delariviere. There is a four year gap between the date of Delariviere's second marriage to Ann Beaumont and the birth of their first child. A Thomas born in 1632 would fit the picture perfectly.

To complicate matters even further, Thomas Burdett, son of John Burdet of Purston Jaglin, had returned to Denby by 1630, when he can be found acting as executor to his unmarried, younger brother, John. He must be the same man recorded in a document relating to the transferring of rents out of his lands at Denby to George Burdett in 1620. He could also be the Thomas Burdet referred to by Adam Eyre in 1647, though it is certain that he was dead at the time of the Hearth Tax in 1672.

The only other Thomas Burdet we have details of was the son of George Burdet who returned from Thorne to Denby Hall. This Thomas was born circa 1665 and was subsequently only seven years old at the time of the Hearth Tax. He lived far too late to be associated with any of the latter.

THE LATER BURDET'S

Samuel, the son of Tobias Burdet was born in 1660 and died in 1732. He was a clothier and married a woman we know only as Martha. It is now that we take a final return to the subject of Denby Hall, as Samuel's second son, George was known to be living there in 1720 when he married Johanna Ivy. We have argued that George Burdet and his son Thomas had returned to Denby by 1673/4 and that they may have taken up residence at the old Hall, or at the recently built , Denby Hall Farm. We have even seen that in the Hearth Tax there are two Thomases mentioned and a George living in separate households. Here the genealogy ends for the direct ancestors of the old Lords of Denby.

This second George was born in 1690 and lived until 1779. At the time of the Hearth Tax, 1672, George's father, Samuel would have been only twelve years old and living with his father Tobias. It is likely that Samuel never left the village, likewise his son. The other George, a direct ancestor of the old lords had died in 1687, when his son, Thomas was still young enough to be an apprentice in York. If Thomas returned to the Hall then the stay was not an over long one. The Saviles would have been keen to re-lease the building and not leave it standing vacant though whether it was Samuel Burdet who took it over, say sometime around the late seventeenth century or someone else is unknown. That George was here in 1720 would not seem to be open to doubt, therefore the scenario would seem to be thus:

1617-1642/3 - Denby Hall and Manor sold for £1500 to the Savilles. As lands at Austerfield were included in the deal and the fact that Richard Burdet was the first to live here would imply that he was responsible for the sale. It is possible that his father, George lived at the Hall afterwards, as a tenant of the Savile's until his death. Though for Richard to have sold the manor one would presume that, first, he should inherit. This he could only have done if George had died.

1672 - William Cotton is leased the Hall by the Saville family. Who had lived at the Hall in the intervening years is unknown.

1673/4 - George Burdet and his family return to Denby from Thorne. They may have lived at the old Hall, alongside the Cotton family or at a recently built structure Denby Hall Farm near the old Hall.

1687 - George Burdet dies, his son Thomas is an apprentice in York, he either does not return to Denby or returns for only a short period. The Cotton family still reside at the old Hall.

1690 - Thomas Burdet is known to have lived at Denby Hall. In 1672 he dwelt at the second biggest house in the village which lends support for Denby Hall farm being a separate structure to the original Denby Hall. Alternatively he may have moved to the old Hall between 1672 and 1690.

1699 - Eleanor Cotton, wife of William Cotton dies, perhaps now, the Cotton family leave Denby for Haigh Hall.

1720 - George Burdet son of Samuel is known to be living at Denby Hall, either his father had taken on the lease or he himself had. George dies in 1779 at the ripe old age of eighty-nine, the Burdet family hold on the Hall and/or the farm is now over.

We have explored the possibility that there were two sites known respectively as Denby Hall and Denby Hall Farm, through analysis of maps and road names it would seem to indicate that the two sites were very close in proximity to each other. The above chain of events is only my hypothesis based on an interpretation of the facts and I know it will be open to much conjecture. Whatever the truth, George was almost certainly the last Burdet to live at the Hall. His burial entry in the parish registers of Penistone in 1779 notes that he had lived at Denby Hall, and by now his family had probably moved on to lives of their own. Johanna his wife died in the same year, and it was a natural end to their occupancy of the Hall. Whatever the truth, if the Burdetts were living at the Hall in the eighteenth century, they were not alone, for we know that Elias Micklethwaite was living here in 1735, just prior to his death and burial at Penistone.

No such misfortune had affected the Bosvilles of Gunthwaite, as Burdet influence receded to

Denby Hall Farm in 1907. *Author's collection.*

almost negligible, their family continued to flourish. They even began taking an interest in former Burdet lands, as in the following details dated 1706 (Samuel Burdet's time). A petition was made for the inhabitants of Denby, Silkstone, Hoylandswaine and the neighbourhood regarding the condition of the wooden bridge at Denby (now Denby Dale). The bridge which crossed the Dearne by the corn mill, was used daily by pack horses, but floods destroyed it in 1706 and trade was thus being hampered as other longer routes had to be taken. It was decided that a new structure should be built, this time of stone and the sum of £7 10s was paid to Godfrey Bosville to begin the work, though a further £40 was needed raised by the local people to complete the task.

Originally the river Dearne had to be crossed by a ford at the bottom of Miller Hill and one can still see today how steep the road must have been before the bridge was built. This has been a busy little area for centuries, near here is Revel Bottom, which takes its name from a French, Huguenot family of wool merchants and clothiers dating from Elizabethan times. There was also an important dye-house, run by Thomas Brierley & Son, sited where the gas holder used to stand.

The first corn mill was situated at the side of the river on a level with the stream and was powered by a water wheel. This was fed from a dam sited where the youth club now stands on Sunny Bank. At one time a number of blacksmiths' shops were close to here though another one existed at the end of Dearne terrace at the bottom of Bank Lane. In time this first mill became inadequate for the needs of the village and a new and larger one was built near the corner of Wakefield Road. A new dam to supply the water power for this mill was situated at the bottom of Chapel Hill, on today's main road, where a petrol station used to stand. The first mill building, whatever was left of it, was later buried by waste soil from Kenyon's textile factory in the village when they enlarged their works and built a new brick chimney in 1917/18.

After the corn mill had ceased to function as a mill the Kenyon family installed a water turbine inside it to generate electricity. Long before the Y.E.B. brought a supply to the village, this turbine provided electricity to light houses belonging to the Kenyons, the Wesleyan Methodist chapel and the Salvation Army building.

The mill buildings were eventually demolished in 1975/6 but remnants were left and by 1978 the area was something of an eyesore. Nothing now remains other than the old photographs as the whole site lies buried under the Brookside estate of modern housing.

There is a possibility that Samuel Burdet had become a Quaker, his marriage to Mary Ann Beaumont a Quaker of High Flatts strengthens the possibility, this would also seem to lend credence to Francis Burdet's grandfather being Samuel's own father's brother. That this alternative religion had gripped one element of the family is not in doubt though whether George and Johanna were convinced is unknown, though they must surely have had significant contact with Thomas, Phillip and Francis at Lower Denby.

George's son Delariver, born, presumably at Denby Hall in 1724 not only had the distinction of carrying on his Great Great Great Grandmothers maiden name, he also seemed to inherit some of his even older ancestors profligate ways.

On 7 May 1754 he married Mary Gaunt, though on the preceding 14 April he had, by a woman called Ann Hawcroft had an illegitimate child which was named Dally River Burdett Hawcroft! One can only wonder at his audacity, not only this, but as Mary Gaunt bore him a child on 3 November she must have been pregnant before Ann had given birth. This created a hundred-year feud, with the family of Dally River Burdet Hawcroft continuing to use the Burdet name, which they felt rightfully, should have belonged to them. Evidently Delariver had been over amorous with the two women in his life and had been forced to choose which he should marry. Ann must have felt not only disappointment and grief but anger at his decision and therefore clung to his name, perhaps as much to embarrass him as to improve the fortunes of her illegitimate offspring. Whilst these ex-lords of the manor were adjusting to more ordinary lives the villages in the manor of Denby were expanding rapidly. Many of the buildings extant today can trace their heritage back to the mid-eighteenth century and earlier. Farms such as Denroyd and Gunthwaite Gate were constructed, and cottages were built to house the expanding population.

Pinfold House is another example, this was built in 1795 on a site where

Corn Mill buildings at the bottom of Miller (Ranter) Hill, Denby Dale, prior to demolition in 1975. *W H Senior.*

Corn Mill after demolition at the corner of the Miller Hill, Wakefield Road junction. The site is now occupied by the Brookside estate. *W H Senior.*

Manor Farm cottage built by Joseph Mosley in 1677. *Author's collection.*

there were once two pinfolds. The term pinfold is of ancient origin. In old English, 'punfald', which gave its name to the pinder, the man responsible for rounding up stray cattle and impounding them until their rightful owners arrived, when after paying a toll they were allowed to take them away. Although today this might seem a slightly quaint thing to do, in fact, the animals could inflict great damage to crops which directly affected the livelihood of the local farmers. The Wakefield Court Rolls record that in 1309 Peter de Cumberworth (6d) and Robert de Denby (4d) were fined for escapes. A second pinfold existed in what is now Denby Dale where the site of the Springfield Mill car park now stands.

All of Delariver and Mary Gaunt's children were baptised at Denby and most of their siblings also stayed local. Their grandson Thomas, can be found in Denby employed as a joiner and

Rock House on Bank Lane, built in 1684. *Author's collection.*

wheelwright, he was also the landlord of the *Star* public house in 1830, when he was thirty-eight years old. The family had over the years spread around the whole district, cousins lived at Penistone, Barnsley, Huddersfield and nearly all the villages in between at some time or other. Many of them would have been ignorant of the exact details about the family's illustrious past but I am certain that they knew that the name Burdet was something to be proud of. Today the name has dwindled in its regularity in the area but some of these direct ancestors of the Lords of the Manor of Denby and High Hoyland do still live in Denby and Denby Dale and would be surprised, but probably very pleased if you called them Sire or M'Lady. Genealogical tables for the later branches of the family can be found in the appendix section at the back of the book.

Closely intertwined with the Burdets at Denby, as we have seen were the Bosvilles of Gunthwaite. The second Godfrey, the Civil War Colonel, died in 1658 and was succeeded by his son William. He was followed by his son, Godfrey III, born in 1654 and who became known as Justice Bosville. He married Bridgett, daughter of Sir John Hotham of Scorborough near Rudstone. Sir John married five times and enriched himself with five dowries but paid the ultimate price when he was executed by Charles II for his activities during the Civil War. Godfrey also built the farm buildings on the north side of the Hall and over the doorway on one of these buildings are carved the initials 'B. G. & B. 1685'. In Penistone church there is a stained glass window commemorating the marriage of Godfrey and Bridget. Godfrey died in 1714 and was succeeded by his son William who died of a 'four hours sickness'. In time the fourth Godfrey inherited, as we have noted he was a keen historian and it is mainly due to him that we have so much detail of the families activities today. Born in 1717 he was placed in the hands of trustees until he came of age, one of whom was Robert Blackburn of Papist Hall. They acquired for him the last part of Gunthwaite not owned by the family, Broad Oak. He married Diana Wentworth, eldest daughter of William Wentworth of West Bretton and in 1773 inherited a large estate at Rudstone near Bridlington, called Thorpe Hall from Thomas Hassell, a relative of Diana's. The question of residence now reared its head. Godfrey had made plans to re-build Gunthwaite Hall which stood on the site of the present day farmhouse. The stone West wing was the end of the old Hall and the centre of the building was half timbered like the barn with another stone wing at the other end. According to the plans it was to have been a splendid mansion, with terraces and porticos on the frontage. This would have involved a huge amount of money and as Thorpe Hall was both more fashionable and modern it became the Bosville family residence. The Hall at Gunthwaite was from now on let out to tenants. Godfrey died in 1784 and was succeeded by his eldest son, William who died without issue. This meant that the succession passed to yet another Godfrey, the son of his sister Diana who had married Sir Alexander McDonald in 1768. Godfrey McDonald assumed the name Bosville in 1814 and after the death of his brother in 1824 became third Lord McDonald and eleventh Baronet McDonald. He married Louisa Maria, daughter of the Duke of Gloucester. In approximately 1830 the old Hall at Gunthwaite was demolished by an agent named Earnshaw. His exact reasons for demolition are unclear, maybe he was struggling to modernise the ancient structure, or perhaps as W H Senior suggests 'he went mad', whatever the reasons, nothing now remains of this building which matched the existing barn. However, he did erect the present day farmhouse.

To pay for repairs at Thorpe Hall many estates held in and around Gunthwaite were sold in 1830. The Denby estate was kept until 1870 when it was sold to Walter Norton of Rockwood House in Denby Dale. Finally, the end of the Bosville hold on Gunthwaite came in 1953 when it was sold for £45,000 to Messrs. Lockwood, Elliot of Woodsome Sanitary Pipe Works, Ferry Bridge,

Bosville Genealogical Table

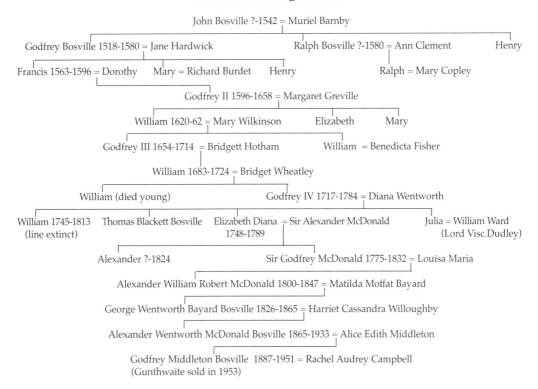

John Bosville ?-1542 = Muriel Barnby

Godfrey Bosville 1518-1580 = Jane Hardwick   Ralph Bosville ?-1580 = Ann Clement   Henry

Francis 1563-1596 = Dorothy   Mary = Richard Burdet   Henry   Ralph = Mary Copley

Godfrey II 1596-1658 = Margaret Greville

William 1620-62 = Mary Wilkinson   Elizabeth   Mary

Godfrey III 1654-1714 = Bridgett Hotham   William = Benedicta Fisher

William 1683-1724 = Bridget Wheatley

William (died young)   Godfrey IV 1717-1784 = Diana Wentworth

William 1745-1813   Thomas Blackett Bosville   Elizabeth Diana = Sir Alexander McDonald   Julia = William Ward
(line extinct)   1748-1789   (Lord Visc.Dudley)

Alexander ?-1824   Sir Godfrey McDonald 1775-1832 = Louisa Maria

Alexander William Robert McDonald 1800-1847 = Matilda Moffat Bayard

George Wentworth Bayard Bosville 1826-1865 = Harriet Cassandra Willoughby

Alexander Wentworth McDonald Bosville 1865-1933 = Alice Edith Middleton

Godfrey Middleton Bosville 1887-1951 = Rachel Audrey Campbell
(Gunthwaite sold in 1953)

Gunthwaite Hall in 1908, re-constructed on the site of the Elizabethan manor house. *W H Senior.*

near Huddersfield who wanted to use it for digging the natural clay, essential for their business. The estate had fifteen farms, some tied cottages, 1150 acres of land and a rental of £1,407. Six hundred years of occupation was finally over, the saddest relics to survive the destruction at Gunthwaite are the keys to the old Hall, which lie on a table at Thorpe Hall, clearly labelled, lest their former use be forgotten.

Before we leave these philanthropic families we must look at the most famous man ever to have borne the name Burdett.

SIR FRANCIS BURDETT of RAMSBURY

Born in 1770, he was living in Paris at the time of the French Revolution returning to Britain in 1793. In 1802 he was elected as an MP for Westminster. He was noted for being outspoken and radical in his policies, he was imprisoned in 1810 for breech of parliamentary privilege and again for his comments about repression at Peterloo in 1819. He became a supporter of Peel in his latter days until his death in 1844. His daughter, Angela Burdett Coutts became the richest heiress in Europe, being also the granddaughter of Thomas Coutts the banker, she was a close friend of Charles Dickens and of the Duke of Wellington. What have the latter to do with Denby.

In the first edition of this book I recorded that according to oral evidence, handed down, this remarkable and noteworthy man occasionally visited Denby and its districts to see his relatives. I also speculated that the connection might involve the Birthwaite branch of the family.

The first Francis of Birthwaite had three sons, Francis II, Thomas and Robert. I was in receipt of information which led me to believe that Thomas was knighted in 1619 by King James I and given the title Sir Thomas Burdet of Bramcote. In actual fact the Thomas who was knighted was a completely different person. The heralds visited Warwickshire in 1617 and met up with Thomas. He told them that his father was Robert Burdet and his mother Mary Wilton. He was at the time married to Jane Francys and had five children, the eldest being Francis at eight years old. He signed his pedigree which was published in 1619, prior to his wife inheriting estates at Foremark and his being knighted.

Thomas's son, Francis built and endowed the church at Foremark in Derbyshire where both he and his wife were buried. He was succeeded by his son Robert who outlived his own issue, whereupon his death in 1716, his grandson Robert inherited. This Sir Robert Burdett held his titles for eighty years and also outlived both his sons, and it was the Sir Francis mentioned above who took over the Baronetcy and lands. Thomas appears to have succeeded his lands and titles from the earlier Thomas who married Mary Throgmorton (Throckmorton) in 1540.

There would appear to be no connection with the Denby Burdets of this time at all. The only evidence I have been able to find connecting him to anybody with probable links to the Denby area is as follows:

13 June 1831 Claythorpe
Draft receipt for £36,250 paid by Sir Francis Burdett of Foremark, Co. Derby and John Hall of Scarborough esq. (trustees under will of William Bosville esq. of Thorpe Hall) *to Rev. Charles Drake Barnard of Lincoln* (devisee and trustee for sale under will of Harrington Hudson of Bessingby esq. Deceased) *for purchase of Manor of High and Low Claythorpe.*

The document deals with a village in East Yorkshire and although Bosville had lived at Thorpe Hall he would have had good knowledge of the Gunthwaite estates, as we have already remarked, the keys to the old hall at Gunthwaite still survive here.

The oral evidence may be nothing more than wishful thinking on the part of the contemporary Burdets in Denby, perhaps even untruthful boasting, but this is about as near to Denby relatives that Sir Francis was to get. If ever the original genealogy of the Burdets who came over from France in the eleventh century is discovered then perhaps an ancient link between the two families could be made, but for practical purposes, there was nothing between the families of Denby and Foremark.

For these purposes alone we will leave the rest of Sir Francis's history in this book, though the story still merits interest of its own.

Sir Francis inherited his Ramsbury estates in 1800 following the death of his mother's sister, Lady Jones. Under the terms of the will he was compelled to take the name Jones and for a few months was known as Sir Francis Burdett Jones, but he quickly reverted back. The line continued thus:

Descent of Sir Francis Burdett of Ramsbury

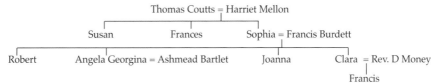

Thomas Coutts = Harriet Mellon

Susan — Frances — Sophia = Francis Burdett

Robert — Angela Georgina = Ashmead Bartlet — Joanna — Clara = Rev. D Money

Francis

In 1801 Sir Francis was a wealthy landed proprietor owning both Ramsbury and Foremark, receiving £40,000 per annum from lands alone, quite apart from his wife's fortune.

Sophia Burdett Coutts died after a long invalidity in June 1844. Sir Francis died in January 1844 and they were buried in the Burdet vault in Ramsbury Church. His son Robert succeeded but died unmarried in 1880 and the son of Sir Francis's brother, Jones Burdett inherited.

Harriet Melon married Thomas Coutts in 1815, he died in 1822 and afterwards she remarried to the Duke of St. Albans. Thomas Coutts left his great wealth to Harriet who between 1822 and 1831 gave each of their daughters £10,000 per annum. Harriet died aged sixty when her husband, the Duke was only thirty-six. She had taken a liking to Angela Burdett Coutts and left her whole fortune to her and her son if she had one. Unfortunately Angela and her sister both died childless and it was Francis, the son of Clara who inherited the family titles.

Angela Burdett Coutts was born in 1814 and married late in life to an American, Ashmead Bartlet, under the terms of her grandmother's will she could not now inherit the Coutts fortune leaving Clara's son Francis as the sole heir. By a family arrangement two fifths of the Coutts income was left to the Baroness for her lifetime.

Diana Orton wrote the biography of Angela named, *Made of Gold* before the Baroness died on 30 December 1906. She was buried under the floor of the nave inside the west door of Westminster Abbey. The book highlights her relationships with some of the most influential figures of her time and relates her endeavours towards charity projects, particularly with regard to the poverty in London, spurred on by her friend Charles Dickens.

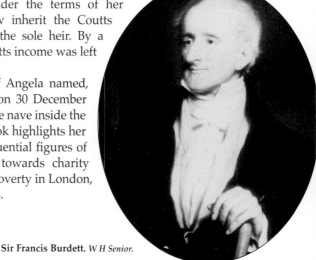

Sir Francis Burdett. *W H Senior.*

Chapter Five

Witchcraft

Between the years 1533 and 1712 more than 4000 men, women and children stood on trial, accused of witchcraft, or of being in league with the Devil. King James I even wrote his own guide book on how to deal with this menace, entitled *Demonology*. An act was passed in the early part of the seventeenth century against conjuration, witchcraft and dealing with evil and wicked spirits and consequently 'witch hunting' became a popular and frequently beneficial sport. Evidence to bring a person to trial was not easy to obtain and so the Courts relaxed the rules to a large degree in order to obtain results. In England, torture was not technically a part of the judicial system, but an unpleasant time was bound to ensue. Across Europe witches were burned, in England they were usually hanged, but these were the end results after barbaric forms of torture had obtained confessions from those on trial, many given whether it was the truth or not just to gain the relief from torture brought about by death. Generally females were accused, being considered at the time to be more susceptible to the charms of the Devil, they would then be stripped and searched for the 'Devils Mark'. Mathew Hopkins, the 'witchfinder general' between 1644 and 1646 used sleep and food deprivation and binding his victims in painful positions for hours as a means to extract a confession. The name Cuckstool Road in Denby Dale, survives to this day to remind us of another activity, probably carried out at the bottom of the hill, at Heywood

Bottom utilising the River Dearne. I am assuming that there is confusion here regarding the two quite different practices involved with the Cucking Stool and the Ducking Stool. The Ducking Stool would see the near naked accused woman, bound to a chair, or in some cases to the centre of a rope. She would then be immersed in the water, if she sank, she would be adjudged innocent, though drowning was a real possibility. If she endeavoured to stay afloat and thrashed around in the water, then she was presumed guilty and hanged. A Cucking Stool, was simply a chair placed outside an offenders home where the accused would be required to sit and endure the taunts and jibes of the villagers for the whole day. Sometimes the person involved would be carried shoulder high, sitting in the chair, throughout the township before being placed outside their home.

Matthew Hopkins 'Witchfinder General' between 1644 and 1646. *Author's collection.*

Against this somewhat hysterical background two women from Denby found themselves accused and were taken to a Barnsley gaol to wait for their hearing at Wooley before Darcy Wentworth Esq. to answer for their alleged indiscretions. The two were Ann Shillitoe (wife of Thomas) and Susan Hinchcliffe (wife of Joseph). Their accuser was Mary Moor, a spinster aged sixteen.

Fred Lawton in his 'Historical Notes. of Skelmanthorpe and District' gives the following transcription of the evidence brought before the Court: Mary Moor gave the following evidence;

That Susan said to Ann, 'If thou cans't but get young Thomas Haigh to buy three pennyworth of indico, and look him in the face when he gives it thee, and touch his locks, we shall have power enough to take life.'

Susan also said, 'Nanny, wilt thou not go today and make hay at Thomas Haigh's?'

Ann answered, 'If thou cans't but bring nine bits of bread away and nine bits of butter in thy mouth, we shall have power enough to take the life of their goods. They need not be in such pomp, for we will neither leave him cow nor horse at house.'

Ann asked Susan, 'Mother, did you do Dame Haigh any hurt?' Susan replied, 'That I did, for after I touched the edging of her skirt, she stepped not many steps after. I shortened her walk.' Mary Moor continues, with details of a previous conversation between the two accused.

Susan said to Ann, 'I think I must give this Thomas Bramhall over, for they tie so much wighen, (the rowan that the witches hated, formerly used by the Druids in ancient tines) about him, I cannot come to my purpose, else I could have worn him away once in two years.'

Ann replied, 'Thou are too far worn Susan' then said to her daughter, 'Nanny, did not thou hear that Timothy Haigh had like to have been drowned I'th Water hall dyke?'

Mary Moor didn't hear her answer, Susan then said, 'I led him up and down the moor, with an intention that he should either have broke his neck or have drowned himself; but at last his horse threw him, and he then went over the bridge, and I had a foot in. How he got over the bridge I cannot tell, except the Lord led him by the hand. I had him not at that time. But the next time let both the horse and him look both to themselves.'

Ann then asked her mother if she had ever done John Moor any hurt, her mother replied yes and said, 'I took the life of two swine and did hurt to a child.' Mary Moor also heard Susan say to Ann that if her father had but touched Martha Haigh, before she had spoken to him, they could have had power enough to take away her life, to which Ann replied, 'There is no time bye-past.'

Mary Moor also said that about the middle of July last past, going to borrow a linewheel, she heard Ann say to Susan, 'I saw my father play such a trick last night as I never saw in my life, he asked for butter, and their came butter onto his knee in a wooden saucer.'

Susan replied, 'That was but a little. Hast thou lived in this house so long, and never saw any of thy father's tricks? Dost not know that thy father went to John Walkers to steime (order) a pair of shoes, and he would not let him have them without he had money in his hand; but he never made pair after. Likewise he went to George Copley's to steime a waistcoat cloth, and he would not let him have it without he had silver in his hand; and because he would not let him have it he never made piece after but two. If anybody would not let them have what they wanted they would take the life of anybody.'

Susan said to Ann, that Joseph Hinchcliffe was as ill as they, but would not be seen in it. He bore it far off. Ann also said that if they were known they might be hanged, but Susan replied that no hemp would hang them. Ann said they might be burnt to which Susan answered, 'Nay, they would never tell until they died.' Mary Moor also heard Ann say, 'I'll warrant ye thou shall say little when thou comes before the bench.'

To make matters even more complicated another statement was taken from Timothy Haigh of Denby which said: he was present when Mary Moor, (the chief witness!) did vomit a piece of bended wire and piece of paper with two crooked pins in it, and 'hath at several other times seen her vomit crooked pins.'

One has to wonder what the villagers and indeed their Church curate, Timothy Kent, made of all the latter! A mother and daughter arrested for alleged crimes of witchery because of the evidence of a sixteen year-old girl. A girl who had also implicated the husband and father Joseph, only to be accused of evil machinations herself.

The drama could have initially been played out in Lower Denby, the Haigh family living for many generations on the site of the *Wagon and Horses* public house. It is also possible that the Shillitoe family came from Upper Bagden, the 1841 and 1851 censuses record numerous individuals living here but occupation of a site for over one hundred and sixty years without supporting evidence can only be a guess at best. It seems highly likely that a neighbourhood feud had developed between the Hinchcliffes, Haighs and Moors, malicious gossip, government propaganda and the relaxed requirements for evidence by the Courts made this a very easy time for people to settle disagreements by eliminating the other parties involved. Of course, Denby could perhaps have played host to two of the 'Devils Brood' but the evidence points more to the latter rather than the former.

The last execution for witchcraft in England took place in Exeter in 1682, though trials continued until 1712. In Denby a little common sense prevailed and a petition was raised, signed by more than fifty people and addressed to the Magistrates of the West Riding:

Some of us have well known the said Sussanna and Anna by the space of 20 years and upwards, others of us for 15 years and upwards, others of us for 10 years and upwards. And have by the said space observed and known the life and conversation of the said Sussanna to be not only very sober, orderly and unblameable in every respect but also of good example and very helpful and useful in the neighbourhood according to her poor ability. That she was a constant frequenter of public ordinances while she was able, and to the best of our understanding made conscience of her ways in more than common sort. That we never heard, or had the least ground to suspect her, or her said daughter, to be in any sort guilty of so foul a crime, but do fully believe that the said information against them both is a most gross and groundless (if not malicious) prosecution. And this we humbly certify as our very true apprehensions, as in the sight and presence of Him who will judge the secrets of all our hearts. And as touching the said girl who now informs, some of us could say much concerning her of a quite different nature, but that we judge recrimination to be but an indirect way of clearing the innocent.

The two women were committed for trial in York at the next assizes, although nothing survived in the records to tell of the outcome. The record itself when last seen, was torn in two, which would seem to indicate that the charges were thrown out. Brian Elliott in his book *The Making of Barnsley* supplies the answer, he discovered a note in *Hunters – Life of Oliver Heywood* which completed the story.

Apparently Joseph Hinchcliffe, who was bound over with his wife and daughter, committed suicide on the morning of Thursday 4 February 1675. He was not discovered until the following Sunday. Meanwhile, his wife, Susan had died praying on her deathbed for her accusers.

It is possible that the statement of Mary Moor was ripped in two because two of the three accused parties had died within six months of their appearance at Wooley and that the case had

A witch begging raw materials from a gravedigger. *Author's collection.*

Torture, using forced drinking, to try and gain a confession. *Author's collection.*

not yet been heard at York. Given the petition of the villagers it would seen that the shame of the accusations had claimed both their lives, and that the case had been dismissed, yet why had Susan Hinchcliffe died praying on her deathbed for her accusers if the case really had been thrown out?

The last witch in the area of which any record was made was also an inhabitant of Upper Denby. Betty Roberts was alive during the early nineteenth century, she is described by Fred Lawton, in his *Historical Notes of Skelmanthorpe and District* thus:

She was very peculiar looking, and wore a tall peaked bonnet or hat, and a long, dark cloak - something after the familiar pictures of Mother Shipton. She lived in a lone hut, which the boys were terrified to pass, although there was a strange attraction to try and peep in, for they were taught they might see the 'posnet' or small cauldron on the fire, in which she brewed the 'stuff' by which she was enabled to fly up the chimney or through the keyhole. When she was teased she made strange cabalistic signs, as if she were calling the stars to avenge her, at the same time uttering some strange gibberish. As she had no relatives, it was supposed that at one tine she had belonged to a wandering tribe of gypsies.

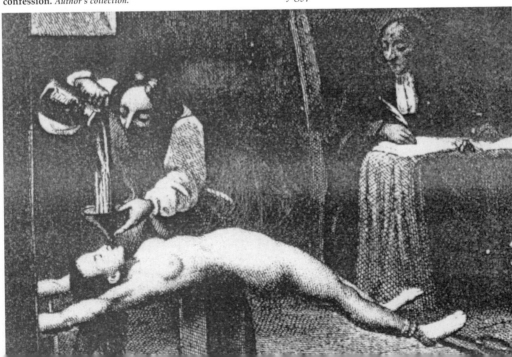

Chapter Six

Religion and Worship

THE CHURCH

Only one church is mentioned in the wapentake of Staincross in the *Domesday* book and it was sited somewhere near modern day Silkstone. Confusion has arisen between this location and the possibility of the edifice being at Cawthorne. This is usually explained by the fact that a part of Cawthorne once belonged to Silkstone, but as the two villages are only a couple of miles apart it could even have been almost central to the two. The family of Ailric, as we have already noted were great church builders, and as they lived at Cawthorne it seems only natural that a chapel arose there during Ailric's son, Swein's time, circa 1090. Silkstone became the mother church for the whole wapentake and has even been known as the 'Minster of the Moors', a title also possessed by Ecclesfield Parish church near Sheffield.

A local church with an even greater claim to antiquity is that of High Hoyland. A Saxon cross, dated to approximately 800AD was found here whilst restoration work was being undertaken. Re-founded by either Ailric, Swein or Adam fitz Swein, the ancient structure has long since gone, today the tower is the oldest part, dating to 1679. Only one memorial of note lies within, that of Francis Burdet of Birthwaite (son of Thomas), dated 1637.

Penistone Church was not founded until after the conquest, again the Saxon family of Ailric were responsible, most likely around the year 1200, indeed it was Adam fitz Swein who was responsible for re-founding Penistone after it had been destroyed during the Harrying of the North. After the male line sired by Ailric died out the right of presentment of the vicar lay in the hands of the Burgh and Neville dynasties. The earliest masonry of the present day church dates from circa 1300.

Denby was originally incorporated into the extensive Parish of Penistone, all services, including baptisms, marriages and burials would have taken place here. The Lords of the Manor, the Burdets would have had the option of using churches in other areas of their manor. As to where the early Lords were buried who can now say. Robert Burdet, died 1451 was buried at

Anglo Saxon cross, dated to approximately 800 AD, found at High Hoyland church during restoration work. *Author's collection.*

Penistone. His direct ancestor, generations later, Richard Burdet was also buried here in 1617. Where lie the remains of Robert and Idonea Balliol, Sir Robert de Denby or Aymer and Nicholas Burdet? They are probably at Penistone, could be at High Hoyland, or at the outside, Silkstone or Cawthorne. The monuments left to commemorate these people, such as they were, are long gone, their last resting places forgotten forever. We cannot even be sure as to the extent of the old churchyard boundaries, ancient burials could lie under today's roads and housing.

The ordinary villagers of Denby had to walk or travel in carts to facilitate their desire for worship and for all the usual services provided by the establishment. In the winter months it was difficult, indeed, nigh on impossible to cross the flooded waters of Scout Dyke in order to reach Penistone. In 1626 the waters of the dyke claimed the lives of thirteen parishioners on their way to church, a tragedy, which further resolved the villagers to petition Archbishop Tobias Mathew for a licence to erect a chapel. He agreed and on 12 December 1627, at York he formalised the agreement. Although he was unable to comply with their requests for him to consecrate it, he did allow them licence to perform religious ordinances here without prejudice to the Vicars of Penistone, and also granted them the choir offices. It was Godfrey Bosville (whose father Ralph had bought the advowson of Penistone Church from Elizabeth I) who built it. Why it was Bosville and not the Burdet family is unknown. They were still Lords of the Manor of Denby at this time, indeed Richard Burdet was married to Mary Bosville so they must have been involved, though evidently not with the financial side. The siting of the church not only reflects its nearness to Gunthwaite and Bosville lands as opposed to Nether Denby and Burdet lands (indeed they probably had the furthest to travel) but also that it commands views out over towards Penistone. The community living around the church probably began to increase from this time explaining why today, Upper Denby has a larger population and subsequently more buildings than most of its near neighbours, excepting Denby Dale which was a product of the industrial revolution. Unfortunately the only surviving record to tell of the size or design of this building is the tiny

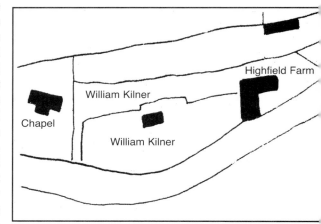

Author's freehand copy of the enclosure map of 1802 shows the shape of the chapel thus. *Author's collection.*

representation made on the Enclosure map dated 1802, though the chapel continued in use until 1844. This building was known as a Chapel of Ease or District Chapel under the diocese of Penistone.

After Ralph Bosville had bought the right of presentation of the Vicar, or advowson, for the rectory of Penistone it passed through his family line by way of his sisters and it was their husbands who were responsible for naming the Vicar.

In 1602 Godfrey Copley, presented Francis Oley, in 1619 John Savile presented Jonas Rook, in 1633 George Burdet, presented Mathew Booth after the death of Jonas Rook. In 1635, after the resignation of Booth, Peter Toothill was presented by Edmund Ogden, of Bullhouse, by the grant of George Burdet (Ogden was his father-in-law), Toothill died around 1642.

Hunter, noted that there was probably an irregularity in the double presentation of George Burdet but it is clear from the above how closely involved Penistone Church was with Denby and Gunthwaite and its most prominent families the Burdets and Bosvilles.

The foundation of the Chapel at Denby was therefore guided by very strong hands, probably encouraged by the growing spirit of Puritanism which swept the country during the reigns of James I and Charles I. Since the Bosvilles were puritans it was natural that they should appoint a puritan minister and they chose Charles Broxholme.

The following extract is taken from Dransfield's *History of Penistone* and is an extract of the *De Spiritualibis Pecci of Bagshaw*:

He was a gentleman born, and so one reckons of the lesser (and lower) nobility. His brother was a Parliament man, in and for some place in Lincolnshire. Providence brought him into the ministry ; and in the exercise of it, unto Belper in Derbyshire, Gunthwaite in Yorkshire and Denton in Lancashire, and so to Buxton, noted for its bath, but never so honoured as when he and some of his excellent successors were as preachers and pastors there. It hath been said that in his time, as there was violent imposition by some on one, so there was violent opposition by some on the other side. This must be said of him, though his principles hindered him being an active conformist, they led him to be a passive and patient non-conformist. As another great man said he might say, his head was too big for a Church door ; till near his end he placed in Chapels : such were those I have named. The violence of those called Cavaliers who too many of them did as one said, hate all manner of purity whatsoever, drove him into Derby, where under Sir John Gell the father, his life was secured.

Broxholme was succeeded by Daniel Clarke in 1635. Clarke was educated at King's College, Cambridge, where he took his BA degree in 1631 and MA in 1634. Whilst at Denby he married a daughter of George Burdet. Clarke was favourable to the cause of Parliament during the Civil War, he was appointed by them on the 14 March 1643 to leave Denby and officiate in Kirkburton Church and to 'receive the profits of the said vicarage for his paynes, till further orders be taken by both houses of Parliament'. His predecessor at Kirkburton, Gamaliel Whitaker, was an ardent Royalist and the son of the rector of Thornhill. He was arrested by parliamentary troops, deprived of his living and taken as a prisoner to Manchester where he died within a month of 'grief and ill usage'. On the day of his arrest his wife had been shot dead on the vicarage staircase, not deliberately but in the scuffle which developed during the arrest of her husband. It was Lord Fairfax who appointed Daniel Clarke to take over from Whittaker who had actively supported the Royalists with men, money, horses and arms (see Quakers). In a Parliamentary survey, Clarke was described as a 'painful preacher', which meant that he took pains with his preaching unlike many others who preached other men's works or printed sermons. He left Kirkburton in approximately 1649.

Up to now no provision had been made for the minister at Denby, but on 6 January 1648 this changed. The diary of John Hobson records in 1733,

At church. Mr Perkin, minister at Denby chapel told me that Oliver Cromwell builded and endowed that chapel out of a Royalists estate, which he had seazed on.

It was actually Colonel Godfrey Bosville who was instrumental in initiating that the heirs of Sir Edward Osborne (a Royalist) of Kiveton (deceased), should pay £25 per annum to Denby Chapel and the same sum to Seaton Ross in the East Riding. The money was paid irregularly, but eventually £1000 was paid by the heirs of Osborne to Colonel Bosville.

Daniel Clarke was succeeded by a man named Miller, it is just possible that this was the preacher whom Adam Eyre mentions in his diary of 1647,

Sunday, 12 December - *This day I went to Denby Chapel and heard an old fellow preach both forenoon and after.*

Miller was followed by John Crooke, from Sheffield. He settled in Denby whilst acting as its curate. He was a puritan and non-conformist who lived during turbulent times. The restoration of Charles II as King of England in 1660 signalled the end of Puritanism and in 1662 all clergymen were expected to subscribe to the new prayer book and to make other changes to their services. Those that refused to comply with this instruction were removed from office by the *Act of Uniformity*, which led to over 2000 members of the clergy being ejected from their livings throughout the country. Reverend John Crooke MA was one of these, he left Denby and retired to Wakefield where he died in 1687. Henry Swift, Vicar of Penistone was another, though he continued to preach in his church and was imprisoned three times for this offence. He died in 1682 and was followed by Reverend Edmund Hough who did conform. This led to well known puritans such as the Wordsworths of Water Hall, the Riches of Bullhouse and the Bosvilles of Gunthwaite leaving the church and holding services at Bullhouse Hall. The *Act of Tolerance* was passed in 1689 which allowed dissenters and non-conformists to have their own places of worship, within three years these local gentlemen had built Bullhouse Chapel which opened on 18 April 1692.

Some time after 1662, the Vicar of Cawthorne, Christopher Wallbank, attempted to gain the curacy of Denby by forging a nomination. A certificate recommending him to the people of the village was allegedly signed by Sir Gervase Cutler, Thomas Barnby, Loy Kett (Vicar of Silkstone), Henry Bubwith, Henry Lewis and others. He was found out and promptly deprived for his efforts. Timothy Kent took over in 1665 and continued up until his death in 1691. His stone epitaph survives in the Church, written in Latin.

The monument in Denby church commemorating the Rev. Timothy Kent. *Author's collection.*

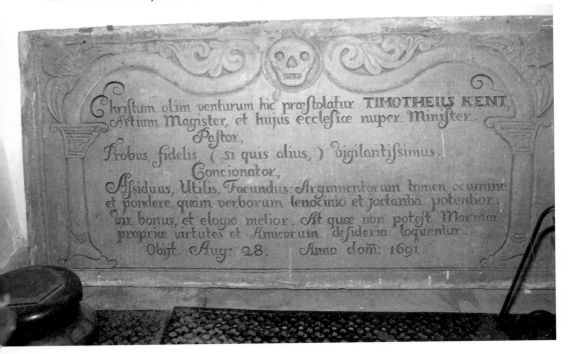

The following translation comes from a booklet produced to mark the centenary of the Church in 1945 :

Here Timothy Kent awaits Christ's future coming;
Master of Arts and of this Church a recent minister.
A pastor, honourable and steadfast ; most watchful lest any should wander.
A popular orator, constant, beneficial, and eloquent
His arguments weighty, yet cunning ; how alluring of speech, yet mightier in actions.
A good man, yet greater in writing. Though stone cannot express
his peculiar excellences,
The longings of his friends will yet constantly speak.
Died, 28th August 1691

He is also probably the same Tim Kent who witnessed the following deed dated 21 November 1676,

In £40 John Morton of Dembye, husbandman to Godfrey Bosville, Lord of the Manor of Gomuldthwayt esq. John Morton to pay Godfrey Bosville annuity of annual rent of 4d and to do suit at Gomuldthwayt Manor Court.

The Chapel was augmented in 1738 with £200 given by Reverend Jonathan Perkins (whom we shall return to) to pay for its expenses and provide a salary for the incumbent. In 1739 a further £200 was granted, allocated from the fund known as 'Queen Anne's Bounty'.

The revenues for this had been transferred from a Papal taxation known as 'First Fruits and Tenths', whereby a person appointed to a living was obliged to pay 10% of his first year's income to the Pope. The proceeds were handed over to the Church of England by Queen Anne in 1704 to provide a fund for the relief of the poorer Anglican clergy, by making grants to livings with incomes of less than £10 per annum (raised in 1788 to £35). From 1809 it was paid by Parliamentary grants, after which, in 1816, Denby received a further £1200.

During the eighteenth century some of the Masters of Penistone Grammar school acted as curates at Denby. Historian W.H. Senior noted in the book *A History of Denby Dale Urban District* that in 1764 Archbishop Drummond found a Jonothan Perkins acting as master of the Grammar school and curate. There appears to be some confusion about an incumbent at Denby with this name. Reverend Moore noted in 1729 a Jonathan Parker, Joseph Hunter named the man Jonothan Parkin and the trade directories of the nineteenth century note a Jonothan Perkins.

In 1743 Thomas Cockshutt, Vicar of Penistone reported to his Archbishop about matters relating to his parish. It was Jonathan Perkins who supplied the following information:

1. We have 130 families in chapelry of Denby of which 9 are Quakers. No papists or other kind of Dissenters.
2. We have one licensed meeting house for Quakers who assemble every Lords Day to the number of 80. One Elihu Dickinson teaches.
3. We have one Charity School endowed with £5 a year for teaching poor children. Sufficient care is taken to teach then in the principles of Christian religion, according to the doctrine of the Church of England, and to bring them duly to Church.
4. Denby being in the Parish of Penistone, I being Grammar School master there reside in the schoolhouse, having no house or lands belonging to the chapelry of Denby.
5. I do all the duty of the Chapelry myself.
6. I know of none that come to Denby Chapel that are not baptised but I believe that a 100 of

competent age come who are not confirmed.

7. Every Sunday and Holy Day and twice on every Lords Day, Divine Service is performed.

8. The first Sunday in every month I catechise in the Chapel and every Saturday in the Grammar School by which means most children and servants in these parts are sufficiently instructed in their catechism.

9. I never administer the Sacrament in the Chapel of Denby, though I believe that there are 200 communicants in our Chapelry most of which receive at different times in the Parish Church.

10. I give open and timely warning of Sacrament being administered at the Parish Church the Sunday before I and the inhabitants take it at Penistone.

The latter was signed by Jonathan Perkins. Adm. 19 July 1731, Deacon, Chester, 26 October 1729. Priest 18 July 1731. Christ's College, Cambridge.

In approximately 1751 Samuel Phipps became curate, before becoming Vicar of Penistone, being presented by Godfrey Bosville in, 1761. There is also evidence to suggest that by 1780 he was Vicar of Silkstone, where he died in 1799 aged eighty-five. The Churchwardens presentment for the Denby Chapelry has the following to say, dated 15 June 1750:

All is well. Our schoolmaster is efficient but we have no ministers house. John Horsfall, Joseph Gaunt, Joseph Rhodes and Wm. Earnshaw, Churchwardens. 1721, July 29th – I Phillip Mitchell, Churchwarden of Penistone, do certify that John Goldthorpe presented at the last visitation for profaning the Sabbath and for not repairing to his Parish Church hath since the visitation duly frequented the said Church as witness my hand Phillip Mitchell.

Francis Haigh became master of the Grammar school in 1751, he was later to acquire the curacy of Denby and those of Bolsterstone and Midhope. Although these curacies supplemented his income they also caused him to neglect his school duties. In addition to this he became blind during the last ten years of his life, until he died in 1776. Joseph Horsfall became the next master of the school, though he was negligent in the extreme and was eventually made to resign, whether he preached at Denby is unknown.

Joseph Wood of Nantwich succeeded Horsfall as master until his death in 1836, but his activities at Denby were limited. By at least 1822 John Brownhill had become curate of the Chapel at Denby. This man is almost certainly the same as the one buried in Cumberworth churchyard in 1857 aged sixty-four. His family lived at Cliff Hall, Shelley until at least 1855, and was probably the father of the dynasty who founded Brownhill and Scatchard the textile manufacturers at Inkerman Mills in Denby Dale in 1868. He was followed by Brice Bronwin who was the incumbent at the time of Bishop Longley's visitation in 1839. Bronwin was recorded to be fifty years old in the 1841 census returns and so was born around 1790.

The Bishop found the Chapel to be in such a, 'filthy and ruinous state' that he ordered it to be pulled down and money raised to rebuild it. In 1844, under Bronwin, a building committee was formed. John Ellis, a builder from High Flatts was paid £1170 to construct a new and bigger Church, which was completed in 1845. This building forms the major portion of the present Church, but consisted of a tower and nave only. The altar was at the east wall of the nave and a gallery surrounded the other three walls; box pews filled the nave, after only a short time the porch was added.

On 12 December 1853 an order in council was signed by Queen Victoria making Denby into a separate Parish, to include the villages of Gunthwaite, Ingbirchworth, High Flatts, Birdsedge and Denby Dykeside (now Denby Dale) all of which were previously under Penistone authority.

Denby church in 1958, the structure had only a tower and nave in 1845 but has been much altered. Note the gravestones still in situ before removal for maintenance purposes. *Author's collection.*

Job Johnson of Huddersfield had become curate in 1851, but became Vicar in 1853. He was responsible for the construction of the Vicarage in 1873 at a cost of £1800, though £2000 is also quoted.

Before the construction of the vicarage the curates had lived in one of the cottages which formed part of the site of 'Highfield Farm'. Though these were probably the late eighteenth and early nineteenth century incumbents, the Masters of the Grammar school most likely having lived in Penistone. According to the booklet *A Stroll Around Denbi* these cottages were originally owned by a J. Micklethwaite, possibly a descendent of the Lords of Ingbirchworth. They were bought in 1781 for £43 by William Kilner, who redeveloped the site. His farm and lands as can be seen from the Enclosure map were the closest to the Chapel.

In later years the adjacent farm, called 'Highfield Farm' and at least one of the cottages became the home of the Charlesworth family. The farm site has been redeveloped in recent times by local building contractor, Joe Price, the name Highfield Farm being dropped in favour of Upper House Fold, which reflects the residential properties created here.

Rev. Orr requests a meeting at the vicarage in 1887. *Author's collection.*

Denby Scouts with flat capped Vicar, Rev. Tibbits. Taken in either 1928 or 1929.
From the back, left: G Booth, C H Roden, F Grange, F Mathews, J Senior, F Booth, vicar Rev. G O Tibbits, M Dearnley, H Kilner, E Turton, J Dronfield, G Hudson, E Dronsfield, D Buckley, D Rusby, D Barber, D Haigh, E Gelder, A Beever, J Fawcett, C Schofield, J Lockwood, H Turton, S Schofield, L Shaw, R Taylor. *Author's collection.*

Rev. Job Johnson, Denby's first vicar with his wife, circa. 1878. *Author's collection.*

Job Johnson was succeeded by the second Vicar of Denby, Alexander Barrington Orr, of Trinity College, Dublin. In 1887 Reverend Orr formed a Church Council 'in order to promote the harmonious co-operation of Priest and people'. A meeting was held at the Vicarage on Saturday 3 December 1887 to constitute the same. It was during Reverend Orr's time that a large part of Denby Dykeside was ceded to Cumberworth Parish, this occurred in 1892.

Romeo Edwin Taglis became Vicar in 1894. He was responsible for a large renovation and rebuilding operation about the Church during 1900/1901. The interior of the nave was almost entirely rebuilt. The gallery was taken down, stone pillars and arches were raised, dividing the centre aisle from the North and South portions of the nave. A barrel roof was placed over the centre aisle and a new chancel was built with a crossed rafter roof. The interior of the Church was now a copy of one which the Vicar had seen in Italy. A vestry was added to the south side of the chancel and new pews replaced the old-fashioned box pews in the nave. The organ, which had been in the gallery was now put in the chancel against the vestry. Thus rebuilt, the building was re-opened and consecrated on Wednesday, 19 June, 1901. Reverend Taglis ended his days at Denby, his grave is inscribed 'Romeo Edwin Taglis, Priest, for 32 years Vicar of Denby, died 24 September 1926 aged 67. Also, Margaret his wife, died 11 April 1940 aged 78.'

Gervase Tibbits and Reginald Sheard followed Taglis, both becoming integral parts of the community, leading the choir, taking Scout troops and raising money for Church funds.

In Norman Moore's first year of office, 1944, the men of the Parish entirely re-decorated the interior of the chancel and nave. The following year saw the centenary of the construction of the Church and a booklet, written by Reverend Moore was produced.

Local newspaper cutting reporting the installation of a new clock probably dating from the mid-1950s. *Author's collection.*

Bishop Dedicates Church Clock at Denby

ON Saturday, the parishioners of Denby Parish Church, including members of the local Urban Council, saw an eighteen-month-old ambition fulfilled when they took part in the dedication by the Bishop of Pontefract (the Rt. Rev. A. H. Morris) of a clock in the tower.

The clock, which is an eight-day one, has two dials, each five feet six inches across. It has cost £270.

Subscriptions to date are about £20 short of the total. Two sisters, Mrs. Annie Haigh and Mrs. Lucy Kaye, have spent the past eighteen months in house-to-house collecting for the clock fund.

A pull on a long cord by the

Picture shows (left to right): Mr. J. Turton (churchwarden), Clr. Kaye, Mr. White, the Bishop of Pontefract, Mr. Colin Crossland (churchwarden), the Vicar and Mr. Waldie.

oldest member of the congregation—eighty-three-year-old Mr. J. R. Waldie—in the ancient porch set in motion the striking mechanism of the clock.

After he had dedicated the clock "in thankful remembrance of the benefactors of the parish," the Bishop, accompanied by the Vicar (the Rev. N. A. Moore), the verger (Mr. R. White), Clr. J. H. Kaye and the churchwardens (representing the subscribers), returned to their places in church to continue a prepared form of service.

Front cover of the booklet produced to mark the church's centenary in 1945. *Author's collection.*

Numerous gifts to the church were donated over the years, the bell is the oldest and most interesting, dated 1678 and inscribed, 'The gift of Dame Mary Beaumont, eldest daughter of George Burdet, Esq. Of Denby Hall'

The Bishop's sanctuary chair was given by Miss M. Hinchcliffe. It is one of a pair, the other (larger and more elaborately carved) is in Wakefield Cathedral and bears the arms of the City of York and was the chair of the Lord Mayor of York in 1617. Paintings on the pulpit are also worthy of mention, these were painted by the Cawthorne based artist Roddam Spencer-Stanhope. Cawthorne church had been largely rebuilt in 1900 and they had installed a new pulpit which Stanhope had carved in Florence whilst studying with Dante Gabriel Rosetti. Their old pulpit was sent to Denby and remains here to this day. It has recently been restored to its original dark wooden finish after being painted a gaudy white colour for a time.

Paintings on the pulpit in the church painted by Rodham Spencer Stanhope, previously in Cawthorne church. *Author's collection.*

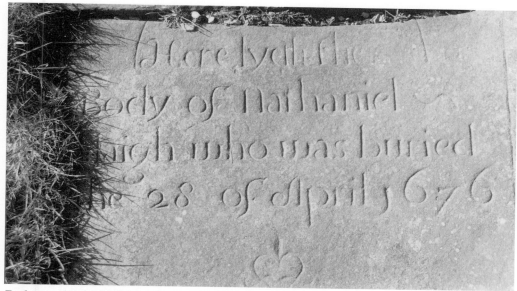

Tombstone of Nathaniel Haigh, at Denby, died 1676. *Author's collection.*

Finally the electric lighting was subscribed for by the parishioners of Denby, in memory of their Vicar, Reverend Tibbits who died in 1939. Inside the Church there are two memorials of note. The first is in memory of Charles Kilner, a professor of music who died in 1858, the second is the war memorial, it contains the following names:

Denby choir, circa. 1935., Rev. Tibbits is at the far right on the third row. *Author's collection.*

Rev. Sheard, circa. 1940.
Author's collection.

Names on the War Memorial in the Church

1914-1918:	James Moore	Charles Edward Jelfs
	Edwin Jackson	Herbert Norton Jackson
	John Ellis Broadhead	Charles Kilner Barraclough
	Noah Green	Fred Firth
	Thomas Hodge	Arthur Williamson
	Gladstone Beever	George Clement Boothroyd
	John Walshaw	Joe Hirst
	Charles Godfrey Hinchcliffe	John Wright
	Archie Roberts	Keble Thomas Evenett
	Henry Sheard	Joseph Bottomley Rotherforth
	Albert Jackson	Frank Cook
	John Cook	Charles Ralph Douglas Bell
1939-1945:	Cyril Schofield	Ernest Roebuck

Denby was in the diocese of York until 1836 when it was transferred to the newly formed diocese of Ripon. Another new diocese was formed in 1888, that of Wakefield, and Denby was transferred here, under, whose jurisdiction it remains today. The Parish registers begin as follows:

Baptisms *12 January 1851 (before this date Denby baptisms were performed and recorded at Penistone)*

Marriages *22 February 1854*

Burials *2 January 1851 (though tombstones in the churchyard prove that in fact burials had been taking place here for some time. For instance, Nathaniel Haigh's tombstone is dated 28 April 1676, Mary Woolsind, 14 April 1723, Isabell Haigh, 26 December 1672).*

William Couldwell died on 30 July 1783. His tombstone has a most interesting inscription, described as a clothier, the following transcription is almost complete, save for words which are illegible due to cracks and weathering:

Frail is the vestment once I made,
Death hath -?- this human thread,
My frame I thought to firm so-?-,
Was but a clothing for the soul,
The cloth and thread I wove and spun,
By time and weather were undone,
The stronger texture of my frame,
That web of nerves was just the same,
And now the fates that spun the chain,
* Have cut the thread of life again.*

More modern times have seen the clearing of the stones from the front graveyard, sometime in the early sixties, because of its overgrown and generally poor condition. The stones were positioned all around the boundary walls of the churchyard where they remain today. I was informed by the late Mr. Jack Waldie that not a single complete gravestone had been taken away so genealogists need not despair.

In 1993, mainly due to vandalism, a number of gravestones and crosses were broken and desecrated, signifying the change in moral attitudes inherent in today's society when compared to our God fearing forbears. In 1990 Denby Dale became a separate parish leaving St. Johns at

Denby and St. Nicholas's at Cumberworth to form a United Benefice. In 1994 a festival of flowers celebration was held inside the church and in the school, where an exhibition of village memorabilia was displayed. A commemorative plate was also commissioned, the funds from this event helping to pay for a kitchen.

The future of Denby church is at present uncertain. A leaflet dropped through letter boxes around the village during 1998 forecasted a shortfall of £4000 per annum, and stated that unless other funds could be found, the costs would become prohibitive by the year 2003. The sale of the church house enabled necessary repairs and replacements to be paid for, but when one considers that the new organ, installed in 1997 cost £9200 and that attendance figures had dropped to an average of just fifteen in 1998, it is difficult to see how the church can survive. Indeed attendances throughout the 1990s serve to illustrate attitudes to religion and spiritual fulfilment throughout the decade when compared to earlier centuries, when peoples lives centred around the holy calendar. Average attendances: 1990-20, 1991-21, 1992-23, 1993-22, 1994-21, 1995-19, 1996-16, 1997-15, 1998-15.

It is to be hoped the church will survive, it has been an integral part of the village of Upper Denby for over 350 years and does not deserve to deteriorate and become neglected to the same extent as its near neighbour at High Hoyland.

The Clergy (this is not a complete listing)

Charles Broxholme	1627-1635	John Brownhil	-
Daniel Clarke	1635-1643	Brice Bronwin	1830 -
- Miller	-	Job Johnson	1851-1887
John Crooke	1657-1665	Alexander Barrington Orr	1887-1894
Timothy Kent MA	1665-1691	Romeo Edwin Taglis	1894-1926
Gamaliel Battie	-	Gervase Orton Tibbits	1926-1938
William Norris	1698-17??NB	Reginald Jackson Sheard	1939-1944
Bryan Allot	-	Norman Aubrey Moore	1944-1982
Jonothan Perkins	1729-	Norman Stanley Fox	1982-1984
Samuel Phipps	1751-1761	Robert Christopher Shaw	1985-1990
Francis Haigh	-	David James Clarkson	1991-Present

NB: *William Norris seems to have left Denby before he died. He was buried at Penistone in 1733 aged 74, but we know that Jonathan Perkins had taken over by 1729.*

QUAKERS

The movement begun by George Fox (1624-91) because of dissatisfaction with the normal form of worship probably arrived in High Flatts around the year 1652. When a person was converted (or 'convinced') he became a 'friend', of which a number belonged to the village of Denby – John & Henry Dickinson (High Flatts), John Turner, Richard Priest and Thomas Crowder (Denby), John Swift and Arthur Brooksbank (Gunthwaite), John Blackley (Gunthwaite Hall) all belong to this 'Quaker Dawn' during the 1650s.

Fred Lawton and W H Senior relate the following story about the early origins of the Quakers of High Flatts.

An entry in the Kirkburton parish registers records the birth of John Firth, son of James Firth of Leak Hall in Denby Dale in 1597. In 1624 he married and went to live at Shepley Old Hall. In 1642 he joined Colonel Bosville of Gunthwaite's troop of soldiers to fight in the civil war against the King. After training, Firth was posted to Nottingham castle to guard prisoners held there, one of whom was George Fox, founder of the Quaker movement. Fox would preach to prisoners, guards, indeed anyone

Quaker Bottom cemetery, present day. Note the uniform size of the gravestones. *Author's collection.*

Quaker Bottom, High Flatts, present day. *Author's collection.*

else who could hear and he eventually converted John Firth, who went 'AWOL' from the army as soon as he could and returned to Shepley.

Here he began holding small meetings in his house along the lines of Fox's beliefs, i.e.: pacifism, non-bearing of arms and non payment of tithes to a church they did not believe in, but, of course, all this was against the law, and he was holding himself up for persecution. A detachment of soldiers were sent from Halifax to arrest him, but he was warned and fled to Skelmanthorpe where he hid in the old town quarry. The soldiers followed him forced him from hiding and arrested him. He was placed on the back of one of the soldiers horses and was led back to Halifax facing imprisonment, but as they proceeded over Shelley Bank towards Kirkburton, Firth managed to slide from the horse and escape into the thickly wooded Box Ings wood. Naturally the soldiers went after him, but night was falling and reluctantly they abandoned the search.

Resigned to returning to Halifax without their prisoner, the soldiers set off towards Kirkburton. Spying a light in the window of a house near Kirkburton church the Captain of the troop, either in a fit of rage or in the belief that it might have something to do with Firth's escape, loaded his musket, pointed it at the window and fired.

Though not usually accurate this bullet ran true and smashed through the window killing Hester Whittaker, who was passing the window with a lighted candle in her hand. She was the wife of Gamaliel Whittaker, Vicar of Kirkburton. The Vicar himself was taken to Manchester for his Royalist sympathies where he died within a fortnight of his wife 'of grief and ill usage', or to put it another way, torture! Whittaker had been at Kirkburton since 1615 though of late the villagers had tried to get rid of him, a petition sent to parliament said that, 'he is of a scandalous conversation, a frequent drunkard and ale house haunter, and hath lately forsook his said cure and betaken himself to the Popish army of Cavaliers.'

He is also reputed to have sent information regarding his local knowledge to the Earl of Newcastle at Wakefield. His removal took place only days after the petition was read out in parliament and he was replaced by Daniel Clarke, curate of Denby.

After things quietened down a little, John Firth returned to Shepley and began his meetings again, but his home in the middle of the village was too public and so a relative who lived at Shepley Lane Head allowed him to preach there. This also proved too public as the house was on the main road and the 'friends' could be seen coming and going. Another relative made his home available to him, this building was sited in a secluded valley and was sheltered by trees, and became a success, John Firth had come to High Flatts. He died at the age of 86 in 1683.

As to whether the latter is all true I am unable to say, what I can offer is that Hester Whittaker was shot on the night that her husband was arrested, 12th Jan 1644. But according to Emley historian, Rev. Pobjoy she died in the scuffle which developed whilst the soldiers tried to arrest Gamaliel. This coupled with the village of Kirkburton's appeal to parliament for him to be removed would suggest that the soldiers came for this purpose alone, perhaps John Firth's story grew in the telling, maybe we shall never know for sure?

Whilst in its infancy the participants in the movement were persecuted for their beliefs. Acts were introduced to prevent meetings taking place, for not conforming with the established church, for not paying church tithes or swearing the Oath of Allegiance. For example, for being at a meeting in 1660, Richard Priest and John Marsden of Denby (amongst others), were imprisoned for three weeks. The term of imprisonment varied from days to years. In 1684 Joshua Green of Denby and Mathew Burdett of Nether Denby had been in prison for over two years for refusing to take the Oath of Allegiance. Burdett finally took the Oath and was released, Green remained in prison for some time. Refusing to pay church tithes also warranted severe punishment, John Crowder of Denby had his goods taken in kind on thirteen occasions between 1675 and 1683 valuing over £6. Crowder was a farmer and usually wheat, oats or barley were the items removed. The Quakers had a tradition for poor relief and charity work, not just within their own circles but in the 'outside world'. In 1826 an operation was mounted to help the people in the township of Denby. The problems in the village had been caused by the changes in the textile industry. At a meeting convened in May chaired by Elihu Dickinson, it was reported that in Denby there were 127 poor families, consisting of 664 individuals, this was roughly half the population of the village, of which fifty-five were wholly employed, 145 partially employed, 208 unemployed and 256 children under ten years old. The average earnings of these people was calculated to 1s 7.5d a week, the meeting resolved that a subscription should be raised to help.

As the movement grew and gained solidity, particular families and individuals gained in importance. The Dickinsons regularly turn up in records as not only staunch supporters of the movement but major landholders as we shall see later when we examine the Denby Enclosure Map of 1802. One other 'friend' from High Flatts worthy of note is Joseph Wood, a man of great character and an illustrious preacher and believer, his success and the records he left during his lifetime (1750-1821) are a testament to the ideal Quaker of his time. For more details on the Dickinsons and Joseph Wood see the book *Plain Country Friends* by D. Bower and J. Knight. In 1764 there were eleven Quaker families living at Denby which met each Sunday (along with others numbering over 100), under Henry Dickinson at the 'Friends Meeting House' at High Flatts.

As we have already seen meetings traditionally began to take place here during the time of Oliver Cromwell's republic (1649-1660), these were in a barn on the site of the present meeting house. This was converted in 1697 into a purpose built 'Meeting House', which was almost completely rebuilt in 1754 at a cost of £89 3s 0d. The present day graveyard was first used in 1790 (a smaller one at the front of the Meeting House was now full).

This hamlet at High Flatts was for many years populated by Quakers and became known as Quaker Bottom. At its peak High Flatts was probably one of the largest country meetings in this part of Yorkshire.

In 1886 a home or sanatorium was opened for 'the restoration of inebriate women of the working and middle classes' in Mill Bank House, built by Elihu Dickinson at High Flatts. This home for women was run by women. Due to the support of the 'Yorkshire Women's Christian Temperance Union' the home continued to run into the early years of the twentieth century. Inmates suffering from alcoholism were aided in keeping away from temptation, although shut away, many managed to kick their habit and indeed returned to help the inmates at the home after their own release. In 1901 the manageress was a Mrs Peace.

An interesting aside to the latter is the story that the *George* public house is also reputed to have been a sanatorium running along similar lines before it became a tavern.

Today this sleepy hamlet is largely untouched by modern development, the cobbled paths, the stately meeting house and the ordered graveyard evoke memories of these Quakers of the past.

CHAPELS

A Wesleyan Reform chapel was built in 1911 (next to what was the Post Office until the 1990s), its life was short-lived being closed in 1930 and converted into a private dwelling by J W Heath. This chapel was a break-away from the Denby Dale Wesleyan Reform Chapel, perhaps better known as the Zion chapel, which was built on Barnsley road in 1860. This chapel proved popular, so much so that a new building was commissioned, completed in 1908. The roof and south gable of

The old and new Zion chapels on Barnsley Road, (K-line) in Denby Dale, circa. 1950. *Author's collection.*

this newer building were severely damaged by high winds in 1962. The older building served as a Sunday school until it was demolished in 1979 to make way for new housing.

As an aside, it is interesting to note that the old chapel building once bore a 'fire mark', sited on the wall at the top of the building. In the days before the modern fire service (pre-1939, when it was part of the duties of the police force) the only men and equipment available to tackle blazes were at the disposal of the insurance companies. The fire mark denoted which company had insured the building and only they would attempt to put out a fire. Even if other brigades attended they would not have lent aid at a property not insured by them.

The chapels community activities included the staging and performance of plays. The following photograph above gives a flavour of the type of costume worn for these.

Taken in front of the older chapel. A group of amateur performers line up for the camera, circa. 1923. *Author's collection.*

Wesleyan Methodist chapel, Cumberworth Lane, Denby Dale, in the late nineteenth century before the Victoria Memorial hall was built. *W H Senior.*

ORIGINS OF OTHER LOCAL CHURCHES & CHAPELS
Wesleyan Methodist Chapel, Denby Dale

John Wood, a woollen manufacturer from Denby Dyke had been a member of the Shelley Methodist congregation but after a split in 1797 when Shelley went over to the New Connection he began to hold meetings in his textile warehouse, at Field House in Denby Dyke. Later he purchased land on Cumberworth Lane in the village on which he had a purpose built chapel erected which was opened in 1799 according to the date stone. Alternatively, W.H. Senior recorded that a man named Joel Mallinson was under the impression that the chapel actually opened in 1801. The ministers house was erected on land which adjoined the chapel, the total cost being £729. Denby Dale was at this time a part of the Barnsley circuit, separating in 1813. John Wood's firm is mentioned in the trade directories of the time as John Wood and Sons and it was two of these that emigrated to Australia in 1846. James and Tedber Wood returned to the village on holiday many years later and provided money to build the first Denby Dale school in 1874.

Victoria Memorial Hall Denby Dale

The Hall was built adjacent to the Methodist Chapel on Cumberworth Lane in 1903 at a cost of £4000. Its initial function was that of a Sunday school and a meeting hall but the outbreak of the First World War hailed a new function for the building.

128

The main room in the Victoria Memorial Hall which was used as a convalescent hospital during the First World War. *W H Senior*

The Wesleyan Methodist church and Victoria Memorial Hall provide the background to an unknown religious gathering around the early twentieth century. *W H Senior.*

Demolition of the Victoria Memorial Hall in 1977. *W H Senior.*

W H Senior noted that it was converted to a makeshift convalescent home for injured soldiers and sailors, housing forty beds. It was officially opened in 1916 as the 'Denby and Cumberworth, Skelmanthorpe and Clayton West Military Auxiliary Hospital', which it remained until 28 February 1919, having received 924 patients during its life. The death toll for the Denby and Cumberworth District was forty-five.

Throughout the twentieth century the hall continued as a Sunday school, housed various different sports clubs, such as badminton and billiards and also held concerts. Unfortunately, this beautiful building cost a great deal of money to maintain and heat, coupled with the cost of the chapel it became financially untenable to continue to use both buildings. It was eventually decided to sell the hall and the land it was sited on to a builder for £9,500 in 1976. The building was demolished in 1977, yet, one cannot help but wonder, whether it would have better served the village had it been retained and renovated. New housing now occupies the site.

Inbirchworth Chapel

Ingbirchworth old chapel was erected in 1832, though in approximately 1890 the members applied to Captain Jessop of Honley for land adjoining these premises. This land, comprising 576 square yards, was given to the chapel along with a donation of £25. A new chapel was built, which opened on 14 May 1894.

Cumberworth Church

The present Cumberworth church, dedicated to Saint Nicholas was built in 1870 but we know that some kind of church had existed here since at least 1255 though very little is known about it. It grew in importance over the years, indeed the living was presented by no less a person than Mathew Wentworth of Bretton in 1650 to Timothy Bradley who had been evicted from Penistone church. A year later Cumberworth became very notable as it had a Bishop as incumbent. Bishop Henry Tilson had been ejected from his see in Ireland and had ended up living in Dewsbury where he was given the living of the church. He rode on horse back each Sunday to preach in the village where, the Bishop recorded, 'the people were barbarous and uncouth'. He presented the church with a silver chalice dated 1651 which was used in communion until relatively recently.

Cumberworth became, along with Denby, the burial ground and parish church for Denby Dale.

Denby Dale Church

The first church in Denby Dale was built in 1893, curiously, of tin. As a child I remember remnants of this structure, rusty lengths of corrugated iron, broken, collapsed and totally overgrown. Thankfully it once looked much more impressive as can be seen below. The present day stone church in the village was built in 1939.

There are two other local places of worship worthy of mention in our area. The **Primitive Methodist Chapel** was built half way up Miller Hill at the top of Cuckstool Road in Denby Dale and opened in 1837. It had a relatively long life before closing its doors for the final time in 1962. The building was re-used soon afterwards by Lewis Craven & Son Printing works, who indeed, remain to this day. Interestingly, the Primitive Methodists were responsible for changing the name of Miller Hill, at least unofficially. If you ask any older resident of Denby Dale they will have heard the name 'Ranter Hill', this became a common substitute for Miller Hill, due to the style of worshipping that took place in the chapel half way up.

Denby Dale Tin Church at around the turn of the nineteenth century. *Author's collection.*

General Booth with local mill owners amist large crowds on Wakefield Road in 1907. *Author's collection.*

The Salvation Army began life in a wooden hut again in Denby Dale. A new building was erected across from the old corn mill in 1927, the corps disbanded and closed in 1970. The building is now occupied by a number of flats. General William Booth (1829-1912) who founded the Salvation Army with his wife, Catherine, visited Denby Dale in July 1907 and August 1909 where he was received by huge crowds waiting to listen to him preach.

Today, congregations at most churches and chapels are dwindling, yet in the past these organisations were the pivotal supports of society around which everything was organised. Without them, village history would be much the poorer and although people today used them mainly to perform Christian ceremonies, and to celebrate major religious festivals, their loss would be a severe blow throughout the parish.

General Booth arriving on Cumberworth Lane in Denby Dale in August 1909. *W H Senior.*

Chapter Seven

Education

The first detail we have concerning education, regards a donation made by William Turton of Denby. In 1443 he gave £3 9s 4d out of his lands to the school at Penistone. Penistone has one of the oldest schools in the country, it was founded in 1392 by the Lord of the Manor, Thomas Clarel inside the church as the Chantry school of Our Lady, St. Mary. When Chantry properties were seized by the Crown in 1547, Penistone was protected by its isolation, the school survived and held on to its grants and endowments, though it moved to a new site, near the church. It continues today, again re-sited, on Huddersfield Road, as Penistone Grammar School.

The schoolhouse, Lower Denby, circa. 1895. Mrs Challenger and her daughter lived in the first half of the building. The second half still retains the distinct appearance of a school although, by this time, it was uninhabitable. *Author's collection.*

The old schoolhouse has undergone a number of face-lifts, this picture dates from approximately the 1970s. *W H Senior.*

Long before education was made compulsory a school was in operation in Lower Denby. According to the Victoria County History, Francis Burdet, of Denby Hall, (as we have already seen) left £200 in his will, dated 24 June 1731 to provide for this and for the poor of the village. The sum was finally invested in 1769 in a cottage, barn and ten acres of land at Hoylandswaine. This site was let for £12 6s per annum, half of this sum was paid to the school master and the other half provided for six free places for local scholars. It is interesting to note that until only a few years ago, the land at Hoylandswaine was still owned under the details of this ancient grant, though plans were afoot to sell it to provide funds for the present day school at Upper Denby.

The provision of education before 1870 was very much dependent upon religious efforts and voluntary bodies. For the working class children of Denby, Sunday schools, Charity schools and Dame schools were the options available. Along with the school at Lower Denby, there was also a boarding school run by Joseph Shaw at High Flatts during the mid-eighteenth century. This was closed between 1877 and 1899 due to a fall in numbers. Dame schools were run at Pogstone House in Denby Dale, just behind today's bowling green and another from a house mid-way up Miller Hill. Interestingly, the one storied room that has been built on at this property, once housed the village/public mangle where people could take their clothes and pay a fee for them to be run through it. Dame schools were more common in the eighteenth century, usually run by an elderly woman, they provided a limited education for children before they reached an age when they became economically useful to their parents and prospective employers.

In 1849, the Denby vestry meeting decided to repair the school at Lower Denby. New shutters and doors were erected, being paid for by the poor rates. The 1851 census notes that David and Elizabeth Hoyle, both from Marsden were the Master and Mistress at this time. Owing to a decline in numbers the school was closed for two or three years before 1861. An attempt was

Denby national schoolchildren in 1872. The master behind them is probably Charles Hargreaves. *Author's collection.*

Denby schoolchildren, presumably in fancy dress for May Day celebrations, 1907. *Author's collection.*

Denby schoolchildren, 1934. Back row: Terence Windle, Dennis Walshaw, Barbara Roebuck, Freda Knowles, Joyce Schofield, Winifred Jackson, Betty Cartwright, Joan Miller, Marjorie Walshaw, Ruth Jones, Donald Beldon.
Middle row: Denise Dronsfield, Lucy Coburn, Zena Herbert, Betty Drew, George Jackson, Joan Hinchliffe, Audrey Dransfield, Madge Roebuck, Betty Roebuck.
Front row: John White, Derrick Morris, Jack Thorpe, Harry Heath, Stanley Barber, John Stanley, Derek Greaves, Gordon Hinchliffe, Gordon Blacker. *Author's collection.*

made to revive it, but the building was old and now unfit for teaching purposes, this led to its final demise in 1876. The endowment (now lost) became applicable for a prize fund under a scheme dated 5 August 1880. The building was later converted into a private home and has now been enlarged, but one of the old round windows from the original property still remains and the name 'The Old Schoolhouse', survives on the wall to remind us of the establishment which was created long before the introduction of compulsory education.

In 1864 the Church day school was built at Denby for the education of all in the township. The land was given by Thomas Kaye of Bradford, the cost according to the nineteenth century trade directories was £750. The state became more involved with education from 1870 when an act was passed which paved the way for free and compulsory education by 1880. Children were required to attend school from the ages of five to ten when providing they had reached a certain educational standard they would then be allowed to work part time whilst still attending school. The earliest Master I have been able to find is one Charles Hargreaves along with a schoolmistress, Miss Roberts. It is likely that he is the Master behind the cluster of children in the photo on page 134, dated 1872, he was certainly the Master in 1881.

Scholars came from the surrounding villages of Denby Dykeside, Ingbirchworth, Lower Denby, High Flatts, Fray Royd and Broadstone to name a few. It is probable that the creation of this new state supported school, known as Denby National, helped signal the demise of the charity school in Lower Denby. Another new school, opened in 1874 in Denby Dale would also have contributed to this. Built chiefly due to the financial efforts of its Chairman, Tedbah Wood, who had made his fortune in Australia, the school was founded by public subscription. A school was also run by the Quakers of High Flatts at Birdsedge in what is now the village hall. A purpose built school was opened in 1911.

Taken at the front of the school, well before the construction of the present day porch, Mrs Jelfs and her class, circa. 1924. *Author's collection.*

Upper Denby schoolchildren around 1928. Back row, left to right: Jack Fawcett, L Miller, S Beever, Hilda Howlands, Marion Heath, Stanley Schofield, John Gaunt. Middle row: Gwen Herbert, H Armfield, Doreen Barber, Mollie Kilner, Bessie Heath, Sylvia Rusby, W Todhunter, Daisy Charlesworth. Front row: George Harley, Eric Moxon, and ? Beever. *Author's collection.*

In Denby in 1877, one page of the register notes that there were thirty children attending, ages ranging from Harry Taylor who was thirteen to Edith Haigh who was four years six months old. It can only be surmised that the Master and Mistress must have struggled with the differing levels of maturity within their classes. Though the standard of teaching at this time was basic, the three 'Rs' and religious studies comprising much of the syllabus, and classes were regularly depleted because of truancy, which in many cases was brought about by parents keeping their sons and daughters away, to work and bring some money into the household.

Denby schoolchildren prepare for May Day in 1959. Christine Martin is the May Queen. *Author's collection.*

Christine Martin being crowned as the May Day Queen in 1959. Other people included on the picture are: John Bower and his sister Janet, Judith Crossland, Paul Whitehead, the Roe sisters, Gordon Pickford, Martin Ryan, Winifred Crossland and Richard Dearnley. *Author's collection.*

The register also shows the previous schooling of a child. In many cases the answer was either none at all or that he or she was being re-admitted. There are though some interesting examples, such as James Taylor, whose family had moved from Manchester to Denby. His father was noted to be a labourer. Why he had moved from the city where jobs were more commonplace to settle in Denby's quiet backwater will always remain a mystery, though it does seem a little odd.

Denby school children, 17 December 1956: Back row: Mrs Moore, Michael Schofield, ?, John Gibbons, Ronald Barber, Lawrence Redman, Arthur Crossland, Jim Beaumont, John Bower, John Barber, Roderick Schofield, Stuart Holmes, Gordon Pickford. Second row: Keith Buxton, Maxine Hill, Christine Martin, Robin Shaw, Janet Bower, Susan Wilson, Margaret Blacker, Susan Ryan, Christine Town, Rosemary Blacker, Judith Crossland, Jean Rusby, Trevor Beacroft, Mrs Gibbons. Seated: ?, June Beacroft, Angela Dearnley, Pat Buxton, Megan Wilson, Janet Saville, ?, Janice Robinson, Diane Goodison, ?, Anne Tyas. Sitting cross legged: Ralph Barber, Tony Hynson, David Redman, ?, Martin Ryan, Robert Barber, Paul Whitehead, John Mosley, Peter Bentley, Alan Robinson. *Author's collection.*

May Day Queen crowning festivities. *Courtesy of Kirklees Cultural Services. Approx. 1960.*

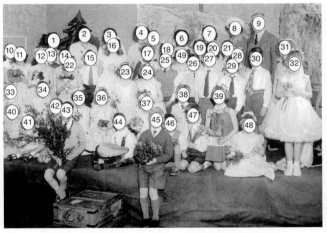

1. Judith Crossland	25. John Slater
2. Janet Bower	26. Rodrick Barber ?
3. Susan Ryan	27. Philip Ineson
4. ?	28. Barbara Pavoloski
5. Christine Martin	29. David Firth
6. Janet Saville	30. David Tyas
7. ?	31. ?
8. ?	32. Karen Jones
9. ?	33. ?
10.?	34. Susan Priestley
11. Jane Hill	35. Jane Haigh
12. Helen Walker	36. ?
13. David Hoyland	37. Judith Haigh
14. ?	38. ?
15. Peter Bentley/Brian Auckland	39. Celia Crowther
	40. ?
16. Pat Buxton	41. Jean Bentley?
17. Angela Dearnly	42. ?
18. June Beecroft	43. Richard Dearnley
19. Winifred Crossland	44. Charles Crossland
20. Sandra Crowther	45. David Redman
21. Robert Fish	46. Steven Slater
22. Vanda Sildasky	47. Andrew Crowther
23. Caroline Walker	48. Susan Liles
24. Katherine Emmott	49. Glynis Harrop

A column entitled 'Reasons for Leaving' is also very illuminating: 'working full time under age' , 'lives over two miles off', 'went to another school because I, (the Master, presumably Mr Hargreaves) wanted 10 school pence' and other variants on this theme. It is also very interesting to note the occupations of some of the local fathers at this time: Farmer, Joiner, Stonemason, Porter, Weaver, Collier, Saddler, Besom (Broom) Maker, Road Surveyor, Tailor, Delver, Publican, Coachman, Mechanic, Hawker, Gypsy, Gardener, Designer, Spinner, Railways, Grocer, Shoemaker and Policeman to name but a few.

It is possible that by 1885 a Mr Milnes had become the Master of the school, the register notes a Herbert Milnes whose father was a schoolmaster but although they lived in Denby it does not say where his father taught. Abel Jelfs became schoolmaster around the turn of the century, working alongside his wife and becoming very well known and respected throughout the village. Mr Jelfs had a seat on the Gunthwaite and Ingbirchworth Urban District Council in 1917 though he held other similar positions at other times. It was Mr Jelfs who organised gardening classes across the road from where the Church gates stand today. Children would be sent to collect leaf mould from Swift Wood, which was used to fertilise the ground. These classes resulted in striking floral displays, which some of the older residents still remember today. These gardens were later turned into allotments, which are now buried under two new houses.

In 1928 a *Sale of Work* booklet was produced, which contained quotations and recipes such as: 'One swallow does not make one summer; but one pin maliciously inserted in the bottom of a chair does certainly make one spring'! This quote came from Mrs J Jelfs, although it is nice to see she had a sense of humour after learning that she used to have a stick that would reach from the front of the classroom to the back, enabling her to sort out troublemakers with the minimum of effort.

The Jelfs moved from Denby to Bromsgrove around 1930, Abel being followed as Master by Arnold Jackson. Mr Jackson was a native of Denby and subsequently found it difficult to settle in, he eventually moved on to Thurgoland where he remained for many years. He was succeeded by a Mr Taylor from Barnsley who stayed throughout the 1930s and early 1940s. Subsequently Miss Thompson was to take over, along with other teachers whose names will still be familiar to older residents, such as Miss Close, Miss Kitson, Miss Hardcastle, Miss Wood and Miss Heath. Miss Thompson, the Headmistress lived in the schoolhouse which was connected to the school via a door and porch as did all the previous Masters or Head teachers. Miss Close, who lived at Plumpton began her spell at Denby during the late 1930s. Miss Heath may not have remained at Denby for long as she can be found teaching in Denby Dale in 1934.

In 1918 the school leaving age was raised to fourteen, almost dispensing with the school/work ethic after a child was ten years old, this was followed by a division of schools with a transfer between tiers at the age of eleven. In 1944 the leaving age was raised to fifteen and free secondary education became available to all children at either Grammar, Technical or Secondary Modern schools, selection for these was decided by the 11+ examination. Denby students moved on to either Penistone Grammar school or Skelmanthorpe Secondary Modern (now Scissett Middle School). In 1973 the leaving age was again changed, to sixteen years old where the situation stands today.

Denby C of E school was under threat of closure during the 1980s, but has survived and is still a very important part of the township. Extensive refurbishment was completed in the 1990s updating the building and creating a modern day village school, though externally the building has little changed. The long arched window, facing towards the common now extends to the floor of the playground and a porchway has been constructed at the main entrance. Though heavily reliant on fund raising ventures the school seems to have a secure future.

Chapter Eight
The Nineteenth Century

We are now into a century from which far more written records survive, enabling us to create a fuller picture of the inhabitants of the village and their occupations, which we will consider later.

We start in 1806 with the village militia. By this time the militia was largely voluntary and was never called upon to resist an invasion. It essentially balanced the standing army and aided in local politics. Of particular concern in 1806, was the prospect of a French invasion by the forces of Napoleon, though the members of Denby's force could have been called upon at this time to dispel Luddite activists but to date I have found no direct evidence to confirm this.

MILITIA FOR THE TOWNSHIP OF DENBY First Class, (men under thirty having no children)

Name	Age	Occupation	Name	Age	Occupation
Armitage Joshua	23	weaver	Hanson John	26	weaver
Armitage Isaac	21	weaver	Haywood Benjamin	19	weaver
Barlow Joseph	21	weaver	Haywood Thomas	22	weaver
Barraclough James	19	weaver	Horn William	18	weaver
Barraclough John	19	weaver	Helliwell Joseph	23	weaver
Blachell James	20	servant	Hough John	21	cotton spinner
Beaver Benjamin	19	servant	Hudson Benjamin	23	weaver
Bedford John	18	weaver	Kaye James	19	weaver
Bedford Joshua	21	weaver	Kilner William	18	weaver
Beaumont Joshua	22	farmer	Kirk John	19	weaver
Biltcliffe Amor	19	weaver	Lockwood Thomas	21	weaver
Blackburn Amos	22	farmer	Lummax Joseph	27	weaver
Boothroyd Benjamin	21	tailor	Mallinson George	19	cloth manufacturer
Brown Benjamin	18	weaver	Marsden Benjamin	21	weaver
Brown Thomas	26	weaver	Marsden John	29	weaver
Brown William	21	weaver	Marshall Francis	29	tanner
Burdett Christopher	20	weaver	Mosley Benjamin	18	servant
Burgess David	26	weaver	Mosley Thomas	19	weaver
Burgess Francis	23	weaver	Moxon Thomas	21	weaver
Crowther James	18	weaver	Pattrill (Irishman)	28	shoemaker
Crowther Jonas	20	weaver	Richardson Charles	24	weaver
Dalton John	20	weaver	Revil George	28	weaver
Dickinson Elihu	24	farmer	Revil Jonathan	18	tanner
Dickinson Jonothan	21	weaver	Sagar Joseph	20	weaver
Dickinson Joseph	19	weaver	Shore John	28	weaver
Dickinson Richard	29	tanner	Stephenson Jonathan	21	slubbin
Ellis John	27	cloth manufacturer	Thorp William	22	weaver
Gaunt Joshua	19	labourer	Tinsdale Joseph	22	weaver
Gaunt Miles	20	dress manufacturer	Tyas George	18	shoemaker
Gaunt William	27	drysalter	Walker Charles	20	servant
Graham Joseph	27	servant	Watson John	20	tanner
Green Edward	20	weaver	White Amarous	23	servant
Green James	20	servant	Willard Cornelius	20	weaver
Green Joseph	28	labourer	Wood Joshua	19	weaver
Haigh John	28	weaver	Wordsworth John	20	weaver
Haigh Thomas	18	weaver	Langley Joseph	21	weaver
Hall Charles	19	weaver			
Hanmerton Henry	21	tailor	Exemptions: Elihu Dickinson (tender eyes), Francis		
Hanson Edward	24	weaver	Marshall (lost an eye), John Marsden (knock knees).		

Militia Second Class (men above thirty having no children)

Name	Age	Occupation	Name	Age	Occupation
Burdett William	35	weaver	Sagar James	35	cloth manufacturer
Ellis Thomas	33	cloth manufacturer	Shaw Jonathan	38	cloth manufacturer
Haigh James	30	farmer	Taylor James	30	labourer
Haigh Thomas	37	farmer	Tyas David	37	shoemaker
Marshall John	39	tanner	Tyas Jonathan	30	cloth manufacturer
Marshall Michael	37	farmer	Wood William	40	cloth manufacturer
Mitchell Thomas	41	farmer			
Priest John	39	farmer	Exemption : Jonothan Tyas (substitution).		
Priest Joseph	33	cloth manufacturer			
Robinson Benjamin	40	cloth manufacturer			

Militia Third Class (men between eighteen and forty-five having children but none under fourteen)
None.

Militia Fourth Class (men between eighteen and forty-five having children under fourteen)

Name	Age	Occupation	Name	Age	Occupation
Addy Thomas	25	weaver	Kilner Thomas	25	weaver
Beaumont William	23	weaver	Lockwood Joseph	30	weaver
Biltcliffe George	29	weaver	Mosley Joshua	24	butcher
Biltcliffe Mathew	24	weaver	Morton Simion	30	weaver
Broadhead George	24	weaver	Peace George	19	weaver
Corkhill William	26	weaver	Rusby Samuel	40	butcher
Dickinson Joseph	24	weaver	Robinson George	37	shoemaker
Ellis John	24	weaver	Shaw Giles	31	cloth manufacturer
Gartside Firth	29	dyer	Shaw Samuel	37	farmer
Gaunt Joshua	25	cloth manufacturer	Tunnicliff Thomas	29	labourer
Grayson William	25	weaver			
Hinchcliffe Charles	43	cloth manufacturer			

Appeals against the list were to be heard at 10.00 am on the 17 September at the *White Boar Inn*, Barnsley. The list itself was compiled by John Shillitoe (Constable) and dated 12 September 1806.

The following year saw the freeholders of the township having to travel to York to vote in the great election, the names below can also be found in the above Militia list.

THE YORKSHIRE POLL 5 JUNE 1807

The following people had to travel to from Denby to York to vote for either William Wilberforce – Independent, Henry Lascelles – Tory or Lord Milton – Liberal. Indeed people from the whole county had to travel to Castle Green, below Clifford's Tower in York to vote. The voting itself took place in small booths and was open for fourteen days. Corruption and bribery were rife, though the publicans of the city increased their turnovers substantially by staying open day and night.

Name		Occupation	Wilberforce	Lascelles	Milton
Barraclough	James	(Yeoman)			1
Burdet	William	(clothier)			1
Dyson	Daniel	(clothmaker)			1
Dalton	John	(clothmaker)			1
Dickinson	Henry	(clothier)			1
Dickinson	Elihu	(clothier)	1		1
Dickinson	Weightman	(miller)			1
Ellis	John	(clothier)			1
Firth	Jonothan	(farmer)			1

Name		Occupation	Wilberforce	Lascelles	Milton
Graham	John	(innkeeper)			1
Gaunt	Joseph	(farmer)			1
Gartside	Firth	(dyer)			1
Haigh	Thomas	(Gent.)			1
Haigh	William	(farmer)			1
Haigh	John	(labourer)			1
Heywood	Christopher	(farmer)		1	1
Horn	Francis	(Yeoman)			1
Kendrew	William	(butcher)			1
Morley	Joshua	(butcher)			1
Parker	Thomas	(farmer)	1	1	
Robinson	William	(clothier)	1		
Revil	Jonothan	(clothier)			1
Sleigh	Thomas	(clothier)			1
Senior	John	(husbandman)			1
Wood	William	(manufacturer)			1
Wood	Joseph	(farmer)			1
			3	2	24

The election result, announced at the Castle until 1885 was: Wilberforce 11808, Milton 11177, Lascelles 10000.

Though Wilberforce stood for the abolition of slave trading, he wasn't the popular choice of the people of Denby. They opted in the main for Lord Milton, perhaps believing that he offered them, the 'abolition of slavery' closer to home. They were to be disappointed, as Wilberforce continued his winning run which had begun in 1784.

These twenty-six people represent the more affluent members of the village at this time, though the labourer John Haigh would seem out of place. Perhaps he was a direct relative of the Thomas, noted as, Gent? It is also tempting to speculate that John Graham could have been the landlord of the *Star* public house but this is undetermined. What is most readily apparent are the amount of people involved in textile work, from manufacturers to weavers and this will be considered later.

Voting for Members of Parliament was very much the preserve of the rich. Prior to 1832 a man had to possess freehold property valued for land tax at 40 shillings or more, per annum to be entitled to vote. In 1790, forty English counties supplied only eighty representatives, as against English boroughs which supplied 392 out of a total of 558 MPs. This is reflected in the percentage of the population able to vote, in 1831 only 5% and in 1867, only 16%.

The situation was very similar in 1741 when a general election was called. England's first Prime Minister, Robert Walpole was under huge pressure, following a badly mismanaged war against Spain. His parliamentary majority was reduced to only twenty when the results were published and he resigned in early 1742.

The population of the township of Denby in 1741 is unknown at present, but in 1801 there were 1061 people recorded in the census. One would presume a lower figure for the earlier year, but even so, only ten men from Denby are recorded as having voted.

The first page of the printed returns proclaims :

The Poll for a Representative in Parliament for the County of York. In the Room of the Right Honourable Henry, Lord Visc. Morpeth, Deceased. Begun at the Castle of York on Wednesday the 13th of January, 1741.

The candidates were George Fox and Chomley Turner, and as with the election of 1807, the men of Denby who were qualified had to travel to York to take part. Whether all those qualified attended is unknown, travel was neither easy nor inexpensive and occupational commitments might have caused difficulties, not to mention the inclement weather possibilities in mid January.

The men of Denby were split seven to three in their preferences:

THE YORKSHIRE POLL begun 13 January 1741

For George Fox:	For Cholmley Turner:
Thomas Armitage (Breastwell)	William Gant (probably Gaunt)
Samuel Haigh	Joseph Gant
Thomas Haigh	John Wood (Shilitoe)
William Horsefall(Huddersfield)	
Joseph Oates	
Joseph Pool	
Thomas Woofendin	

(**NB:** *names in brackets indicate places of freehold*).

Until 1872 there was no such thing as a secret ballot. Following an act of 1696, which was created to try to prevent fraud orchestrated by returning officers, local printers were allowed to print copies of the poll books, showing the persuasion of every individual that had taken part. Changes in the system came thick and fast after the Secret Ballot Act of 1872. In 1918, all men over twenty-one and women over thirty became entitled to vote. In 1928 the age for women was lowered to twenty-one. In 1969 both ages were lowered to eighteen. Subsequently the percentage of the population entitled to vote grew accordingly, in 1918, 74% and in 1928, 97%.

DENBY WORKHOUSE

Generous provisions for the poor had been made by the more affluent members of local society over the centuries. For instance, a John Mitchell of Nether Denby had lodged 50s into the hands of Robert Booth of Denby in 1640 for the use of the poor in Denby quarter, yearly, at St. James Tide. Unfortunately these sums of money were irregular and offered little security to their beneficiaries.

As the country's population continued to rise during the eighteenth and nineteenth centuries, many workhouses were built or converted from other buildings to house and employ a growing army of paupers. The following extract is taken from Dransfield's, *History of Penistone* and concerns the one at Denby:

Memorandum of Agreement made this 1st day of October 1827, at a meeting convened for that purpose between the inhabitants. of Denby Township in the Parish of Penistone and the County of York on the one part, and Jonathan Shaw of the above written Township and County on the other part, viz.:

The said Jonothan Shaw doth agree to take all paupers of the said Township into his house in form of workhouse upon the following terms, viz.:

The rent, three pounds per year, to be paid half yearly by the overseer of the poor of the said Township. When wheat is under 25s per load the paupers maintenance to be 2s 9d per head, per week, and when 25s and under 35s per load the paupers maintenance to be 3s per head, per week, and 35s and upwards to be 3s 3d per head, per week, with the addition of 1s a week for coals. And at any time there should be no paupers within the said workhouse, deduct the 1s for coals. And the said inhabitants doth agree to the above statement and also to furnish the said workhouse with such bedsteads and bedding and other furniture as may be agreed upon by the said parties at this or any other time, and the said inhabitants doth also agree to furnish the said paupers with necessary clothing and paid for by the Overseer of the poor.

And the said parties doth agree to give each other three months notice in writing previous to the giving up of the said workhouse, and everything according to the inventory to be accounted for and given up peaceably and free from damage at the expiration of the three months notice. As witness our hands this 27th day October 1827.

Signed in the presence of - William Turton and John Gaunt by
Richard Mallinson (for John Mallinson) - assistant overseer.
Jonothan Shaw.

The following is an inventory of goods placed in the workhouse by Richard Mallinson, 27 October 1827: 2 bedsteads and cords, 2 beds with straw, 2 long pillows, 2 coverlids, 2 long pillow cases, 4 forks, 1 round table, 1 long pillow case, 1 twill tick bed and chaff, 3 sheets, 4 blankets, 1 tub, 3 stools, 4 knives, 3 spoons, 2 blankets (new), 1 coverlid (new).

Shaw's building was situated at the back of what is now the Southcroft housing estate, a little way down Gunthwaite Lane on the left and was part of a smallholding called Robinson Lathe. The remains, which comprise a grass covered mound with odd stones poking out of it, are probably those of the workhouse though most of the site has gone forever. Robinson Lathe, probably a property owned and named by a family called Robinson in antiquity, and there are numerous mentions of such a family in this book, was an enclosure, inside which were a barn, outbuildings and a cluster of dwellings. Denby band used to practice in one of these old buildings before moving to the wooden hut further down the lane. One presumes that the workhouse, Shaw's residence, must have been the original farmhouse, as it had to be a building with a fair number of rooms.

In 1834 the Poor Law Commission queried the Overseers of the poor of Denby about the following particulars of the workhouse :

Q : State for what number of persons there is room in such poorhouse or workhouse or other houses, and also the greatest number which have been in the workhouse or other houses at any one time.

A : The premises occupied by the contractor for the reception and maintenance of the poor are pretty large and might accommodate twenty paupers. The greatest number that he has had at any time has been seven paupers.

Details contained in the 1841 Census taken in the Township of Denby list the occupants of the workhouse:

Elizabeth Beardsell, aged 15 (born 1826), fancy weaver.
Ruth Battison, aged 51 (born 1790), farm servant.
Martha Battison, aged 11 (born 1830).
James Burgess, aged 14 (born 1827), agricultural labourer.
Jeremiah Homes, aged 86 (born 1755), former clothier.
Ann Senior, aged 58 (born 1783), bobbin winder.

Jonothan Shaw is also listed in the survey as Master of the Workhouse. Born in approximately 1770, Shaw was seventy-one years old when these details were recorded. I am at present unaware of the year that the workhouse closed. Shaw died before the next census was taken in 1851, and the census details do not record anybody dwelling at the workhouse in Denby. It would, at present, be reasonable to assume that closure occurred soon after the event of Shaw's death. The Penistone Union was formed in 1849 to care for the poor and soon there were fifteen townships in the Union. In 1860 they erected their own workhouse at Netherfield (opened 25 July 1861) this was the natural successor to the one at Denby and may have been another reason for the latter's closure. None of the above occupants are listed in the census of 1851, though Jeremiah Homes was probably dead. Evidently the others were moved on to other premises, perhaps to Netherfield, poverty giving them little say in such matters.

A detail from *Baines* Trade Directory of Yorkshire dated 1822, lists some of the occupants of the village who could possibly have attended the meeting mentioned above, to inaugurate the workhouse:

Amos Barraclough (Star public house)
James Barraclough (blacksmith)
John Bentley (grocer & flour dealer)
John Wood & Sons (fancy weavers)
Joseph Langley (grocer)
Joseph Dalton (corn miller)
Joshua Dyson (grocer & draper)
Joshua Moxon (miller)
Rev. John Brownhill (vicar)
Ward & Haywood (scribbling millers)
William Hague (Wagon & Horses)

The list is somewhat longer, though small compared to the total population of the township at this time, which was 1412, an amount recorded in the following table for 1821:

From the Victoria County History (Volume iii)
Table of population, Penistone Parish:

Village	Acres	1801	1811	1821	1831	1841	1851	1861	1871	1881	1891	1901
Whole	22773	3681	4231	5042	5201	5907	6302	7149	8110	9094	9482	11160
Denby	2885	1061	1132	1412	1295	1690	1709	1813	1637	1559	1661	1765
Gunth.	952	111	119	86	99	66	77	81	83	70	68	57
Huns'lf	2465	327	429	436	531	578	729	1150	1283	1404	1559	1680
Ing'wh	1105	170	264	367	371	419	393	368	303	335	321	274
Langst.	4914	204	235	325	320	303	296	280	246	271	263	922
Oxsp'g	1202	219	255	247	283	241	278	346	370	350	322	397
Penis'n	1134	493	515	645	703	738	802	860	1549	2254	2553	3073
Thurls.	8116	1096	1282	1524	1599	1872	2018	2251	2639	2851	2735	2992

The population expansion at Denby reached a peak in 1861 but remained fairly constant thereafter. It is interesting to note the dramatic upward trends of Langsett and in particular,

Penistone. Until 1881 its population was less than that of Denby, yet due to the arrival of new industry, the total doubled between 1871 and 1901.

THE 1851 CENSUS

The census returns for the township of Denby list 1709 inhabitants though these include people from Birdsedge, Ingbirchworth, Denby Dale and many others. The returns list a person's address, fore and surname, marital status, age, occupation and birth place, enabling genealogists to flesh out the lives of their ancestors. The occupations make for interesting reading as does their frequency :

Occupation	No.	Occupation	No.	Occupation	No.
Domestic	34	Wife	4	Rag Sorter	4
Scholar	83	Cook	1	Pauper	4
Woollen Engineer	1	Shawl Knotter	1	Handloom Weaver	2
Stone Mason	8	Fancy Waistcoat Weaver	16	Rtd. Farmer	3
St. Masons Lab.	2	Tailor's Son	1	Burler	3
St. Masons Son	1	Tailor	3	Landlord	5
Fancy Manufac.	1	Shoemaker	4	Shopkeeper	3
Farmer's Wife	4	Cotton Dyer	6	Builder's Son	1
Fancy Weavers	102	Cart Driver	2	Visitor. Sawmill	1
Piecer	7	Teacher	3	Building Master	1
Miner/Collier	6	Woollen Weaver	3	Worsted Dyer	3
Woollen Dyer	1	Invalid	1	Tailor & Inn	1
Fulling Miller	8	Cordwainer	4	Corn Miller	1
Carder	3	Visitor	2	Governess	1
Slubber	5	Carpenter	4	Warehouse Man	1
Fancy Finisher	2	Warper	3	Farmer	31
Labourer	9	Carpenter's Wife	2	Farmer's Son	4
Bobbin Winder	37	Farmer's Daughter	.2	Inn & Shop	1
Blacksmith	4	Carpenter Assistant	2	Pattern weaver	1
Bob.Wndr. Home	1	Power Loom Weaver	7	Butcher	1
At Home	11	Errand Boy/Girl	8	Gas Maker	1
Blacksmith Assistant	2	Carpenter's Son	1	Woolcomber	1
Dressmaker	4	Beer Seller	1	Saddler	1
Road Labourer	6	Twist Winder	1	Laundress	1
Shawl Knitter	2	Winder	1	Whiskey Maker	1
Railway Labourer	3	Plumber/Glazier	2	Shawl Fringer	2
Agricultl. Lab.	35	Cropper	2	Woollen Spinner	1
Plate Layer	3	Glazier	1	Mechanic	1
Drawer	1	Collector Ric.	1	Stone Gritter	1
Washer Woman	1	SKRV	1	Washer Woman	2
Annuitant	1	Dress/Bonnet Maker	3	Steam Loom Weaver	1
Land Holder	4	Nurse	1	Machine Joiner	1
Wool Willower	1	Prop. Herbs	1		
Farmer's Son	4	Bakery	1		

Again, as we have already noted, much of the work in the township was textile oriented, add to this the farming community and its dependants and only domestic suppliers and workers remain, with the odd exception.

It is also interesting to note the numbers of people living in places, which still exist today, for instance :

Surname of family and number of people on Rattan Row, 1851: Beaumont 3, Blacker 2, Boothroyd 2, Gaunt 6, Hanwell 12, Hirst 2, Lees 2, Moors 2, Morton 3, Newsome 3, Senior 2, Wood 2, Barraclough 1, Burdett 1, Moore 4, Robinson 1, Weetman 2, Horton 1, (fifty-one people).

Surname of family and number of people at Denby Hall, 1851: Gaunt 7, Haigh 1, Lockwood 11, Mayon 1, Lockwood 10, and servants, Armitage, Askey, Fenwick, Mahon, and Whitaker, (thirty-five people). (**NB**: *two separate Lockwood families*).

The *New Inn*, **Rattan Row and Bank Lane, circa. 1910.** *Author's collection.*

I have been asked questions concerning the antiquity of Rattan Row. It is not recorded in the 1841 census returns, but is highly significant in 1851. It may just be that the name was ascribed to the row within that decade. Ratten means 'to practise sabotage against', or, alternatively, Rattan was a name ascribed to various climbing palms, from which canes and wickerwork were made. I believe that the latter rather than the former is the more likely explanation, particularly in a village such as Denby, where one can easily believe that a street in which there were many basket makers could lead to a new nickname for the road. Unfortunately, Rattan Row's occupants in 1851 were mainly weavers, there were no basket makers, therefore the name 'Rattan' may have been orally remembered from a more ancient time.

TRADE DIRECTORIES

The Trade Directories of the nineteenth and early twentieth centuries were similar to the telephone books of today, of course without the telephone numbers as Alexander Graham Bell didn't patent his machine until 1876! They supply a few short details concerning the history and geography of the village and the names of all the noteworthy persons who lived and traded there. The earliest one I have discovered for Denby, is, as we have already seen dated 1822. Others exist in local libraries for the years; 1838, 1857, 1861, 1866, 1867, 1881, 1889, 1901, 1904, 1912 and 1917 though there are likely to be a few others.

These directories enable us to follow the progression of family businesses and their subsequent transferrals of ownership or closure, the following are extracts taken from the directories up to the beginning of the twentieth century :

White's Directory 1838 (Vol. 2).

Name	Occupation	Name	Occupation
George Houldon	(Gent)	George Wiley	(Registrar)
Joseph Turton	(Schoolmaster)	Jas. Barraclough	(Blacksmith)
Thomas Turton	(Surgeon)	Joshua Shaw	(Blacksmith)
Thomas Whitehead	(Schoolmaster)		

Post Office Directory - Yorkshire 1857

Private Residents:

Herbert Cam Dickinson Esq.	Miss Dickinson
Mrs Mary Firth	Mrs Hunter
Rev.Job Johnson MA	George Norton Esq.
Thomas Turton Esq.	John Wilkinson Esq.

Commercial:

Name	Occupation	Name	Occupation
Thomas Turton	(Surgeon)	Aaron Hanwell	(Shoemaker)
James Armitage	(Farmer, Coal Owner)	Joseph Haigh	(Farmer)
Elihu Barraclough	(Blacksmith)	John Milnes	(Wheelwright)
Benjamin Boothroyd	(Tailor, Tanner)	George Micklethwaite	(Shopkeeper)
Francis Burdett	(Shopkeeper & Joiner)	George Norton	(Quarry Owner)
John Ellis	(Stonemason)	Miles Moore	(Stonemason)
Joshua Dyson	(Farmer)	George Tyas	(Shopkeeper)
John Gaunt	(Farmer)	Thomas Shillitoe	(Farmer)
George Firth	(Chairmaker)		

Whites Directory 1866:

Name	Occupation	Name	Occupation
Francis Burdett	(Joiner)	John Wood	(Tillage Merchant)
William Laundon	(Saddler)	John Hargreave & Co.	(Coal Owners)
John Wood &		Thomas Turton	(Surgeon)
Charles Homes	(Corn Millers)		

Kelly's Directory 1881:

Name	Occupation	Name	Occupation
Joseph Barraclough	(Blacksmith)	George Micklethwaite	(Shopkeeper)
Ellen Barraclough	(Farmer)	John Hargreaves	(Farmer, Upper Bagden)
Henry Boothroyd	(Tailor)	James Moore	(Stonemason)
John Boothroyd	(Tailor)	John Kilner	(Shopkeeper)
James Burdet	(Shopkeeper)	James Slater	(Farmer)
Francis Burdet	(Shopkeeper/Joiner)	Joseph Milnes	(Farmer)
Gideon Dixon	(Farmer, Hall)	William Priest	(Farmer)
Thomas Ellis	(Clerk to Local Board)	John Turton	(Chemist)
Charles Hargreaves	(Nat. Schoolmaster)		

Kelly's Directory 1889:

Name	Occupation	Name	Occupation
Aaron Wood	(Farmer, Denby Hall)	John Turton	(Surgeon)
Joseph Barraclough	(Blacksmith)	John Heath	(Wheelwright)
Martha Barraclough	(Shopkeeper)	John Horn	(Farmer)
Charles Bedford & Son	(Rope Manufacturer)	Henry Lockwood	(Farmer, Denby Hall)
Henry Boothroyd	(Tailor)	Arthur Priest	(Farmer, Shopkeeper)
James Burdet	(Shopkeeper)	Charles K. Hanwell	(Collector to Local Board)
Mark Gaunt	(Farmer)	John Micklethwaite	(Quarry Owner, Farmer, Post Office)
Henry Haigh	(Farmer-Tenters)		
Alfred Thorpe	(Farmer, Fall Edge)		

Kelly's Directory 1901:
Lord Savile - Lord of the Manor
Post Office - John Micklethwaite (Sub postmaster)
Council meetings take place in council room at Denby Dale on the 2nd Thursday in the month at 7pm.

Members: Chairman - Thomas Norton JP DL
Vice Chairman - John Hinchcliffe
Clerk - Wilfred Barns of Denby Dale
Treasurer - Frederick Crawshaw of Penistone
Medical Officer of Health - Duncan Alistair McGregor of Clayton
Surveyor - Charles Hinchcliffe of Denby Dale
Sanitary Inspector - George William Moxon of Denby Dale

Abel Jelfs is schoolmaster (max. kids at school 200 - average attendance 140).

Name	Occupation	Name	Occupation
Delarever Burdet	(Farmer, Denby Common)	Harry Heath	(Wheelwright)
James Burdet	(Shopkeeper)	Elizabeth Lockwood	(Threshing Machine Owner)
William Challengor	(Blacksmith)	Turton Turton	(Farmer, Fall Edge)
Henry Firth	(Farmer)		
Aaron Hanwell	(Shoemaker)		

The latter listings are only representative samples and yet they supply the names of the people and families involved in the different occupations considered later in the book.

LOCAL GOVERNMENT

Until 1895 the administration of Denby was in the hands of the vestry which was mainly concerned with roads and the poor. Their records were preserved in a Town Chest, a fact noted by historian W.H. Senior who discovered a record from 1849 ordering the chest to be repaired and 'three locks and keys provided for three rate payers to hold'.

The Denby and Cumberworth Urban District Council was created in 1895. This body remained until further reorganisation took place in 1938 when the four old councils were united to form the Denby Dale Urban District Council. The council was divided into four wards, those of Emley, Skelmanthorpe, Clayton and Cumberworth & Denby Dale.

The Denby Dale Urban District Council was finally absorbed into the new borough of Kirklees in 1974.

TURNPIKE ROADS

Used by traffic including, stagecoaches, wagons and carts the turnpikes were roads maintained by tolls collected from travellers. By the 1830s there were more than 20,000 miles resulting in tolls in excess of £1.5 million annually, though 80% of the nations roads were not subject to this system. The introduction of the railways led to the dissolving of the turnpike trusts due to the significantly reduced traffic and responsibility for the roads was transferred to local authorities.

A few years before 1810, John Metcalfe of Knaresborough constructed two miles of road over Birdsedge and High Flatts being paid £340, these new roads began to replace the old dirt tracks, preparing the way for today's road network.

John Metcalfe, or 'blind Jack' as he was known was born in 1717 and lost his sight at the age of four, he was a military musician, playing troops into battle at Falkirk in 1745, where he was taken prisoner. He made his name as a builder of houses, roads and bridges and it is reputed that he made the trans Pennine road from Huddersfield to Manchester. He died aged ninety-three in 1810.

William H Senior noted that the Denby vestry held a meeting in 1845 to consider the proposal to build a turnpike from Barnsley to Shepley Lane Head. They decided to oppose it in Parliament with the help of the Barnsley Canal Co. and to meet legal costs from the highway rate, unfortunately, for them, they were defeated and the road went ahead. Another was built between Wakefield and Denby Dale, and by 1850 there were three turnpikes running along the boundaries of Denby and Cumberworth. Tolls were charged at CatchBar, Denby Dale and at the *Star Inn* at Upper Cumberworth up until 1875 when the roads were dis-turnpiked but although these tolls were collected a significant amount of Parish funds were still required to maintain them. These roads became necessary to facilitate deliveries of raw materials and improve communications to remote markets for the blossoming textile industry.

RAILWAYS

The first sod for the Huddersfield and Sheffield Junction line was cut by Lord Wharncliffe at Penistone on 19 August 1845. Surveyed by Joseph Locke, construction was very labour intensive as many tunnels, embankments, cuttings and viaducts were necessary along its thirteen mile length. The first, wooden, viaduct built at Denby Dale was begun in 1846 and completed in 1847, but before its completion a great storm blew down twenty-seven of its forty perpendiculars. On completion it measured 112 feet high and 400 yards long and was opened on 1 July 1850.

Being constructed of wood fire was obviously a high risk and it was the job of one of the junior porters to go over the viaduct each day to fill the fire buckets with water. These could only be

The first viaduct built at Denby Dale was made entirely of wood and opened in 1850. *W H Senior.*

Building work in progress on the stone viaduct between 1877 and 1879. *W H Senior.*

filled half full as the vibrations caused by the trains caused most of the water to spill out.

Negotiations began in 1867 to replace the viaduct with a stone built structure, villagers were becoming alarmed that the present edifice was unsafe, but progress was slow and nothing was resolved until, finally, Naylor Brothers won the contract to build it in August 1877 with their tender of £27,650. Beginning in 1877, it took until 1879 to build the twenty-one huge arches and the official opening took place on Whit Sunday, 16 May 1880. In 1884 Naylors removed the wooden structure which was estimated to contain 80,000 cubic feet of timber.

In Denby the hollow known as the 'basin' was dug out and sledded into Denby Dale to provide filler for this new viaduct. By 1850 the Lancashire to Yorkshire railway extension was opened and more routes followed throughout the decade, as rail travel opened up opportunities

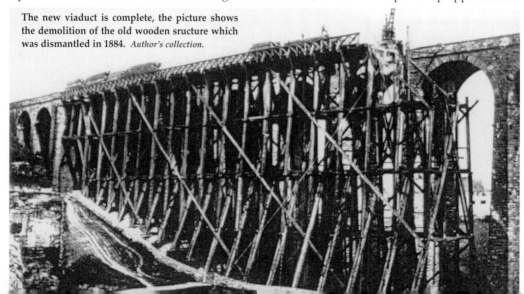

The new viaduct is complete, the picture shows the demolition of the old wooden sructure which was dismantled in 1884. *Author's collection.*

never before considered by village people.

New industry began to arrive and flourish, mills, which needed to be near water for power, were built in the valley below Denby and the foundation of the modern village of Denby Dale took place.

Gradually, due to the effects of the growing road transport system some of the least used lines were closed. During the 1930s until after the Second World War new investment was at a minimum until nationalisation in 1947 but the line which runs through Denby has long been in danger of closure.

STREET LIGHTING

W H Senior noted in the book *A History of Denby Dale Urban District Council* that the Denby board maintained street lighting for the Denby Dale Gas Co., though for more rural areas oil lamps were provided. Acetylene gas replaced these in 1904. Invented by R J Moss & Sons of Birmingham, it is interesting to note that the cover picture of their brochure was drawn from a photograph of William Challenger, lighting one of these lamps in

William Challenger seen at Lower Denby posing for an advertisement for Moss & Sons, inventors of an acetylene gas lighting system. The photograph appeared in the brochure below. *Author's collection.*

Lower Denby, around where the telephone box currently stands.

Town gas was piped from the works in Denby Dale to Denby by the early twentieth century, indeed my own Great Aunt and her brother were responsible at one time for going round the village, ladder in hand, in order to light them.

WATER & SANITATION

Details, again supplied by W H Senior tell us that an outbreak of cholera in 1849 left the district with serious problems over sanitation. Not until 1878 was a medical officer appointed for Denby and Cumberworth. Duncan McGregor was paid £30 per annum by the Denby board and only £11 by Clayton, his first report on the area was very critical.

Doorless privies, defective drains, bad odours, no sink drains (so water ran across gardens, and people emptied chamber pots onto the roads)! Measures were put into place to rectify these problems, though by 1895 only twenty new privies had been built and twenty sinks trapped. A bye-law of 1898 forbade any householder to shake their rugs or mats or to empty chamber pots on the roads. Mr. Senior also noted that the Denby vestry minute books before 1871 record permission to sink wells for water by the villagers. Unfortunately by 1875, many of these had become contaminated by water from Zacheus Hinchcliffe's colliery. The wells were eventually abandoned after agreement had been reached with the Dewsbury waterboard to supply to the village.

GAME TRESPASS AT DENBY

We have already had reason to note details on hunting and forest laws, but trespass was still common during the nineteenth century, as, indeed, it is today. The following report is taken from the *Barnsley Chronicle*, dated 1883.

> *Joseph Roebuck of Denby was charged with trespassing in search of game on land belonging to W. Norton, Justice of the Peace at Denby. Mr. Horfield prosecuted – Thomas Ellis, a game watcher in the employ of Mr. Norton spoke as to seeing the defendant in a wood belonging to his master. He had a gun with him which was capped. When he saw the defendant he called to him and the defendant said,*
>
> *'Hey lad, I have a right to be here'.*
>
> *He also saw him in a field which had just been sown with oats. The defendant said he was never out of the field. It was stated that the wood belonged to Mr. W. Norton and he also had an agreement with the owner of the land to preserve game on the land. Wright Beaumont, the occupier of the field adjoining Calverley Wood, said he had given the defendant leave to shoot small birds. Fined 10s and costs.*

(Calverley Wood, perhaps better known today as Long Lane Wood is adjacent to Broomfield in Denby.)

Before we continue into the twentieth century we will now examine in a little more detail some of the trades and occupations adopted by the Denby villagers during the nineteenth and early twentieth centuries, to try and flesh out and explain much of what has been discussed in this chapter. Small rural villages were generally self supporting, but many of the practices and skills familiar to our ancestors have either changed beyond recognition or become obsolete and many of their workplaces have now been destroyed or modernised changing the face of the village forever.

Chapter Nine

Occupations and Trades

PUBLIC HOUSES

From late medieval times the public house has been a part of English culture. Three basic types existed at this time; Inns, usually providing meals and accommodation, Taverns for 'respectable drinking' and Ale houses for the general public and commoners.

It was during the sixteenth century, after the growth of Protestantism had curbed Church centred social drinking that 'Pubs' became more a part of everyone's everyday life. Figures suggest that there was one alehouse for every 150 people by 1577.

The modern Public house began to emerge during the nineteenth century. Apart from their sign these alehouses looked very much like private homes. As literacy spread and became more common place the name of the pub was added to the sign and also the brewers name began to be shown.

There were originally three 'alehouses' in the modern village of Upper Denby, namely the *Star*, *New Inn* and the *George*, and two more at Lower Denby, the *Wagon and Horses* and the *Dunkirk* or *Junction*. The *Star*, which was adjacent to the buildings that were to become the *George*, was certainly operating by 1822 when we find Amos Barraclough as the landlord.

In 1830 duty on beer was abolished by Parliament which meant that any ratepayer could then sell it for consumption on or off his own premises without a licence. Around 1838 the *New Inn* began trading, being followed by the *George*, around 1857. Free trade in ale was brought to an end in 1869 opening the way for a gradual extension of ownership of pubs by the breweries. This led to a number of closures, particularly during the years 1899 -1904 when an act was passed which raised a levy on the whole licensing trade to provide some compensation for publicans who had lost their licenses. The *Licensing Act* of 1872 gave magistrates the power to grant licenses and check for the adulteration of alcoholic drinks, they also fixed closing time at 11.00 pm. Licensed victuallers thought these too excessive whereas temperance societies conversely thought them too lenient.

The public bar was originally in the kitchen of an Alehouse, which would have had a partitioned off area known as the taproom. More discerning customers used the parlour or best room. It was only when kitchens became private that the public bar was called the tap room. By the 1850s there were three grades of rooms, the bar room (standing), the tap room (sitting), and the parlour or best room. During 1845 because of the repeal of duties on glass the bottling of beer became practicable and signalled the decline of pewter tankards, which were finally replaced by glasses towards the end of the century.

The *George* and the land around it was owned by the Norton's group up until 1877 when it was bought from their trustees. In 1882 it was noted by the Barnsley Permanent Building Society that the pub was owned by Reuben and James Senior and that the property comprised a barn, carthouse, garden, carriage house and one cottage and that it was occupied by George Taylor. Before its history as a pub the building which became the *George* was used as a sanatorium,

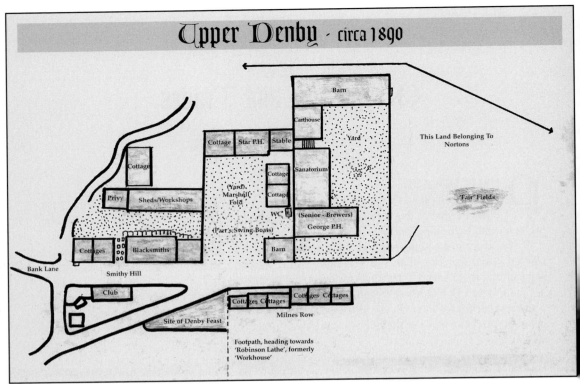

The author's reconstructed plan of the centre of Upper Denby in approximately 1890. Note the *Star* public house and the sanatorium next door which eventualy became the *George* public house. *Author's collection.*

Mill Bank House, built by Elihu Dickinson at High Flatts. The photograph was taken when the building was being run as a sanatorium, circa. 1901. *Author's collection.*

The *New Inn*, with the house known as 'Spion Kop' in the foreground to the left, circa. 1910. *Author's collection.*

presumably upon similar lines to the one at High Flatts as we have already noticed. The building, which is recorded on the Enclosure map of 1802 is probably of eighteenth century origin and was originally a small farmstead.

Seth Senior and Sons brewery began trading in 1829. The story goes that Seth borrowed a sovereign to begin brewing in his own cottage and became so successful he was able to start the business, where he was joined by his sons, Reuben and James. They took over many pubs around the Shepley area, including the *Sovereign* named as a reminder of their humble beginnings. They became owners of both the *George* and *New Inn* at Denby and although not in existence at the pubs origins they were also to take over the *Star*. On 21 November 1946 Seniors were taken over by Hammond's brewery of Lockwood which signalled the demise of their name in pub ownership.

The *Star's* days were numbered when the *George*, next door to it, began trading. In its last year or two should any customer require a drink of beer it had to be hurriedly fetched in jugs from the *George,* after which it was poured straight into glazed pots, complaints about its quality were rare as no one could see whether it was clear or not! It closed around 1904 probably as a result of the compensation made available by parliament. The landlord, Joshua Swainson, went on to take over the *Dunkirk* at Lower Denby and the *Star* was converted to a private residence by J W Heath and Mr Town, the pub sign lying in the old Heath joiners shop for many years.

These pubs were very much different from today's comfortably furnished affairs and ran slightly differently. The floors were either wooden or simply stone flags. A fire would blaze in the hearth and customers would be served at their tables by the landlord after attracting his attention by rapping their pots on the table or ringing bells at the back of their seats. Beer was simply a pint of best or mild, customers often asking for a 'gill of ale', which was supplied in either pewter, or

Denby footballers in front of the *George*, circa. 1909. Note that Joseph Airton was the pub landlord as featured on the sign. *Author's collection.*

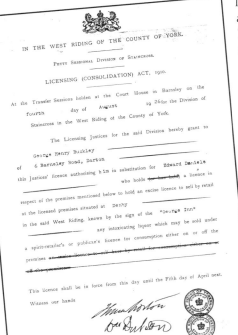

The licence held by George Buckley for the *George* public house, 1926. *Author's collection.*

later glazed, pots. These were places for drinking and talking, not for eating and listening to music. The landlords usually ran their pubs alongside their other jobs, i.e. John Firth (*Star*) was also a shopkeeper and farmer, John Hanwell (*New Inn*), was a cobbler as was his kinsman, Aaron Hanwell (*Star*) and Joseph Airton (*George*) was a plasterer, a fact which he advertised on the sign for his pub.

During the 1950s the *New Inn* was a popular place for a drink, particularly with local farmers. Other than the best and mild brews offered by Hammonds one could also partake of bottles such as *Guards Bitter, Prize Medal* or perhaps *Town Major*. Smith's crisps were sold out of tins of eighteen. The *New Inn* also offered funeral teas, unlike the *George* at this time. The upstairs room would be used for such occasions, a room, which was at this time apparently full of stuffed birds! The steps to the cellar were so badly worn into

The *New Inn*, **looking down the hill towards the** *George* **circa. 1905.** *Courtesy of 'Old Barnsley'.*

the shape of a barrel that one unlucky customer, (perhaps the worse for drink?) fell down them, much to the amusement of the attendant clientele.

A customer walking in would see the best room on the right and the tap room to the left, the bar was straight in front and only the width of the hallway, the privies were outside, round the back. Entertainment was spartan, but on occasion a village lady, Ginny Grange, would gain a free glass of beer to take home providing she sang to the accompaniment of the piano for the landlady. The pub had a darts team, which played in the Penistone league, and the landlady would sometimes offer round steak teacakes as a snack.

In 1963 the *New Inn* closed down. Hammonds had decided that one of its two pubs in Denby should be modernised and the other closed. The *George* had the advantage as it already possessed a car park. The brewery approached the owners of the land across from the *New Inn*, with a view to building one, but were refused permission. The decision was therefore made for them and the house was sold and converted into a private residence.

The hamlet of Dunkirk at Lower Denby is reputed to be named after the Battle of Dunkirk in 1658. The French were at war with the Spanish, though English soldiers fought on both sides. The Duke of York's Royalists for the Spanish and Cromwell's 'Ironsides' for the French, who in fact captured Dunkirk whilst the Spanish looked on.

The *Dunkirk* at Lower Denby was built in 1840 after the Barnsley to Lane Head turnpike was built and opened in sections between 1825 and 1830. In 1866 we find Elizabeth Burgess as the landlady, giving way the following year to Allen Booth. The present building was originally three cottages, the early pub being run from one of them. These were purchased by the Cubley brewery of Penistone in 1887 and were knocked through to create the building we have today. More recently Paul and Michelle Tugwell, who left in 2000 and Rik and Janice Davidson to present, have been the landlords and ladies.

The *Wagon and Horses* across the road was also an early alehouse and important coaching inn.

The *Dunkirk Inn*, Lower Denby, 1905. *Author's collection.*

In 1822 the landlord was a William Hague, he was followed by Joshua Shaw - 1838, Mrs Senior - 1861, John Johnson - 1867 (to at least 1881). From at least 1901-1912 William Challenger ran a blacksmith's shop at the side of the pub.

Within the triangle which still exists between the two pubs used to stand a stone building to which salt was brought from Cheshire and various other places by pack horse. The salt was stored in this

Advertisement for the *Junction Inn* taken from the brochure for the Denby Dale Pie, 1964

The *Dunkirk Inn*, operating under its other name the *Junction Inn* in 1961 during a meet of the local hunt. *Author's collection.*

The old *Wagon and Horses* public house opposite the *Dunkirk Inn*. The road to the right is Miller Hill heading down into Denby Dale, circa. 1890. *Author's collection.*

building waiting to be distributed to local drysalters, shops and farms. The building became known as the Salt Pile later being corrupted to Salt Pie. After demolition the stones were stored behind the *Junction Inn* (formerly the *Dunkirk*) and were subsequently re-used to build a bungalow a few yards further up Dry Hill, or Draw Hill as it was originally called. The *Junction* has since reverted to its original name, the *Dunkirk* but you will find the two

Coach and horses outside the *George*, circa. 1900. *Author's collection.*

Advertisement for the *George* **taken from the** brochure for the Denby Dale Pie, 1964. *Author's collection.*

names locally interchangeable. Only the *George* remained in Upper Denby, the barn and carthouse were demolished to extend the car park and a new toilet block was added.

The spittoons were given by the landlord, Jim Barber to a farmer at the bottom of Cuckstool in Denby Dale to use as pig bowls. Hammonds gave way to Bass Breweries who subsequently sold it on to Century Inns who were in turn bought out by Enterprise PLC of Solihull. The village pub is now just one of approximately 2000 owned by the group. Ownership aside, the pub still retains its traditional village character. At its busiest around Christmas, particularly Boxing Day, when the Rockwood Harriers meet in the car park and crowds of traditionalists turn up to watch them depart before entering the pub, usually frozen cold and ready for a pint.

Chronological Table of Upper Denby Publicans

Year	The Star	The New Inn	The George
1822	Amos Barraclough		
1830	Thomas Burdet		
1838	John Firth	John Brook	
1857	John Firth	John Hanwell	Enoch Taylor
1861	John Firth	John Hanwell	Enoch Taylor
1866	Aaron Hanwell	John Hanwell	Enoch Taylor
1867	Aaron Hanwell	John Hanwell	
1881	Aaron Hanwell	Mary Hanwell	Nancy Taylor
1882			George Taylor
1889	Aaron Hanwell	Mary Hanwell	George Taylor
1901	Wilson Green	Hannah Pearce	Alfred Taylor
1904	Joshua Swainson	Harry Thorpe	Alfred Taylor
	CLOSED		
1909			Joseph Airton
1912		Sam Wing	
1917		Sam Wing	Benjamin Slater
1926			Edward Daniel
1927		Percy Cartwright	Genny Buckley
1930		Percy Cartwright	Frank & Mabel Widdowson
1950 app.		Walt Martin	Frank & Mabel Widdowson
1952 app.		Eric & Joyce Bailey	Frank & Mabel Widdowson
1954		Doug & June Fisher	Frank & Mabel Widdowson
1958		? Fisher	Frank & Mabel Widdowson
1959-1962		? Fisher	Jim & Dot Barber
1963-1970		CLOSED	Jim & Dot Barber
1971-1992			Roy Barraclough
1992			Martin & Carol Brook
1993-1999			Steven & Jill Slater
1999-2000			Ken Hunt
2000-present			Joan Eastwood and Clare Davis

NB: *It should be noted that the dates given are not terms of tenancy but the years known in which the pub was occupied by that person.*

WHEELWRIGHTS, JOINERS AND UNDERTAKERS
The Wheelwright
The masters of this skill were very important to the local farming community, sometimes they worked in tandem with the village blacksmith in a job which involved both wood and metal.

The nave or naff was turned on a treadle lathe (the one from Denby was donated to the Tolson

Museum, Huddersfield), and great precision was required to fit the spokes and felloes (rim). Hard woods were used, though cast iron naves began to appear from 1846. Once the wooden parts were assembled the metal tyre was added with the aid of a tyring plate. The tyre was red hot when forced onto the rim and then drenched to shrink it tight around the wheel. The carts and wagons the wheels were made for varied locally throughout the country. Carts were two wheeled, wagons four wheeled. The dray seems to have been a popular type for Denby farmers being low and strong and suitable for heavy goods.

Denby Wheelwrights and Joiners

John Milnes was the Denby wheelwright in the 1851 census, where he can be found employing four men and two grandsons. His premises were reputed to be in the building at the end of Back Lane, now Coal Pit Lane, just a little way from the Barraclough blacksmith's shop. He was a member of a large family of farmers, his relations working at both Broad Oak, Gunthwaite Gate and Oughtibridge Hall farms.

His grandson, John Heath from Oughtibridge, became one of his apprentices in the late 1840s and was then set on as a full time employee after his apprenticeship ended. In 1868 John Milnes died, aged eighty-eight, it is likely that he had already passed much of his business over to his grandson by this time, but it was now that John Heath inherited sole responsibility. He was also responsible for burying his own grandfather as the business involved undertaking, though it was unusual for a family to bury their own. He was laid to rest in Denby Churchyard free of charge, usual cost £2. John married Ellen Hanwell and had a large family, his sons, Walter, Rufus, John Milnes and Harry all became joiners and wheelwrights, and aided in the family business.

Before the introduction of stone for buildings, timber was the chief source material. The people who built these wooden structures were known as 'wrights'. The Latin word for 'wright' is 'carpentarius', therefore makers of wheels were wheelwrights, and more general woodworkers were carpenters. On the other hand, joiners were involved in the construction of furniture only, which led to friction between them and the carpenters. Today the two terms are interchangeable but originally they were two different professions. John Milnes and the Heath family had no such reservations and wore all three different hats, alongside other maintenance work such as glazing and painting and repairs to just about anything.

The following list will illustrate this and also the prices charged and the clients they worked for.

John Heath's Ledger, 1882 onwards:

Name	Work Undertaken	Cost in £ s d		
Sarah Gaunt	Close Post		1s	
Wilson Green	Child's Coffin		3s	
Denby Local Board	Mattock Shaft			10d
	Barrow Repaired			10d
David Tyas	New Cartwheel	£2	5s	
	New Cart Axle		16s	6d
John Micklethwaite	Manger Repaired			10d
Arthur Priest	Short Ladder			9d
James Moore	New Gate		18s	
John Boothroyd	New Book Case	£1		
	Chest of Drawers	£4	10s	
George Schofield	Pig Sty Door and Hanging		11s	6d
Joseph Barraclough (blacksmith)	New Stool		2s	6d
	Shoeing Box Repaired			6d
	Pattern Making		6s	9d

Benjamin Holmes	Cart Wheel Rimming and 5 spokes	£3	3s	
	Cart Bottom Repaired			8d
Zion Chapel	4 New Doors, Hanging and Locks	£1	2s	3d
Aaron Hanwell (shoemaker)	Last Tops Making		1s	6d
John Kilner	Little Pig Trough		4s	
	Spout Putting Up and Painting		10s	6d
	Table Repaired		1s	4d
Mary Hanwell (New Inn)	Billiard Cush Putting On			6d
	Chair, new rockers		1s	9d
James Burdett	2 shelves, putting up		2s	9d
William Fretwell	Wheels rimming and 4 new spokes	£1	8s	3d
Tom Thackra	New Hawking Cart, springs, fittings, iron work etc	£17	0	0
John Horn	Turnip Chopper repaired		3s	9d
	Plough repaired		6s	9d
John Haigh	Dray undergear repaired		8s	10d
Rev. Job Johnson	Peggy repaired			4d
	Cupboards for Church		9s	
Denby School Manageress	New Desks and Floor rests	£1	18s	6d
	School floor repaired	£1	12s	
	Class room boarding	£3	17s	
	Desk top removing and planing		3s	9d
John Burdett	Cart painting and varnishing		17s	6d
George William Moxon	New Dresser	£4	15s	
Charles Rusby	Cart wheel rimming		17s	
Alfred Gaunt	New cart axle		17s	
Erasmus Smithson	New Dray Wheel	£1	17s	
Church Work	New Belfry Floor	£4	11s	6d
Church Work	New seat in gallery		2s	4d
	Steeple Roof Repaired		8s	9d

Work was also carried out for Zacheus Hinchcliffe and Augustus William Saville to name but two, and clients came not only from Denby but also Denby Dale, Cumberworth, Gunthwaite and elsewhere. The ledger is very long as is the above representative list, but it gives details about the everyday things in villager's lives as well as the financial aspects of woodworking. Of course,

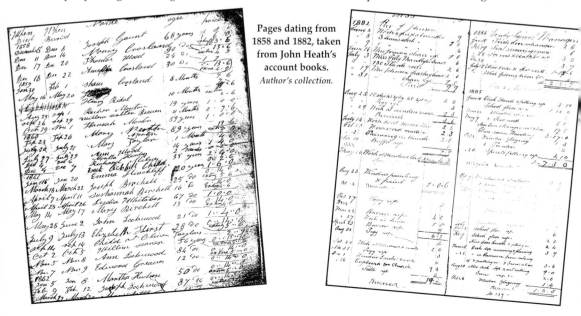

Pages dating from 1858 and 1882, taken from John Heath's account books.

Author's collection.

Barnsley Ct 9

No. of Plaint, 0249

In the County Court of Yorkshire, holden at Rotherham.

Between   *John Heath*   Plaintiff,

and

Henry Brooke   Defendant.

You are hereby informed that the Defendant was on the 24th day of *May* 1887, served with the Summons issued in this Action.

Dated this 25 day of *May* 1887.

F. PARKER RHODES.

Registrar acting as High Bailiff.

To the Plaintiff.

Hours of Attendance at the Office of the Registrar, in Westgate, Rotherham, from Ten till Four, except on Saturdays, when the Office will be Closed at One o'Clock.

A summons taken out by John Heath to recover money owed by Henry Brooke, 1887. *Author's collection.*

even in those days it could be difficult to recoup an overdue debt, as the above summons illustrates, taken out by John Heath to recover money owed by Henry Brooke in 1887.

Undertaking

A ledger has survived dating from 1858 detailing burials undertaken by John Milnes and John Heath. The price of a burial, as now, was varied. A child's burial would be around 5-9s, an adult burial anything from £1 10s and upwards depending on the type of coffin requested and arrangements required. Pitch pine was the cheapest material for these and is consequently the most used. As the ledger moves forward in years so the prices increase, i.e.: Rachel Fish was buried on 24 November 1873 at a cost of £3 17s 6d. It is interesting to note that the linings for the coffins were accounted for in the ledger as '4 1/2 yards of black stuff'! The following breakdown shows the cost of the expenses involved in a burial on 23 April 1870:

John Burgess, 6 1/2 yards of black stuff - 4s 4d, Dress and Hearse - 7s 6d, Grave Digging - 12s, Vault Wall and Stone Line - 13s, Minister charge for vault - 6s 8d, Dues at Church - 3s 6d, Total: £2 7s 0d. Added to the above was the charge made for the coffin which brought the total up to £2 12s.

By the early 1880s John's third son Harry was working alongside him as his partner. The close proximity of the workshop to the Barraclough blacksmith's probably aided in the union between the two families when Harry married Elizabeth Barraclough, daughter of the blacksmith, Joseph. Thus two integral village businesses were drawn together. Two cottages, which used to stand on Smithy Hill, next door to the blacksmith's were the homes for the two families. The houses, demolished in 1972 were of seventeenth century origin.

John Heath died in 1903 aged seventy-three in one of these cottages and Harry was left to carry on. Two of his children, Joe Willie and Ernest were to become joiners themselves, Joe Willie taking over the business after Harry's death in 1922 aged fifty-nine.

Joseph Barraclough died in 1907 and the buildings and land belonging to him were sold to

Smithy Hill, circa. 1960, showing cottages, now demolished. *Author's collection.*

Harry Heath. Presumably it was now that the joiner's shop moved from the end of Back Lane into the outbuildings at the back of the blacksmith's on Smithy Hill, though it is likely, in view of the family union that the two sites were interchangeable.

Joe Willie Heath bought land across from the new site and constructed the present day Joiner's shop in 1926. Today this wooden structure has quite obviously seen better days, though plans were made at one time to rebuild in stone. His son Harry took over the business, after working with his father for many years

Joe Willie Heath, his wife Harriet and family, circa. 191... *Author's collection.*

in 1969, after Joe Willie's death. Ill health and the reduced demand for traditional craftsmanship have all but seen the end of this family business, yet the advent of modern power tools and the 'do it yourself' enthusiasts will never take the place of these craftsmen of the past.

Genealogical Table of Milnes and Heath Families

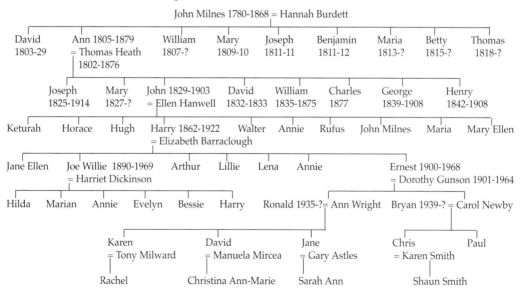

John Milnes 1780-1868 = Hannah Burdett

| David 1803-29 | Ann 1805-1879 = Thomas Heath 1802-1876 | William 1807-? | Mary 1809-10 | Joseph 1811-11 | Benjamin 1811-12 | Maria 1813-? | Betty 1815-? | Thomas 1818-? |

Joseph 1825-1914 — Mary 1827-? — John 1829-1903 = Ellen Hanwell — David 1832-1833 — William 1835-1875 — Charles 1877 — George 1839-1908 — Henry 1842-1908

Keturah — Horace — Hugh — Harry 1862-1922 = Elizabeth Barraclough — Walter — Annie — Rufus — John — Milnes — Maria — Mary — Ellen

Jane Ellen — Joe Willie 1890-1969 = Harriet Dickinson — Arthur — Lillie — Lena — Annie — Ernest 1900-1968 = Dorothy Gunson 1901-1964

Hilda — Marian — Annie — Evelyn — Bessie — Harry — Ronald 1935-? = Ann Wright — Bryan 1939-? = Carol Newby

Karen = Tony Milward — David = Manuela Mircea — Jane = Gary Astles — Chris = Karen Smith — Paul

Rachel — Christina Ann-Marie — Sarah Ann — Shaun Smith

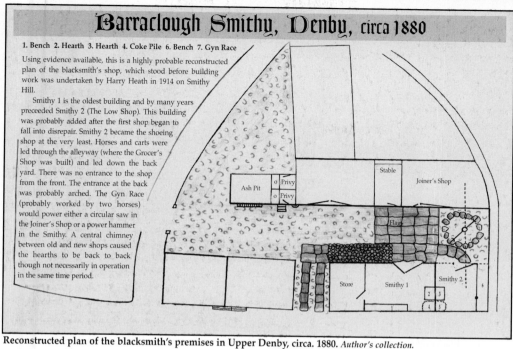

Barraclough Smithy, Denby, circa 1880

1. Bench 2. Hearth 3. Hearth 4. Coke Pile 6. Bench 7. Gyn Race

Using evidence available, this is a highly probable reconstructed plan of the blacksmith's shop, which stood before building work was undertaken by Harry Heath in 1914 on Smithy Hill.

Smithy 1 is the oldest building and by many years preceeded Smithy 2 (The Low Shop). This building was probably added after the first shop began to fall into disrepair. Smithy 2 became the shoeing shop at the very least. Horses and carts were led through the alleyway (where the Grocer's Shop was built) and led down the back yard. There was no entrance to the shop from the front. The entrance at the back was probably arched. The Gyn Race (probably worked by two horses) would power either a circular saw in the Joiner's Shop or a power hammer in the Smithy. A central chimney between old and new shops caused the hearths to be back to back though not necessarily in operation in the same time period.

Ash Pit   Privy   Privy   Stable   Joiner's Shop   Flags   Store   Smithy 1   Smithy 2

Reconstructed plan of the blacksmith's premises in Upper Denby, circa. 1880. *Author's collection.*

BLACKSMITHS

It was reputedly, the year 1600 when James Barraclough opened a Blacksmith's shop in Upper Denby. It is likely that this first building was just a timber structure, which later gave way to a brick built building, which was only demolished in the early twentieth century. It stood on Smithy Hill (not on The Green as reported in the book *A Stroll Around Denbi*), and was not accessed from the front, but through an alleyway, between itself and the two adjacent cottages and round to the back, where there was also a Joiner's shop and at one time, a gin-race. The Barracloughs continued to be the village blacksmiths until 1907, when the last of them, Joseph, died.

Many times employed in tandem with wheelwrights, the blacksmith was an important part of farming life, a myriad of tasks kept him busy throughout the hours of daylight. The following abridged description is taken from *Compton's Encyclopaedia* volume 3:

The glow of the forge, the ringing clang of hammer against anvil, the sizzle of heated iron or steel cooled suddenly in water, and the neigh and stamp of horses were familiar sights and sounds in the shop, as the blacksmith repaired and made carriages, wagons, tools and machinery. Smithing is one of the oldest crafts and became increasingly important with the discovery of iron. In time it was discovered that heated metal could be shaped more easily. Time and experience brought skill to the arts of refining, shaping and tempering iron and steel.

Very few Blacksmiths shops exist today, there are fewer horses to shoe, wagons and carriages have given way to trucks and cars and tools and parts are now mass produced by machines. Tool and die making shops, rolling and forging mills and the steel industry in general have left little for the blacksmith to do other than the farriers task of shoeing horses. Until well into the 20th century the community blacksmiths shop was a familiar sight.

School children on their way home would peer through the open door into the dark, smoky interior.

The village blacksmith, shoeing horses, probably at Lower Denby, therefore it is probably Mr Challenger, circa. 1895. *Author's collection.*

Using a tyring plate to apply a metal wheel rim, at Cawthorne. Probably William Challenger again, circa. 1892. *Author's collection.*

William Challenger and his wife, Fanny, circa. 1896. *Author's collection.*

A leather aproned smith might be thrusting tongs into the forge and pulling out pieces of white hot metal. He would turn quickly to the anvil, put the pieces together and hammer them hard to weld and shape them. Of course the shop was also a gathering place where farmers and others would muse over the problems of the day. The floor space in the shop had to be large, so as to allow the wagons, ploughs and horses enough space to be worked on. A workbench, water tub, anvil, tool table and coal bin would reside against the walls, as well as racks to hold metal rods and sheets used as raw material by the smith. The floor around the forge and anvil would have been either, packed soil or wood covered by sheet iron so that the chips of hot metal that flew when being pounded would not set fire to the floor. The anvil was usually placed about six feet from the forge and was made of steel, its face being hardened. It stood on a block of wood which was sunk into the ground to a depth of about two feet. The tongs a smith would have used varied in shapes and sizes and the jaws were of various kinds, being designed to hold different shapes of metal. For heavier work the smith would swing sledge hammers of varying weights. Other instruments were hot and cold chisels (for cutting hot or cold iron), and shaped instruments called, flatters, sets, fullers and swages, used for flattening or forming special shapes in the metal.

Although none now remain the Barracloughs once populated the township of Denby in enormous numbers, as one would expect for a family that had lived here for 300 years or more.

In 1851 we find James and Elihu both working at their trade, employing two younger members of their families as apprentices, Francis, aged sixteen and William aged thirteen. James and Elihu's father James was also a blacksmith, and it seems to be through this line that the business was handed down. That Elihu was deaf and dumb seems to have been no barrier to practising his skill. Other members of the family were employed in the textile industry, farming and butchery, though it is probable that some of them had a knowledge of some aspects of smithing. The humble family business, expanded over the years, and incorporated a shop in Denby Dale (where the present hardware store belonging to Marsden's now stands) and a shop at Lower Denby, which was taken over by William Challenger. It would seem that Elihu ran the Upper Denby shop, whilst James looked after Lower Denby and that the Denby Dale site was taken over some time in the late nineteenth century.

It was James's son, Joseph who inherited the business, trained by his father and uncle he was the last of a long line in Denby. His will, dated 1907, nominates his son George (also a blacksmith) and his son-in-law, Harry Heath as executors. Arrangements were made to sell the blacksmith's shop in Denby Dale, to Harry's brother, Walter Heath. The shop in Upper Denby was adjacent to Harry's own home, and was bought by him, and demolished shortly after by Allot and Bedford of Denby Dale. The site was re-developed at a cost of £100 10s during 1911/12. As Harry was the village carpenter and undertaker, the outbuildings at the back of the shop, which included a

Joseph Barraclough, the last of the family of Denby blacksmiths, circa. 1898. *Author's collection.*

joiner's shop, continued to be used for many years more until these too were demolished.

The shop at Lower Denby had been taken over by William Challenger, around 1893/4. Married to Fanny Challenger, nee Robinson, the family had moved from Dakinbrook to the old schoolhouse in Lower Denby to allow William to work at the forge which used to be part of the buildings which comprised the *Wagon and Horses* public house. His ledger began in 1894 with a Mr Thomas Fish of Foal Foot. Other clients included the Laycocks of Gunthwaite Hall, Charles Harley of Denby Hall, Erasmus Smithson of Nether End and the Denby and Cumberworth Urban District Council. From his ledger we are able to learn a little of the prices charged and the jobs undertaken by the smith at the time:

Pony, 2 shoes	1s	4d	Repair machine blade.	1s	
Mare, 4 shoes	3s		Foal, 1 remove and foot dressing.	1s	
Brake handle for a cart.	1s		Pair of new plough traces.	3s	2d
Horse, 4 removes	1s	6d	1 shovel,sharpening		6d
Cart wheel bearing	1s		1 muck fork, repaired		3d
2 cold chisels		2d	1 hammer repaired		4d
Key engine wheel	1s		1 coulter laid		10d
1 Mattock		1d	(a coulter was the iron cutter		
1 lock staple and 1 sprained door.		4d	in front of a ploughshare).		
1 dozen studs and putting in.		10d			
1 mattock & shafting					
(a mattock was a kind of pick axe.)		4d			

The majority of the work was undertaken on behalf of the local farmers, and shoeing horses was by far and away the most common activity of the week. Finally it would be useful to note that although most of the accounts were eventually paid, a bartering or contra account system was still very much alive as W H Senior discovered on the page for Mr Cyrus Laycock of Gunthwaite Hall whose bill was made out for £1 6s 7d. He supplied Mr Challenger with pork and pooling fat to the value of 7s 7d to be deducted from his bill, which was settled in February 1902.

Genealogical Table of Denby Barracloughs:

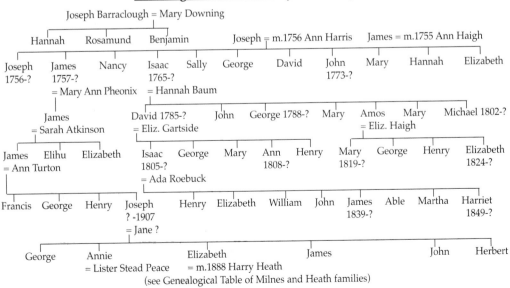

FARMING & TEXTILES
Farming

The art of living off the land is as old as the human race itself, its evolution would take far too long to tell in the context of this book and therefore we will concern ourselves with just the major points, applicable to Denby.

Denby's high elevation and the weather expected in this northern part of England meant that arable farming was never an important part of agriculture in the district. Of course crops were grown, but not on the same scale as those in more southern areas. Livestock became an integral part of life for many inhabitants of the village, sheep in particular, which could graze on the roughest pastures, led to the enormous boom which affected the village at the height of the cottage textile industry.

Crops, cattle and sheep amidst old fields and scattered farmsteads would just about describe Denby during medieval times. Within the fields, villagers would have their own strips of land, fairly proportioned to ensure that each had a fair share of good and bad. The results of the harvest would have been paid in part to Lord Burdet for his allowing them to farm on his land, a system known as 'feudal tenure'.

The Black Death of 1349, followed by other epidemics wiped out over a third of the population of the countryside in England, which led to a shortage of labour to farm the land, undermining the power of the manorial Lords. The peasantry became able to resist feudal obligations and feudal tenure was gradually replaced by rent.

By the late seventeenth century, agriculture had become an industry rather than a way of life. Manorial Lords had almost ceased to be farmers and were now landholders with tenant farmers, the peasantry were earning wages and subsistence economy was gone.

Due to a significant increase in population during the eighteenth century land became a good investment and ownership led to a steady increase in enclosure, which culminated in the enclosure awards made by the government at the turn of the century.

The Enclosure Award

Villages had been dividing up their open field systems long before the *Enclosure Act* was passed by parliament. The larger freeholders gained the biggest allotments, leaving the smaller, cottage farmers, who previously grazed their livestock on the common ground with much less acreage. Miles of dry stone walls sprang up creating a uniformity to the countryside and also paving the way for many of the roads we know today. Land that could not be ploughed or farmed was known as waste and was left for sheep to graze on.

The map, which accompanies Denby's enclosure award, dates from 1802 and a brief read through the names of the landholders soon provides the names of the more affluent members of the village. William Bosville held much of the land around what is now the present site of Upper Denby, he along with William Marshall, Charles Kent, Richard Lumley Saville and the Dickinsons of High Flatts are most prominent. Joshua Mosley held the lands around Manor Farm, John Ellis held lands close to the Pinfold and William Kilner those that adjoined the chapel. Penistone Grammar School also had two plots at Lower Denby.

The following plan illustrates not only the owners of the property in the direct vicinity of today's village, but also details the structures built before or during that time. It may be conjectured that here we have our earliest village plan, of buildings which must have been built in the 1700s and before.

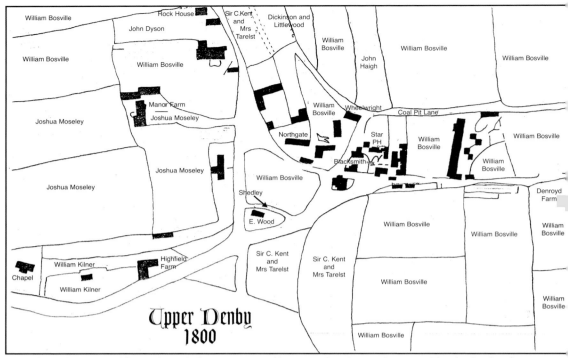

The enclosure award for Denby and Clayton was passed in 1800 and made on 14 June 1804. The plan is taken from the map which accompanied it, dated 1802. *Author's collection.*

The enclosure award book, which accompanies the map, details each landholder's property by number, and also states their responsibility for its upkeep. It was checked on 18 November 1850 by George Wilby, George Rusby, Joseph Haigh, William Thorp, Jas. Peace and Herbert Cam Dickinson.

Field name map of the area around Toby Wood and Square Wood, created by W H Senior. *Author's collection.*

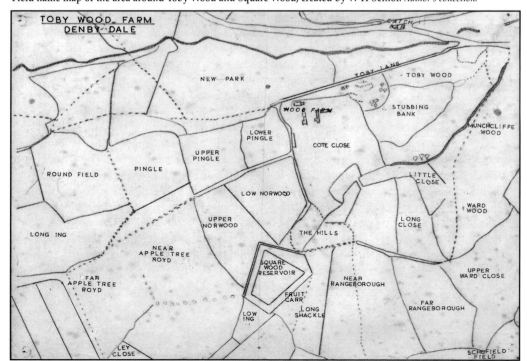

It is also interesting to note that many of the fields that exist today have in former times been christened with a name. A field map exists for Nether Denby, though the one reproduced opposite was researched by William H Senior and refers to fields in and around Square Wood Reservoir and Toby Wood.

Agricultural Revolution

Loosely dated 1750 - 1850 the revolution occurred because of the demands made upon farming by a rapid and constant increase in the population of the country. Ways had to be sought to increase productivity. The hand tools, which had been used up to now, were inadequate and labour intensive and it was a natural progression that the advances in technology should be applied to agriculture. Some of the more important innovations were:

1701	Jethro Tull's seed drill.
1730	The Rotherham plough (wood and iron).
1770	The first all iron plough.
1780s	Patrick Bell's reaping machine (pushed).
1784	Alexander Meikle's threshing and winnowing machines worked by a horse gin, later combined. Winnowing involved separating chaff from grain.
1790s	Iron plough with replaceable parts.
1802	Richard Trevithic's first agricultural steam engine (to drive a threshing machine).
1840	Steam applied to cropping, crushing, threshing and winnowing.
1888	Petrol engines.
1902	Ivel tractor, the Fordson selling 6000 in 1917 and by 1956, 478,000.
1920s	Combine harvesters (developed fully in the 1950s).

The development of the latter gradually caused bitter resentment amongst the labourers who feared the loss of their jobs or reduced wages. The appearance of the threshing machine, coupled with steam power, led to acts of arson and animal mutilation by some labourers in efforts to save their livelihoods. Though no records survive for this in Denby it is certain that feelings ran high.

Power

Oxen were used from the earliest times being followed from at least the twelfth century by horses. Stationary machines, housed in buildings were worked by either horse gins or water power where available. Steam power became widespread during the nineteenth century, both for static machines and ploughing and cultivating with the use of traction engines until it was superseded in around 1914 by petrol and diesel driven engines and electricity for static machinery and dairying.

The *Corn Law Act*, 1815

Innumerable acts have been passed by parliaments, which have affected the farming industry, but perhaps the resolution determined in 1815 is one of the more famous. During the Napoleonic Wars imports of corn from abroad had virtually ceased and British farmers had been encouraged to grow as much as possible to make up the shortfall. At the end of the war the fear was that a sudden surge of foreign corn flooding the markets would reduce the price and ruin the farmers. The above mentioned act was introduced to prevent any imports of corn until the British price

Threshing machine being used by the Pickford family, probably at Gate Farm around 1920. Threshing was usually a communal effort. A group of neighbouring farmers would help each other on their farms utilising the one threshing machine available. Sheaves were fed in to the top with the husks coming out at one end and the grain at the other. Besides the hard work in keeping up to the machine it was a dirty and very dusty job - particularly at the husk end. There was also a high risk of fire when using a traction engine to power the thresher. *Author's collection.*

Traction engine at Gate farm with Clem Pickford aboard it, circa. 1920. *Author's collection.*

Ploughing the old fashioned way. The picture was taken in a field belonging to the Pickfords oft Gate farm. *Author's collection, c.1912.*

had reached 80s per quarter. Although the act protected the farmers, bread prices were very high at a time when bread was the staple diet of the poorer classes. This became a symbol of the oppression of the

Harvesting at Toby Wood farm, circa. 1930. *Author's collection.*

poor until the act's repeal in 1846 under Peel's government. As many will know, in Denby Dale a pie was baked to celebrate the occasion, which is examined later.

Netherend and Manor Farm Barns

These two farms are almost opposite each other on the Barnsley road heading to Cawthorne, at Nether Denby. Manor Farm, on the left has a barn which is dated to 1657, although it is possible that some of the other buildings in the enclosure are even older, possibly back into the sixteenth century and contemporary with the massive barn at Gunthwaite, mentioned in Chapter Two.

The walls of the old cruck barn at Netherend on the right hand side of the road were, according to the gable end, built in 1663. Although there is evidence to suggest that this date on the lintel is inaccurate, it is again likely that a structure was sited on this land in the mid sixteenth century.

Here again we see the antiquity of Nether Denby, we have earlier noted that William Cotton and his family resided at the Denby Hall at Nether Denby, and that the Burdets were also in the locale. We will now turn to the only other family I have references of dwelling here during this time.

Long connected with Denby and Dodworth, the Oates family was certainly at Denby during the latter half of the sixteenth century, where we find William Oates, gent, a freeholder of estates in Dodworth and elsewhere. William's grandson was a partner in the Wortley Iron Works, having bought a share in it from William Simpson from Babworth, though he later sold out to Mr Arthur

Pedigree of Oates family of Nether Denby

Thomas Oates b.1554, Lived in Thornhill Lees   Lawrence Oates owned property at Wooley

William Oates d.1659 of Nether Denby, Gent.
= 1. ?   = 2. Ann Beaumont

John Oates 1632-1709   son2 son3 son4 son5   Josias   Mary Ann dau.3 dau.4
= Susan Brooke   = 1. Eliz. Fenton 2. ? = William   = Rev. John
                                                                          Brooke   Brooke
                                                                          1643-1680 bro. Rector of High Hoyland

Joseph   James   Samuel   William Joseph   Rev.Thos. Brooke MA William Mary Ann Jane
of Denby   of Dodworth   1688- ?   = ?   of Meanwood   1699-1739
= Grace   = Catherine   Emigrated   = Mary Fenton = Mary Cumber
dau.of   Wilson   to Boston,USA
Bartin Allott

James   John   dau.   (8sons) (8 dau.)   ?   George Samuel   John Charles FSA, Somerset Herald,
1723-47 1709-09   = Mr Wilson   = ? = ?   = Mary Hamer Sec. To Earl Marshal of England
= Miss   inf.   Of Broomhead
St Barbe

Joseph Oates   Susanna d.1806   Elizabeth d.1789   Joseph   Samuel Hamer Oates
al.1776 = ? Russell   = William Crowder   = John Crowder   of Westwood Hall, Leeds = Mary Coape

James Poole Oates   Edward   Joseph-Henry   Edward   ?
1770-1863   settled in USA   = ?   1792-?
(served in Peninsula War)   = ?

R H Oates   George William Oates Edward Francis   William Edward Charles George   Emily William Henry
?-1881, died   d.1876   (Frank)   of 2nd W.Yorks BA Trinty Col.   Coape Oates
in Toronto,   FRGS   Militia   Dublin, Barrister   of Longford Hall
no issue   died of   = Caroline Anne at Law, of the Inner   Newark, High Sheriff
                                             a fever   Buckton   Temple, of Meanwood   of Co. Notts 1880
                                             (Traveller & of Meanwood   Side, Leeds
                                             Naturalist) Leeds

Lillian-Mary 1879-?   Lawrence-Edward-Grace (Titus) Oates 1880-1912   Violet-Emily 1881-1966   Bryan 1883-?
= m. 1909   (Died during Captain Scott's failed Expedition to be   = ?
Frederick Ranalow   the first men to reach the Antarctic - *'I am just going outside and may be some time'*

Sheila   Edward

Speight in 1738 and retired. Thus the family had similar concerns as the Cottons.

It would be surprising in the extreme if the Oates family had not, at some time, dwelt at either Manor Farm or Nether End Farm, the two sites are certainly old enough and their close proximity to their neighbours, the Cottons and the two families interests in ironworking only strengthen the argument, besides which, I know of no other dwellings to have ever been built at Nether Denby.

As can be seen from the above, the Oates' family lineage is of very ancient derivation. A member of the family appears on a battle roll commemorating the followers of William the Conqueror at Hastings in 1066, and a Hugh Le Fitz Oates, according to a record dating from the reign of Henry III, was a crusader in 1270, and accompanied Edward I to the Holy Land.

The William Oates of Nether Denby who died in 1659 was probably either the son, or more likely, the grandson of either Thomas Oates, born in 1554, who lived at Thornhill Lees, or Lawrence Oates, his brother who owned property in Wooley.

The family had been reasonably wealthy since the sixteenth century, though as can be seen from the previous chart there were many offshoot branches. One in particular led to one of the most famous men of his, and all, time. Lawrence Edward Grace Oates who was born in 1880, son of William and Caroline Oates, this branch of the family had settled at Meanwood, Leeds, sometime around 1700. He was the Great, Great, Great, Great, Great Grandson of William Oates of Nether Denby.

He lived with his parents at Gestingthorpe Hall, Essex, though his mother was originally from Meanwood. It would appear that Lawrence had inherited some of his Uncle Frank's ideas about exploration. Frank was a great traveller and naturalist who died of a fever in South Africa. Whilst still a child and because of ill health, Laurence travelled with his family to Cape Town, South Africa where they were to stay with their cousins, a family by the surname of Burdett! Can this be a mere coincidence? I would like to believe not, the Burdett family are at present scattered all over the globe, there is little doubt that at least one branch may have emigrated to South Africa, and when one considers the close proximity of the two families whilst at Denby the possibility of an inter-family marriage is not at all unlikely. Though I must state that to date, I have found no record of a Burdett marrying an Oates, it must surely now be just a matter of time until the evidence surfaces.

Lawrence, nicknamed 'Titus', either after one of his horses or after the anti-Catholic agitator of the seventeenth century, completed a successful academic career and went on to serve in the army before being chosen by Captain Robert Falcon Scott to accompany him on his expedition to the South Pole in 1911. In a race against rival explorer, Roald Amundsen, Scott's party, including Oates, began their journey in November, hampered by unusually bad weather, five men reached the bottom of the world only to find that they had been beaten by the Norwegian where they found traces of his expedition. The party were forced to turn back, with a month's supply of food they were well prepared but disaster overtook them. Severe weather conditions hampered their progress, the men were forced to slaughter their ponies for dog meat, and to make matters worse, the severe cold had rendered Titus Oates almost incapable of walking by March 1912. Realising that he was costing his companions any hope of survival he made the supreme sacrifice, leaving the tent he went outside into a blizzard and uttered the immortal words, 'I am just going outside and I may be some time'. He was never seen again.

Captain Scott and the rest of his party died two weeks later of starvation and exhaustion. Oates' body was never recovered, near the spot where he walked to his death a cairn was built and a message left,

Hereabouts died a very gallant gentleman, Captain L E G Oates of the Inniskillin Dragoons. In March 1912, returning from the Pole, he walked willingly to his death in a blizzard to try and save his comrades beset by hardship.

Only one month later, more than 1500 passengers and crew drowned in the North Atlantic, victims of the sinking of the *Titanic*, the First World War began in 1914 and saw a loss of human life on a scale never before imagined, yet the last words of Titus Oates somehow survived the carnage and are still familiar to most of us today.

This man may or may not have known of his links to Denby, albeit somewhat distant, but Denby now knows of its links to him!

A series of letters has survived addressed to John Oates of Denby from a Mr Jessop (commonly known as Judge Jessop) of Sheffield on behalf of Sidney Wortley. John appears to have been the manager of his affairs, and would appear to be the son of the first William on the previous pedigree. It would appear that John Oates was not exactly doing his job to the best of his ability:

> *Sir, - I wonder you did not come over to execute the new counter security when you was last at Wortley. I'm sure Mr Wortley will be very angry when he hears of it, and its well if you do not provoke him to send a writt against you by trifling with him at this rate... I see no reason why he should forbear with you any longer. He tells me he designs to be at Wortley very shortly and what business soever you have or pretend, he expects you will make up your accounts forthwith, for he will be trifled with no longer.*
> *26 May 1698 for Mr John Oates at Denby*

> *Sir, - Here hath been one Thomas Crawshaw with me to complain of you for binding him over to ye sessions about the selling some sheep, and here is one Joseph Beldon, complains you have bound him over to the sessions about some hay... unless you let these poor men rest and cease any further proceedings against them, ...I shall endeavour to pick some hole in your coat and make you smart severely for it and pray let us hear no more of any sessions proceedings against Mr Wortley's tenantry, for I assure you if I hear of any such charges hereafter I shall endeavour to persuade Mr Wortley to deal as severely with you, as you use them. God forbid that I should do anything to hinder you from getting anything due to you in due course of law or in a friendly way, but if you made your applications to me and Mr Ranks we should take care that you had justice done you, and, I believe the money you demand of Crawshaw will be allowed you by Mr Wortley, but to proceed against people in this manner at the sessions is what doth them harm, and can do you no good and looks like malice than any design to right yourself and thereafter I desire of you once more that we may hear no more of these complaints.*
> *5 April 1699 for Mr John Oates at Denby.*

It is also interesting to note that John Hobson records in his diary of 1730:

> *26 September – A jumping match at Brotherton march, of 100l, betwixt Richard the son of Mr Joseph Oates, of Denby and a Staffordshire man. Richard Oates at 20 jumps leapt 71 yards; the other man, 73 1/2.*

This would be the son of Joseph mentioned in the latter table who married Grace, the daughter of Bartin Allot.

Broad Oak and Gunthwaite Gate Farms

Broad Oak was farmed for many centuries by the prolific family of Hawksworth. The name has already cropped up many times throughout the duration of this book. It was originally called 'the Rodes', 'the Roods' or more likely 'the Royds' and was owned by the warrior monks, the Knight's Hospitallers. By the sixteenth century the Hawksworths were in control and were the richest freeholders in the locality, where the centre of activity took place around a one time green. In 1577, during the reign of Elizabeth I, John Hawksworth refused to do suit at the court of Godfrey Bosville for his manor. He alleged that he held his land of the manor of Brierley and not of Gunthwaite. He also had a battle with Godfrey over rights to pasture land near the Hall at

Gunthwaite on common land. Godfrey denied him any rights and turned Hawksworth's cattle back. A William Hawksworth is also recorded as being alive and active in Gunthwaite during the reign of Mary I in 1553.

During the next century the family acquired Wheatley Hill farm in Clayton West where we find Peter Hawksworth the brother of Richard Hawksworth at Broad Oak. Richard was part of a very active puritan group during the civil war years as we have already noted from Adam Eyre's diary. Records exist which show a Richard Hawksworth inheriting Broad Oak upon the death of his father, John in 1617. Whether this is the same Richard or an earlier one, perhaps his father, is currently unknown. The lands at Broad Oak, would appear, at this time, to have been held by George Burdett as Richard had to pay suit at the court of the Manor of Denby. The lands involved were known as 'the roydes' or 'netherroydes', which correlate to Broad Oak and perhaps the demesne sited only a short distance away, now known as Far Broad Oak. One member of the family was also responsible, in part, for the re-building of High Hoyland church. An inscription in the tower informs us that John Moor was the mason and that Thomas Hawksworth was the carpenter involved in the construction, dated 1679.

The family continued to reside here until we reach the year 1726 when we find that the trustees of another Godfrey Bosville (whose father, William died when he was only seven years old) had purchased Broad Oak from them. This acquisition finally gave the Bosville family the whole of the Manor of Gunthwaite. John Hobson records the death of the man responsible:

17 September 1727. *Mr. Richard Hawksworth buried at Barnsley. He formerly owned Broad Oak in Gunthwaite, but had sold it, and spent all his substance, and died at Morton's, at Dodworth bottom, who had married his brother's wife.*

It would seem likely that Richard's wife, Dorothy had pre-deceased him at the age of twenty-five, as a burial is recorded at Penistone in 1709. The sale in 1726 for £1200 could suggest that the families fortunes had turned against them, though Richard's death a year after the sale may imply that he was an old man without an heir.

During the late eighteenth century a Captain Hawksworth is recorded as living and farming at Broad Oak. Probably a relation of the previous owners, but now merely the tenant of the Bosvilles. When he died, two of his employees, Thomas Ingham and his brother-in-law, Nathaniel Priest took over the tenancy and shared the house between their two families. Thomas Ingham's daughter, Sarah married one of the farm hands called Joseph Milnes and united two farming dynasties.

John Milnes of Darton (1750-1819) had taken the tenancy of Gunthwaite Gate farm in 1795. He had six surviving sons and a daughter, the eldest of whom, Richard, was born in 1777. His third son, Joseph Milnes and Sarah Ingham were married in 1811 and initially went to live at Heald Head, only returning to Broad Oak after Nathaniel Priest had left. This could only have been a few months after their marriage as we know that all their children were born at Broad Oak, the first of which, Ingham, named after his Grandfather, was born in November 1811. Thomas Ingham died in 1815, though an entry in the parish registers dated 19 May 1814 refers to Joseph as farmer, Broad Oak, implying that Ingham had relinquished his interests to his son-in-law by then. With his father only just up the hill towards Denby the Milnes family were doing very well. At some unknown date, John Milnes eldest son, Richard had taken on the tenancy of the neighbouring Far Broad Oak, also known as 'Ash Plant' and it may well be that, for albeit a brief period, all three farms were owned by the same family. White's trade directory dated 1852 notes

Genealogical Table of Milnes family.

John Milnes 1704-? = Rachel Stansfield

John Milnes 1750-1819 = Dorothy Rusby 1750/51-1811
Took tenancy of Gunthwaite Gate in app.1795

| Richard 1777-? | John 1780-1868
= Hannah Burdett
1778/9-1846 | Joseph 1782-1858
= Sarah Ingham
1784/5-1854 | Thomas 1785-1867
= Mary Hadfield | Charles 1787-?
= Hannah ? | dau.?-? | William 1797-? |

| David | Ann
1805-1879
= Thomas Heath
1802-1876 *(see other line of descent)* | William | Mary | Joseph | Benjamin | Maria | Betty | Thomas | John
1815-? | Mary
1816-? | Martha
1823-? | Richard
1828-? | Sarah
1828-? |

Joseph Milnes 1782-1858 (Formerly Broad Oak) = Sarah Ingham 1784/5-1854

| Ingham
1811-1892
= Dorothy Pickford
(Quaker) | Ann
1812-1894 | Sarah
1817-1887 | Maria
1820-1858
= James Pickford | Joseph
1821-1905 | Thomas
1823-1898
= Mary Smith | Richard
1825-1860 |

NB.*Joseph Milnes inherited the tenancy of Broad Oak Farm, Gunthwaite from his father in law, Thomas Ingham who died in 1815. Ann Ingham (nee Smith) 1762-1824, Thomas's wife, had a sister, Martha, who had been employed at Gunthwaite Hall until the Bosville's left, she moved on to Oughtibridge Hall as John Woods housekeeper taking with her, her illegitimate son, Joseph When Wood died in 1812 he left the tenancy to Joseph but as Joseph died childless the tenancy of Oughtibridge Hall passed to the Broad Oak family.*

Aerial view of Gunthwaite Gate farm taken in approximately 1970. *Author's collection.*

Aerial view of Springfield Mill, circa. 1975. *Author's collection.*

During the Second World War, most of the looms were kept employed on parachute silks and some khaki shirting material, but after the war the whole mill was considerably re-organised. In 1945 most of the old looms were replaced by modern versions, the engine was dismantled and a twin-diesel electric system was installed. In 1961 the shareholdings were sold to the fabrics division of Qualitex Fabrics Ltd of Colne, Lancashire. The factory at Colne was then closed down and production transferred to Denby Dale. Over the next ten years the company expanded into producing textured yarns, becoming one of the largest producers in the United Kingdom. This side of the business was re-named Qualitex Yarns with plants in Burnley, Ashton, Radcliffe and Manchester. The mill in Denby Dale stayed as the fabrics division producing woven ladies dress goods.

In the early 1970s ICI made a successful take-over bid of approximately twenty-two million for the Qualitex group and along with other acquisitions formed the company Intex. The policy of ICI was not to have a weaving unit, so the factory at Denby Dale became surplus to requirements, eventually the William Reed group based in Nelson acquired the company to complement their operations, the name Qualitex Fabrics being retained.

In 1973 Henry Kayes of Middleton were brought into the group, Kayes were narrow fabric weavers, specialising in curing tape for the hose industries. The factory at Middleton was closed down and production transferred to Denby Dale. Eventually the weaving of ladies dress goods was abandoned and narrow fabrics took over.

Just after the first needlelooms had been installed into the mill (between August 1974 and January 1975), bought from the Swiss company Muller, the company found itself in financial difficulties. On 16 January 1975 redundancies became necessary, forcing the mill to close down its lining and petersham qualities. The unlucky ones were informed by Production Director, Eric Mead. Two months later, following the death of Mr Mead, Gordon Estill became Director in Charge and Bryan Heath, Works Manager (rising to Board of Directors in 1977).

Aside from this blip the William Reed group expanded throughout the 1970s under the

Chairmanship of Stanley Wootcliffe. He was succeeded by Dr John Blackburn, when the name changed (in 1978) to Rivington Reed.

The group ran into serious financial trouble resulting in the appointment of receivers on Thursday 15 May 1980. The Pudsey based company A W Hainsworth took over the assets of Qualitex Fabrics (and indeed its name) on Friday 27 June. Production finally halted at the mill on Friday 28 November 1980, with management and some staff beginning work in Pudsey the following Monday where the company still thrives to this day.

The empty building in Denby Dale was bought by Messrs Wilf Charlton and John Dignan who used much of the mill as a warehouse and furniture showroom, trading as British distributors for the North Carolinian based American company, Broyhill (in England – Broyhill UK). In approximately 1985 the two businessmen were forced to wind up the venture when the cost of importing the furniture from the States became prohibitive. Wilf Charlton took over Springfield Mill, where he began a new venture – Fine Design- again furniture. John Dignan went on to open the Pine Factory in Scissett.

Mr Charlton now had far more space than was needed and so he decided to rent out various parts of the building for warehouse and retail space. Early opportunists were Cellarchoice (now Springfield Wines), Mike Pearson (TV repairs), Roy Morley (car maintenance) and Springfield Books (publishers), who began trading on 14 February 1984, eventually going out of business in 1997. The old mill is now home to a myriad of retail outlets and has become something of a tourist attraction.

Today only one of the three above mentioned mills is still running, that of Z Hinchcliffe, Kenyons having closed down in April 1977. The demise of the industry signalling another change in the occupations of the populace of Denby and its dale.

Although there were craftsman and specialists in Denby from the earliest times the bulk of the population were originally employed on the land, as either farmers or labourers. Their adoption of the woollen industry steadily grew more widespread until its golden years in the nineteenth century. As technology progressed many of the men, women and children involved lost their jobs and were left at the mercy of the poor rates to support themselves and their large families. As we have seen, the Quakers of High Flatts mounted a charity operation to help the poor of Denby in 1826, poor because of the changes brought about in the textile industry. The coming of the mills in Denby Dale did create many jobs, but their decline, particularly in the latter part of the twentieth century has left the area with no specific product to associate with the villages within it.

Many of the old farm buildings have now been modernised and turned into new homes for the changing community and the factories in the valley are now largely retail units and warehousing space for new smaller companies. Yet, the woollen industry will always be associated with this part of Yorkshire and enough relics exist of that time to remind us what an important part it played in the lives of the ordinary people.

OTHER OCCUPATIONS
Denby Post Office
The Post Office, which was founded in 1635 grew steadily throughout the seventeenth and eighteenth centuries until the modern service blossomed, when parliament led by Rowland Hill introduced the penny post in 1840. Telegraph companies were nationalised in 1870 when they were taken under the wing of the Post Office. A telephone was a regular feature of the shops after 1890.

Hannah Wood ran the Post Office in Denby Dale during the 1860s. Letters from Huddersfield would arrive at 7.30 am and 5.30 pm, they were despatched at 7.05 pm. Hannah Wood had given way to John Micklethwaite by 1901. John was also a quarry owner and other members of his family ran a shop in Upper Denby during the latter half of the nineteenth century.

The first Post Office in Upper Denby was opened on 11 March 1914 by Harry Heath, the village carpenter. He had already opened a grocers store in 1907 and so the two were merged. His family continued to run the enterprise after his death in 1922, first Elizabeth his wife who was then followed, in 1947 by her daughter, Annie. Annie retired in 1958, aged sixty, thus the Post Office was closed down, within two years the shop was also discontinued.

Being only a sub-post office, services such as savings were not available, but the shop did possess a telephone in the corner allocated to 'postal services'.

Kathleen Wickam was the last proprietor of a sub-post office in Denby, also combining postal activities with a general store, this being closed in the 1990s, and so leaving UpperDenby once again dependent on the sub-post office in Denby Dale for its services.

Shops

A glance through the trade directories of the nineteenth century provides the names of quite a number of people in this manner of business. For instance in 1881, James and Francis Burdett ran a shop, Francis was also a joiner, though it is possible that the shop was at High Flatts and not in Denby. John Kilner and George Micklethwaite were also described as shopkeepers. The villages self sufficiency becomes even more apparent when one considers the farm produce available, particularly dairy items, the services of John Turton a chemist and the numerous cobblers, joiners, smiths, tailors and masons living in Denby.

Denby's General Store – 1904 to 1960

Harry Heath opened his shop around 1904 in a small structure, recently built between the Barraclough blacksmith's shop and two adjacent cottages, the building sited on the former alleyway through to the blacksmith's workshops round the back. As we have seen, he set up a Post Office here in 1914. His first ledger survives and this can be used to illustrate not only the price of goods in the period 1904-1915, but also to show the type of goods available at the time:

Boots and Shoes

Clogs	2s	6d	Child's Slippers	1s	11d
Slippers	2s	6d	Men's Boots	8s	9d
Leather Lace Boots	6s		Canvas Shoes	3s	3d
Boys Button Boots	7s	11d	Ladies Boots	7s	9d
Tan, Strap Shoes	4s	11d	Sandals	3s	11d

Food Stuffs

Bacolite Lard		3d	Matches	2d
Flour (2 stones)	2s	10d	Eggs (1/2 dozen)	2d
Rabbit		11d	Tea	8½d
Butter	1s	3d	Treacle	5½d
Potatoes		3½d	Tobacco (Bacco)	1½d
Vinegar		1d	Oatmeal	4½d
Tomatoes		6d	Biscuits	3d
Candles		5d	Rice	2½d

Currants		4½d
Sugar		4½d
Coffee		2½d
Yeast		5d
Apples		3d
Jam		8½d
Camphorated Oil		2d
Onions		2½d
Ham		5d
Marmalade		4d
Pepper		1½d
Salmon		8½d
Mustard		1d
Bacon		4d
Nutmeg		½d

Oranges		3d
Sago		3d
Beef		7½d
Tongue	1s	2d
Ammonia		1d
Blacklead		1d
Jellies		2d
Beef paste		1d
Magnesia		2d
Figs		4½d
Soda		2d
½ stone of wheat	1s	5d
Cheese	1s	2d
Cocoa		1½d

Hardware and Fabrics

Stockings	1s	3d
Brush		4½d
Floor Cloth		2d
Laces		1½d
Needles		1d
Garters		2d
Paint		6d
Hairpins		½d
Apron		9½d
Emery Paper		1d
Soap		2½d
Starch		1d
Rope		1d
Buttons		1d
Pins		1d
Comb		3½d
2 Men's Shirts	2s	2d
2 pairs of knickers	2s	4d
Teapot		6d
6 pieces of paper	1s	5d
Collar		4½d
Shawl	6s	6d
Blouse	2s	6d
Pair of Towels	1s	7d
Blankets	3s	6d
Scarf		5½d
Broom	1s	
Hand Bag	1s	
2 pairs of Bloomers	5s	

Men's trousers	8s	
Men's braces	1s	
2 night dresses	9s	6d
A Child's Doll	4s	6d
Box of chocolates	2s	3d
Corsets	5s	3d
2 men's vests	7s	6d
Smock	6s	6d

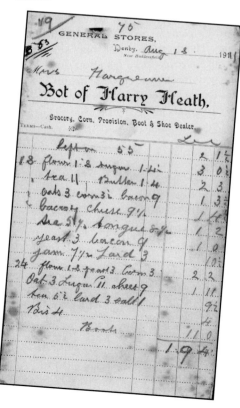

NB: *it should be remembered that foodstuffs were sold in old weights and measures and the above are only representative samples.*

Mrs Hargreaves weekly shopping bill, dated 18 August 1911. *Author's collection.*

Note the absence of some of the foodstuffs that today we expect to find on supermarket shelves, bread, cakes, soup, etc. These, of course, all being made at home. Coffee beans were bought and ground down on the premises with the use of a grinding machine powered by an engine, previously owned by Norman Peace. The silver paper linings of the chests that tea arrived in was used for Christmas trimmings .

A license had to be obtained to sell fireworks for 5 November, Annie Heath making sure that as many children as possible received a bag full with their name on it, usually more bangers for boys and snowstorms for girls. The names 'Little Demon', 'Thunderflash' and 'Jumping Cracker' evoke smoky memories of delighted faces. Toys were also sold although the store was definitely not a toy shop. In the early days stock was transported to the shop in a horse and cart later deliveries were made by company vans.

There were numerous other shops locally, notably that of Lucy Travis in Lower Denby which ran upon similar lines to the Heath shop described above. A number of people also sold produce from their homes, vegetables, salad and other home grown items, and sweets, usually sold off a trestle table in the kitchen. The general store at Lower Denby run from Landon House eventually ceased trading and was turned into

Annie Heath who became sub-postmistress in Denby after her mother's death in 1947. Photographed here in 1915. *Author's collection.*

Annie Heath with an unknown merchant, circa. 1925. *Author's collection.*

Delivery van above the cottages on Smithy Hill, circa. 1935. *Author's collection.*

The Huddersfield and Yorkshire school of singing at Landon House, Lower Denby, in the 1960s. *W H Senior.*

something that sounds altogether more grand – 'The Huddersfield and Yorkshire School of Singing, Piano Forte and Opera'.

Run by a Mr Henry Crowther, it was a relatively short lived enterprise. It is also interesting to note the triangle bay windows had not yet been built when the photograph, below left was taken.

The Co - Op

Founded in Rochdale the Co-Op grew steadily bigger from around 1844. The one in Upper Denby was sited on Rattan Row and is still apparent, though now converted into a private dwelling, by the large front window, formerly the shop window. During the 1940s and 50s it was run by Teddy Higson. The big supermarket chains began to take over during the 1970s signalling the end of many Co-Op outlets and indeed village shops. The Co-Op closed in 1963.

Besom Making

This was the art of making brooms from twigs, which were tied to handles, typical of the stereotyped witches broomstick.

The White family were responsible for this craft in Denby during the nineteenth and early twentieth centuries. Fred White retired in 1923, after following in the footsteps of his father, Charles and his grandfather, John. The besoms were sold to a number of sources, notably farmers and industrial factories.

Fred White had liberty to collect heather twigs on Honley Moor, Boardhill, Cannon Hall Park and all the moors around Denby. He used small oak poles, torn into thin strips to tie the heather to the poles, these were known as lappings. A report in the *Huddersfield Examiner* dated 1936 commemorated his golden wedding and he was quoted as saying:

> I once made one (a besom) *for a sovereign in three minutes and it was another besom maker who bet me I couldn't do it. I had got my seventh lapping on when he was doing his second. Its grasp that you need in besom making, for holding the heather and tying the lappings round.*

The White workshop used to stand as an outbuilding which backed onto Northgate, a usual weeks output was ten dozen besoms.

Genealogical Table of the White family

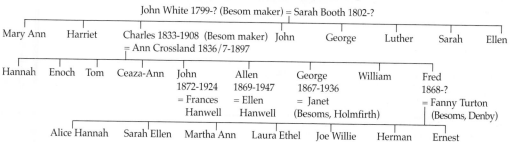

Tanning and its Offshoots
Tanning was the practice of turning animal hides into leather. The skins were soaked in 'tannin', which was derived from tree bark or vegetable extracts, later mineral salts were used. Once soaked the skins were hung in sheds to dry before being passed to the 'currier' who dressed or treated the leather before being sold. The Post Office directory of 1857 notes that the village tanner was Benjamin Boothroyd, who was part of a large family of tailors.

Cordwainers, Shoemakers and Cobblers

The origin of cordwaining comes from the goat skin leather (cordovan) manufactured in Spain. The cordwainer originally made shoes without heels, and later high boots. This archaic term was the forerunner to shoemaking, which incorporated many types of the leather available. The sole leather was hammered to make it hard-wearing and the boot or shoe was constructed with the aid of a last and a half moon knife. Originally a cottage industry, mechanisation saw its gradual demise in the late nineteenth century.

Genealogical Table of Denby Hanwells

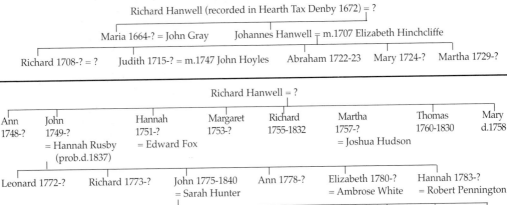

Richard Hanwell (recorded in Hearth Tax Denby 1672) = ?

Maria 1664-? = John Gray   Johannes Hanwell ⊤ m.1707 Elizabeth Hinchcliffe

Richard 1708-? = ?   Judith 1715-? = m.1747 John Hoyles   Abraham 1722-23   Mary 1724-?   Martha 1729-?

Richard Hanwell = ?

| Ann 1748-? | John 1749-? = Hannah Rusby (prob.d.1837) | Hannah 1751-? = Edward Fox | Margaret 1753-? | Richard 1755-1832 | Martha 1757-? = Joshua Hudson | Thomas 1760-1830 | Mary d.1758 |

Leonard 1772-?   Richard 1773-?   John 1775-1840 = Sarah Hunter   Ann 1778-?   Elizabeth 1780-? = Ambrose White   Hannah 1783-? = Robert Pennington

Hannah 1802-? = John Marsden | Thomas 1805-? | John 1807-1872 = Harriet Norton (Morton) 1807-1840 | Elizabeth 1809-? = Wright Cooper | Martha 1812-? = William Fort | Maria 1814-? | Richard 1816-? | Leonard 1819-1869 = Sarah Turton | Charles 1821-1897 = Ann Firth | Harriet 1823-?

Mark 1829-1835 Luke 1831-1834 John 1832-? Ann 1832-1873 Aaron 1834-? Ellen 1836- Allen 1838-? Richard 1840-1905 Thomas 1843-1885 John 1845-? Ann 1850-? Ellen 1854-? Anthony Leonard 1857-? Sarah 1863 Henry 1850-? 1864 Harriet 1853 1853 Fred 1859 1866

Harriet Firth 1833-71 = John Heath

= Ann Rawnsley

= Jonothan Crossland

Alice 1857-? = Tom Jackson Mark 1858-? Annie 1860-? Harry 1862-1922 = Elizabeth Barraclough (+9) Harriet 1862-? = Job Ward Louisa 1863-? Phyllis 1864-? Elizabeth 1866-? Luther 1866-? Frances 1872-1908 = John White Sam Rawnsley (Racket) Mary Ellen = Allan White

It would seem that John Hanwell 1807-72, re-married after the death of Harriet Norton in 1840. He remains at Denby and appears to have begun a new family after marrying Mary Kilner. The first child of the marriage is born in 1842, just about right considering that Richard (Harriet's last child) was born in 1840.

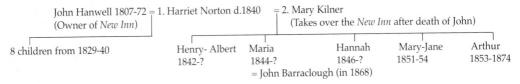

John Hanwell 1807-72 ⊤ 1. Harriet Norton d.1840   = 2. Mary Kilner
(Owner of *New Inn*)   (Takes over the *New Inn* after death of John)

8 children from 1829-40   Henry- Albert 1842-?   Maria 1844-? = John Barraclough (in 1868)   Hannah 1846-?   Mary-Jane 1851-54   Arthur 1853-1874

to last, it would appear, though no date is currently known, that Thomas died before his father. These must have been depressing times for the elder Thomas, his wife, Amelia, had given birth to their last child in 1844, but appears to have died soon after as Thomas took a second wife, a woman we know only as Rebecca.

Thomas Turton, the elder, died in 1868, in his last will and testament he left all he had to his wife Rebecca including an annuity of £10 per quarter. He left one of his violins (noted earlier, which he played with the Bishop of Ely), to his son John, the other went to his Grandson, Francis (Frank - William Walter's child). His daughter, Clara was left his pianoforte. His library of medical books were left to be split between his sons, John and William Walter (chemist and surgeon respectively), and Thomas Bedford, Clara's husband. He left Thomas Turton, his grandson from his late son, Thomas, a monetary sum. Ingham Milnes of Gunthwaite, farmer and Erasmus Smithson of Nether End, farmer also received gifts, but other than these two, money was split across the family.

The main Denby line of the family would seem to have run down through Thomas's fourth son, John. Noted as a chemist, it states plainly on his gravestone in Denby churchyard that he was a surgeon. In his last will and testament, dated 1896, he describes himself as of Plumpton House, Denby and styles himself chemist though the witnessing solicitor noted that at first he wrote surgeon and then changed it. His wife Anna Bella and Ralph Smithson were executors. It is possible that Plumpton House was at Pinfold. With his father and eldest brother dead, John may have moved into the ancestral home, which was, after all, where the surgery was. Kelly's Trade Directory of 1889 notes that he was living in Denby working as a surgeon. Alternatively, the death of Thomas Turton senior in 1868 may have signalled the end of the families long stay here, but the name of Turton has carried on to the present day.

Possibly the most curious individual was John's son, Turton Turton. Did he give him the same Christian name as surname to try to preserve the families heritage? Who can now say? Turton was not encumbered by his name as he became a successful farmer at Fall Edge in Denby.

The Turton family are not only numerous throughout the centuries in Denby and its district but are also very integral to it. In 1838 a Joseph Turton was a schoolmaster here, he must have been a relation but only time and further research will take his and their story further back.

As a final, interesting aside, we should remark upon the fact that a Doctor Turton was one of those responsible for trying to cure King George III from his 'madness', or porphyria. Whether he was a direct ancestor of the Denby clan is currently unknown, though it does make one think – was it through this man that the people of Denby got to know about the King's temporary recovery. Is he the reason why the first of the famous Denby Dale pies was cooked and eaten in 1788?

Clay Pits

The clay quarrying activities in Denby took place on the land that is now the Southcroft housing estate. There were originally two pits, the earlier one being across from the former Wesleyan Chapel, the later one being accessed across from Low Fold Farm. Wooden scaffold was constructed to take trucks full of clay along rails, once above the waiting lorries their contents were tipped into them and transported away. Southcroft was built in the late 1960s, though the clay pits had been disused since the 1940s. Villagers had long been using them as rubbish tips by the time the scaffold was dismantled and the remaining pits filled in. The owner of the pits was Alin Ward, who collapsed and died on Northgate after visiting a privy.

A group of workmen, probably from the clay pits, circa. 1925. Standing left to right: unknown, Johnny Kilner, unknown, unknown, unknown, Alin Ward, John Gaunt. Front left to right: unknown, unknown, Clance Morris, unknown. *Author's collection.*

Tailors

The Boothroyd family seem to have been Denby's village tailors for many years. Their job was to cut and create men's clothing, a process possibly brought into the family due to its links with Manor Farm. The family were living here during the textile revolution, and as many farms set up machines for weaving in outbuildings it was only a short step to begin manufacturing clothing from the resulting cloth, though the Boothroyds had acquired this skill long before their residence at the farm began.

Clement aged thirteen and John aged seven went to live with their Uncle Benjamin at Manor farm in 1866 after their father's death, their mother having died earlier. John became a tailor following in his family's wake. His son, Benjamin broke away from the family trade by becoming a highly skilled stone, marble and wood carver. His work still survives to this day, and can also be seen on some of the tombstones in the churchyard.

The premises for their work included a cottage on Bank Lane, which is still owned by a member of the family, Betty Springer. It was mainly in the top floor of the house that the clothes were made, the Boothroyds and their employees, who included Lister Peace, working long hours in a profession now almost totally automated.

Genealogical Table of the Boothroyd family

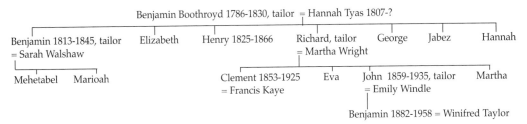

198

John Boothroyd and his wife, Emily, circa. 1930. *Author's collection.*

Miscellaneous

Two ex-slaughter houses exist in Denby today. One is in the grounds of Poplar Villa, the first house on the right heading down Gunthwaite Lane. The other stands detached on the right of Denby Lane just after Upper House. Of course there were others locally, the Barraclough family were involved in this occupation, Isaac working at Exley Gate in 1857. Though the names of Rusby, Morley and Robinson can be added to the list. Norman Naylor ran the detached abattoir on Denby Lane in the mid-twentieth century.

Charles Bedford & Son ran a rope and twine manufacturers in Lower Denby, during the latter part of the nineteenth century.

The family names of Moore and Ellis were well associated with masonry during the nineteenth and early twentieth centuries, indeed they had much to do with many of the nineteenth and early twentieth century buildings which survive to the present day, though by the 1940s Jack Hanwell was the monumental mason.

Finally there were numerous coal and quarrying operations in and about the village, John Hargreave & Co. were coal owners in 1866. James Armitage was a farmer and coal owner and George Norton was a quarry owner in 1857 and as we have seen John Micklethwaite was not only a sub postmaster but also a quarry owner, and farmer! We also have a record concerning a coal mine at Athersley which

Benny Boothroyd, circa. 1910. *Author's collection.*

was bequeathed to Robert Burdet by John Blithman in 1620. I am, at present, uncertain as to whether this is Robert Burdet of Denby or one of his many cousins.

Village Policemen

The village 'bobby' was an integral part of village life in the not too distant past, usually armed with nothing more than a whistle, a truncheon and a bicycle for transport. Their home in the village to which they had been posted also served as the police station, which was decorated with a black and silver police badge hung just above the front door. The first house after the old Co-Op on Bank Lane was certainly used during the 1940s, before a house up the snicket known as 'Shedley' which leads on to Bank Lane was pressed into service. The following list of men who held the post is not complete but it will serve to illustrate these numerous individuals who had to report to Scissett police station, which was their headquarters:

Mr. Storey (app.1920s), Mr Moyser, Mr. Todhunter (pre Second World War), Mr. Pawson (pre Second World War), Mr. Heeley (pre Second World War), Mr. Crabtree (app.1930s – see photograph below), Mr. Fryer (app. Second World War), Mr. Glazebrook (after Second World War to app. Early 1950s), Mr. Potts (after Second World War app. 1950s), Mr. Herbert (1950s to 1960s).

Chris Herbert, the last on the above list had made a house on Falledge Lane his home and police station, he was Denby's last village constable, leaving Denby to move down the valley into Denby Dale.

Probably Constable Crabtree with some of the village tearaways, circa. 1931. *Author's collection.*

Chapter Ten

Leisure and Celebration

Our forbears lives were very crowded, occupations or trades kept the men busy, working from the early hours until after dark. Women spent much of their time giving birth and bringing up large families. Watches, indeed time in general was irrelevant to most, when it was light people got up, when it was dark, they went to bed. They did not live their lives to the clock as we do today.

The people did of course get their free time in these days before wireless and television, village wakes or feasts were very welcome occurrences though employers were seldom pleased at the outcome of such celebrations, for they were known to last many days, resulting in employees not turning up or being unfit for work!

Circuses or fairs were also very popular and traditional excuses for having a good time. Entertainments were varied, but one could usually expect to see ballad singers, gingerbread sellers, jugglers, tumblers, freaks, touring menageries, melodramas, travelling showmen of the gypsy variety and even theatre companies. Popular Bank holidays, i.e.: Whitsuntide, May Day, and Easter would be usual occasions for the appearance of some of the above. Older forms of village entertainment would certainly have included cock fighting and cock squalling (a rather barbaric game whereby the cockerel was tied to a stake and punters could pay for the privilege of throwing rocks at it. The person that knocked its head off was the winner). Bull baiting and bull running were also popular. In 'running' a local farmer would provide a bull, which would then be let loose through the streets, people, then chased it and tried to climb on. Finally it would be subdued when it was led onto a bridge, hoisted over, killed and eaten. 'Baiting' involved tying a bull to a stake and letting dogs attack it. If the bull was weak and allowed the dogs to hurt it, it was considered a poor specimen and left to its fate. If the bull fought back, tossing the dogs into the air then it would be deemed a great beast and set free. Dog fighting was also popular, occasionally men would fight with them and then with each other, all for the sake of their own prowess and the gambling public.

Spa Sunday

In the valley of Gunthwaite, below the Hall there is a mineral spring, which is supposed to have come from an old silver mine at Ronscliff in Cawthorne. The spring is said to have curative properties, particularly for scurvy and liver complaints. Since the middle ages the spring has been revered, and a blessing of the well ceremony in these early times has led to today's 'Spa Sunday', which takes place on the first Sunday in May.

A procession led by a man with a banner displaying a silver cross, chalice and host would have been watched by such dignitaries as the Bosvilles, Burdets and Micklethwaites, with the lower classes gaining vantage wherever they could. The man wore a black tunic with a bugle over his shoulder and a chain around his neck, which held a silver plate bearing the insignia of the Abbot of Pontefract. Two Benedictine monks followed in black gowns and hoods. The Abbot himself followed on a pony, attended by the Vicar of Silkstone, Church officials and more monks. With solemnity the Abbot would reach the spring, dismount and bless the water before a muted congregation.

The tradition continued, in the nineteenth century big gatherings were served by refreshment stalls, the occasion was like a fair, and as many as seven bands have been known there at once. In about 1870, due to rowdiness and trespassing the gatherings were officially stopped, though they did continue into the twentieth century, I have been told of activities such as cock fighting taking place here in the 1920s and 1930s on this special Sunday.

Today the occasion is still observed, mainly due to the efforts of Thurlstone Brass Band who revived the tradition a number of years ago whilst in need of funds. Drinks and snacks and an occasional ice cream van are usually available as ramblers from Penistone, Denby and other areas turn up to listen to the band playing in front of the mill dam.

Coronations and Jubilees

These occasions have always been a popular time for the villagers to party. For instance, after the death of Queen Victoria (1901) it was decided to hold celebrations for the Coronation of Edward VII. Due to his illness in June 1902 the celebrations were abandoned, except for teas given to the old folk and widows at the school and the distribution of mugs and chocolates.

Denby held celebrations to mark the Silver Jubilee of George V in 1935. The day began with the Holy Communion service and continued as listed in the programme below. One event, which began at 11.45 am was the *Hare and Hounds* men's running race which started at the *New Inn*, the runners in the field were as follows:

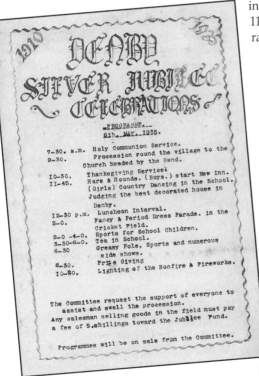

Denby Silver Jubilee (of King George V) programme of celebrations 1935. *Author's collection.*

Gunthwaite and Ingbirchworth Silver Jubilee programme 1935. *Author's collection.*

RUNNERS	TRAINERS	COLOURS
Sam Racket	Rawnsley	Mucky Blue
H N Taylor	B Charlesworth	Blood Red
Eli Turton	Fred White	Tangerine
J Rigget	R Armitage	Black & White
Jimmy Pump	G O Tibbits	Marina Green
Teddy Woodhead	J W Heath	White Label
Walt Bobbiner	H Broadhead	Late Buff
Cam Busking	Bob Waldie	Green Un
G Shaw	Jimmy Moore	Daffy Yellow
M Webster	Johnny Moore	Snow White
Luther Hanwell	Tommy Kilner	Con-blue
Joe Mosley	Arthur Hudson	Black Hoops
Hugh Beever	A Lockwood	Stone Grey

The Clerk of the course was Bill Dronfield, weigher-in T Senior (butcher).
Unfortunately I do not know who won, yet reading through the names would suggest that it must have been an interesting race, without any hint of cheating or gamesmanship! I don't think! Prizes were also given for the best decorated houses in the village, as can be seen from the following photographs. In first place was picture number three, second was picture number two, both overleaf.

Sports events included country running, skipping, flat races, obstacle race, slow bicycle race, egg & spoon, tennis, and even an 'old man's race'. Prizes for which varied from cricket tackle, clocks, sweaters, and watches for the men to compacts, bread knives and handbags for the women. For the girls skipping, first prize was a scent set, second prize was 'William the Gangster', perhaps a prize for anyone who knows exactly what this was? The organisers did seem

Silver Jubilee 1935, Best Decorated House competition entrants. Village shop to the left and 'Holmfield' on Smithy Hill, also known, at one time, as 'Post Office Row'. *Author's collection, 1935.*

The Old Wesleyan Chapel, here pictured with the man who turned it into a private residence - Joe Willie Heath and two of his daughters. *Author's collection, 1935.*

to run out of ideas for the old man's race where both first and second prizes were ash trays!

On 12 May 1937 the village celebrated the Coronation of George VI with an almost similar programme of events, though this time they managed to get a printed programme to sell instead of a type written sheet!

The winning entry! Bank Lane runs off to the left. *Author's collection, 1935.*

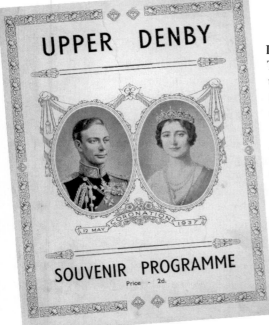

UPPER DENBY

CORONATION 1937
12 MAY

SOUVENIR PROGRAMME
Price - 2d.

Upper Denby Souvenir programme of celebratory events held to commemorate the Coronation of King George VI, 1937. *Author's collection.*

Denby Feast

The feast would appear in Denby in July and set up in one of two fields. The oldest site was at the end of Milnes Row, in the corner of the field as can be seen from the following photograph. The later site was on land, which now plays host to the old folks' bungalows and the council estate. The name 'Fairfields' was supplied by Dot Barber, landlady of the *George* who was asked by Councillor Netherwood for any ideas as to the name of the new site. She suggested that it should reflect the feast or fair, which used to be held there, and the rest as they say is history. The Parr family of Penistone brought the bulk of the amusements and the Porters of Denby added their swing boats, which were kept in the village throughout the winter, until they began touring again the following year. The Porters lived in the row of houses incorporating what was the *Star* public house.

Jabus Battye used to bring his roundabout, which was steam powered. This ride could be the one remembered by Jim Barber, which had motorbikes to sit on whilst travelling round on rails, giving the impression to the young that they were driving a motorbike.

Denby Feast, held in the field above Milnes Row, looking down the lane towards the *George* which is on the far left, circa. 1910. *Author's collection.*

The feast appeared on a Friday night and ran through Saturday, closed on Sunday and continued an Monday before packing up and leaving. It was only a small affair, but the villagers became very involved with it, particularly the children, eventually interest died off and the feast was discontinued due to lack of custom before the Second World War.

In more recent years agricultural shows and steam rallies have largely taken the place of the old village feast. The inaugural Gunthwaite, Veteran and Vintage Weekend took place in 1996, and proved to be a very popular innovation by its organiser, John Ward. Held in fields surrounding Gunthwaite Gate farm, a mixture of vintage cars, motorcycles, lorries and farming equipment, such as threshing machines, and steam engines were displayed, alongside a fairground, various craft and gift stalls, a bar and catering facilities. The show continued until 1999 when its date was brought forward from September to July, perhaps in an effort to beat inclement weather.

Denby Band

The band originally used to practice in one of the outbuildings, which formed a part of Robinson Lathe. The Pickford family were very involved not only on the playing side but also in the administrative aspects. It was Albert Pickford, who applied to Godfrey Bosville MacDonald for permission to build a wooden band hut, a little way down Gunthwaite Lane on land belonging to the Gunthwaite Estate. MacDonald assented though he did insist that this was all that was built and nothing else. Albert Pickford had lived at Gunthwaite Gate farm since 1912, therefore the band hut was constructed after this.

The band won numerous prizes and were frequently called upon to play at village functions, such as the Gunthwaite and Ingbirchworth Silver Jubilee celebrations in 1935 and it is almost certain that they played in Gunthwaite on Spa Sunday a time or two. Rivalry existed, of a friendly nature, of course, between local villages, entering competitions and desperately trying to win and retain village pride. The song below gives a good example.

Song sheet, Denby Brass Band. *Author's collection.*

DENBY BRASS

(Composed by Walter Sm...)

1 Denby is a pleasant land,
And they own a little Band.
But they can't beat Denby Dale,
Tho' they very seldom fail.

2 When they heard about the Contest,
Each man said he'd do his best,
So that they could win a Cup,
And their faces did light up.

3 Johnny Garratt then comes in,
Wiping sweat from off his chin,
And he said to every man,
"Will you do the best you can?"

4 When the Contest day drew nigh,
All the lads began to sigh,
Saying one unto another,
"Oh! this is a lot of bother",

5 Young Jack Dronfield being small,
Tried to make himself look tall,
So he stood upon a buffet,
And he looked just like Miss Muffet.

6 When the Contest day was done,
And the prizes were all won,
Denby Band set out for home,
Leaving Denby Dale to roam.

7 Poor Johnny Garratt never slept,
But stayed awake all night and wept,
Saying to himself in sorrow,
"I will dress them down to-morrow".

8 Denby Dale with all its fame,
Put the Denbyites to shame,
And they all shed many tears,
Both in madness and with fears.

9 "Never mind" said Johnny Haigh,
"They are nothing but a plague,
Wait 'till we have learned to play,
We will beat them any day".

10 If they would just talk to Cook,
He would teach them from his book,
Then like Denby Dale you know,
To big Contests they could go.

11 Let us hope the next time then,
That they will play just like men,
And ins ead of looking sad,
They will go about quite glad.

12 If I tell you the whole story,
You will all be in your glory,
So I think I'll finish here,
And give them just a word of cheer.

Denby United Silver Prize Band, circa. 1930. *Author's collection.*

The band hut was demolished sometime during the early 1960s and the band was no more, the instruments were reported to be kept at the top of Denby common by Clem Pickford. Although the interest in brass bands has abated somewhat, particularly amongst the young it would still have been a pleasure to listen to them play, perhaps in the *George* at Christmas time, tunes such as Swain Hark or Pratty Flowers emanating from their instruments.

Denby band in front of the band hut, down Gunthwaite Lane, circa. 1935. *Author's collection.*

Possibly the starting point for May Day festivities in 1935. Importantly, the long since demolished Denby Band hut can be seen in the background. *Author's collection.*

Regulars photographed outside the club, circa. 1925. Left to right, standing: Kenny Windle, Ben Holmes, Arthur Gaunt, Herman White, Bob Beever. Left to right, seated: Johnny Haigh, Wilson Moorhouse, Ned Beever, Sonny Moorhouse, visitor.*Author's collection.*

Denby Club and Smithy Hill triangle. *Author's collection, c.1915.*

Denby Club

Denby club was situated on what is now the village green. Newer residents in the village would find it hard to believe that this small triangle of land once played host to not only the club, but two houses and some pig stys. The club was not licensed but did house a billiard table for its patrons, it was more a place to gossip and relax than anything else. Of course being sited next to the house belonging to Jimmy Pump there was always the possibility of unforeseen entertainment, for instance, some people moved into the house above his and complained to him about the state of his abode. Jimmy then had to spend time clearing away all his rubbish, including his straw filled mattress much to his uncomprehending disgust.

It is possible that after the club closed, the billiard table made its way up to the band hut on Gunthwaite Lane. The band hut did possess a table during the 1950s, though what happened to it when the band hut closed is unknown.

The photograph above shows the site of the club on the far left, along with the residence of Jimmy (Pump) Gaunt, in the centre of the triangle. His home looks like it should be the clubhouse, but I am reliably informed that this was certainly not so in the early twentieth century. Before this? who knows? The photo also shows the Heath grocers and post office and the new house sited on what was the old blacksmiths shop and is dated around 1915.

Football and Cricket

The earliest football team photograph I have been able to discover was taken by James Henry Gaunt, a photographer to whom I am in debt for some of the best photographs in this book. The photograph appeared in the *Memories of Yesteryear* section of the *District Chronicle* dated 1966. It depicts Denby Park Avenue (their name at the time) who were winners of the 'Millhouse & District Medal Competition' 1909/10. The team have played in various leagues, including Penistone. The photo was taken outside the *George*, as with the one printed earlier in this book in the pubs section.

The football team eventually disbanded and was not re-started until 1955 when Joe Price, Terry Laundon, Frank Richardson and Arthur Crossland (whose family owned the land, which was to become the playing field) re-started it, playing in the Penistone league.

The age old game involving willow and leather known as cricket has long been an activity for small villages and Denby was no different. The pitch was originally on Falledge Lane but has

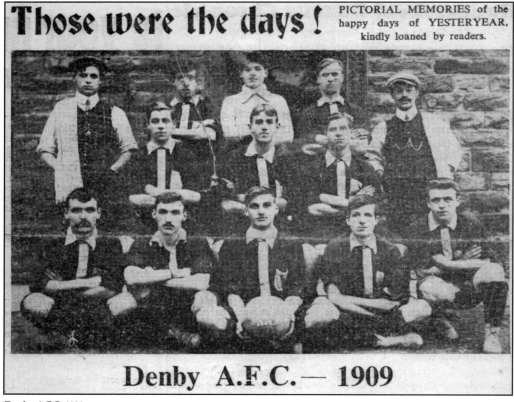

Those were the days !

PICTORIAL MEMORIES of the happy days of YESTERYEAR, kindly loaned by readers.

Denby A.F.C. — 1909

Denby A.F.C. 1909. *Author's collection.*

since moved to the back of the Church, the photograph opposite depicts the 1927 team, when village pride in winning was as strong as it is today.

The earliest match report I have been able to find comes from the *Barnsley Chronicle* dated 29 June 1901. Denby, then known as Denby Utd. were playing at Greenfoot against a team called Craiks, though the match wasn't destined to finish as rain stopped play, the Denby scorecard read as follows:

Woodhead	st. Firth	b Penty	2
Clarkson	c. Whittle	b Guest	2
Dransfield	c. and	b Guest	1
Wood	lbw	b Guest	13
Laundon		b Penty	7
Waldie	run out		12
Beever	not out		1
Gaunt		b Penty	7
Marshall		b Guest	0
Jackson	not out		1
Wommersley	did not bat		
			48-8

From a later season we find Denby playing in the Penistone & District League alongside such other teams as Silkstone United, Hoylandswaine, Thurlstone Old, Crane Moor and the team which beat them on 31 July 1927 where the *Barnsley Chronicle* reports that Denby made 102 runs

Upper Denby cricket club players 1927.
Standing left to right: James Henry Gaunt,
Walt Turton, Jack Waldie, John J (Jack)
Pickering, Jimmy Jackson, Fred Roebuck, Bob
Waldie, Norman Charlesworth.

Seated left to right: Kenny
Windle, Joe Turton, Charlie
Turton, Ray Charlesworth,
Herman White. *Author's collection.*

**DENBY
CRICKET CLUB**

Season 1952

Member's Card

M _____

LIST OF FIXTURES
1952

DATE		NAME OF CLUB	AT	RESULT
May	3	Greenmoor	home	
"	10	Cranemoor	away	
"	17	Millhouse	home	
"	24	Mortomley	home	
"	31	Midhope	away	
June	7	Open		
"	14	Thurgoland	away	
"	21	Pogmoor Sports	home	
"	28	Barnsley Bobbins	away	
July	5	Thurgoland	home	
"	12	Millhouse	away	
"	19	Barnsley Bobbins	home	
"	26	Cranemoor	home	
Aug.	2	Mortomley	away	
"	9	Greenmoor	away	
"	16	Pogmoor Sports	away	
"	23	Midhope	home	

List of Officers

President—
Councillor H. S. NETHERWOOD, Esq.

Vice-Presidents—Messrs. J. N. Peace,
J. W. White

Captain—J. Gaunt

Vice-Captain—P. Wadsworth

Secretary—R. A. Heath

Treasurer—R. W. Nicholson

General Committee—
The President, Vice President, Captain,
Secretary, Treasurer, and Messrs. J. Pell,
R. Mosley, A. Heywood, B. Harvey, J. Waldie,
C. Crossland, D. Pell, H. Turton.

Umpire—A. Heywood.

Subscriptions for Players.
Under 18 years old—3/6.
18 to 20 years old—6/-
Over 20 years old—8/6.

Denby Cricket Club, member's card and
fixture list for 1952. *Author's collection.*

all out but were defeated by Penistone Church who made 104 for 8.

It was unusual to find many runs being scored on a regular basis throughout the cricket teams history but the headline of , 'ONLY 39 RUNS' was a little out of the ordinary, the *Barnsley Chronicle* dated 22 May 1954 gave the following match report:

Crane Moor 19 all out, Denby 20 for 8
One of the most exciting games seen for some time was witnessed at Crane Moor last Saturday, when bowlers on both sides got good figures. In the dismissal of the home team J. Price for Denby took 7 wickets for 11 runs in 9 overs, whilst of the 8 Denby wickets which fell G. Allen claimed 6 for 9 runs in 7 overs. No batsman on either side reached double figures. R.Redmond scored 5, the same score as T. Wigfield for Crane Moor and D. Mosley hit 9 for Denby. Other bowling returns were: for Denby - C.Taylor 3 for 8 runs, for Crane Moor, Redwood 2 for 10 runs.

The 1954 season did not prove to be one of Denby's best, they lost their return match with Crane Moor at Denby, Denby 68 all out, Crane Moor 70 for 4. Denby's runmakers were J Jones 22, C Crossland 21 and D Mosley 11. Even further humiliation was to befall the side when on June 5th they were bowled out for just 16 runs by Millhouse, only D Mosley for Denby reached double figures (10), the wickets that they did take falling to G Senior, J Jones and G Taylor.

Things improved somewhat on 3 July when they posted an impressive 120 runs in their return match with Millhouse. For Denby P Wadsworth made 11, J Jones 9, O Marsh 11 and their matchwinner F Barden who made 45 not out. Millhouse were dismissed for 67, Carl Taylor the main wicket taker with 4 for 23.

Things got back to normal when the side took on the impressive league leaders, Thurlstone on 10 July. After being reduced to 11 runs for 4 wickets, Fred Barden hit 14 but the rest of the side capitulated and were bowled out for 32. Thurlstone easily passed this total making 38 for 1, though their opening batsman, Dennis Hey was the victim of a splendid catch by Joe Price.

The return match did not bring much improvement, set an impressive target of 101 by Thurlstone, Denby were bowled out for 46 with only Dennis Pell reaching double figures with a fighting 29.

On 1 August Thurlstone wrapped up their division B title and were promoted to Division A, unbeaten all season they received the Goldthorpe Cup for their efforts, made all the more remarkable for the fact that this was only their second season in the league after 17 years without a team in the village.

League table with 2 matches still to play:

Division B	*Played*	*Won*	*Lost*	*Drawn*	*Points*
Thurlstone	11	9	0	2	20
Midhope	11	5	2	4	14
Thurgoland	11	5	4	2	12
Denby	12	4	6	2	10
Millhouse	11	3	5	3	9
Hoylandswaine B	12	3	7	2	8
Crane Moor	12	3	8	1	7

There were many ways of spending leisure time in Denby, tennis courts used to be at the back of the Church for those so inclined, home pursuits including crafts of all types have always been popular. Village get-togethers were also welcomed. Denby Ladies coffee mornings and fund raising events such as jumble sales will remain with the village into the twenty-first century and these activities are as popular today as they were in 1916 as can be seen overleaf.

Denby Cricket Team, circa. 1960. Standing left to right: Jerry Holmes, Walt Martin, Arthur Crossland, Dennis Pell, John Mosley, ?, Sam Townsend, ?, Peter Aughty, Robert Gaunt, David Wainwright, Dennis Sampson, ?. Seated left to right: Peter Bentley, Ian Wainwright, ? Hoyland, Morris Bentley, ?, ?, Howard Moxon, Alan Beever, David Gaunt, Frank ? *Author's collection.*

Denby Cricket Club 1st Team, 30 July 1982. Back row left to right: R Gaunt, P Geldart, R Price, S Rodgers, J Gooder, D Meacham. Front row left to right: B Auckland, M Price, D Gaunt, H Moxon, S Geldart. *Author's collection.*

Boxing Day gathering of the Rockwood Harriers in Upper Denby, circa. 1966. *Author's collection.*

Those were the days ! PICTORIAL MEMORIES of the happy days of YESTERYEAR, kindly loaned by readers.

PICNIC AT UPPER DENBY – 1916?

Members of the Wesleyan Reform Chapel, Denby Dale, outside the home of Mrs A Crossland at Upper Denby, circa. 1916, readying for a picnic. In the doorway - Miss N Travis, Mrs J N Peace, Willie Hirst, J A Riggott. Back row: R A Morris, J W Heath, G Boothroyd, H Morris. Centre row: Mrs S Woodhead, Mrs F Broadhead, Mrs H Heath, Mrs A Crossland, Mrs S A Green, Mrs W Haigh. Front row: Mrs Gibson, Mrs B Senior, Mrs A Bedford, Mrs J Hirst, Mrs J E Hirst. *Author's collection.*

Bonfire night has, and will always be popular with people, Denby seems to have been celebrating the occasion for many years, in what are now the playing fields, across from the council estate. Organisation under various guises has seen to it that most years food has been available and that a large bonfire has been burnt to celebrate the occasion, provided that mischief night activists haven't already set fire to it! At present the proceeds from the bonfire are used to help fund the purchase of a village Christmas Tree, an item once supplied free of charge by Kirklees Council, but due to cutbacks, now only possible with the financial support of the villagers.

Boxing Day Hunt

The Rockwood Harriers have for many years been meeting in the car park of the *George* public house.

Throughout the twentieth century, horses, dogs and people have turned up to witness a tradition not always appreciated by today's politically conscious human rights activists, particularly considering the fact that once the horses leave, heading up to Falledge Lane, around dinner time, most are dismounted before actually taking part in a hunt.

The group was founded in 1868 by Walter Norton of Rockwood House, Denby Dale. Mr Norton hunted at his own expense, even the hounds were his own property until 1896. A Mr C S Tinker of Meal Hill, Hepworth was a notable master of the hunt, he built new kennels at Meal Hill around 1900 where the hounds were then quartered.

Denby Church Youth Club

The youth club began around 1950, instigated by Denby children in association with the Vicar, Norman Moore. The Church had shown a couple of films for the benefit of the villages youth and

Denby Church Youth Club, circa. 1951. Back row left to right: Rev. Moore, Dennis Turton, Duncan Knowles, Winston Knowles, Bryan Heath, Alan Kaye, Elizabeth Jones, Melvyn Rusby, Roy Nicholson, Iris White, Dorothy Barden, Robin Moore, June Moorehouse, Mrs Moore, Derek Haigh. Front: Terry Laundon, Frank Burdett, Gerald Kaye. *Author's collection.*

it had been decided that a youth club should be formed with a view to buying a projector to continue this. Members were drawn only from the Church going fraternity, a fact that annoyed some members of the community and were obliged to pay 1s to attend every Friday night in the school. The members of the club engaged in competitions against neighbouring clubs (not all Church oriented), such as Kirkburton and Wooldale. The competitions included sports, such as athletics and table tennis and also handicrafts such as woodwork or model making for the boys or needle craft and knitting for the girls. The group were very successful in competition and won many cups. Dances were also held in Denby school. An offshoot of the club was the friendship created between the members, of which one group decided to build some tennis courts at a family home on Denby common. The Church held an annual 'Sale of Work' in November and it was usual to find members of the youth club holed up in the Vicarage making items to sell.

The club also performed playlets and concerts in the Church. One of these involved a song from *Snow White* called the *Silly Song*, but the words were changed slightly by the Vicar's wife to incorporate a village theme, the following is an incomplete example:

The collection plate was handed round,
Said Colin (Crossland) this is certain,
They can keep their miserly threepenny bits,
What do you say Mr Turton?

We chased a pig on Ratten Row,
A big fat buxom fellow,
It came from Manor Farm,
Cos it kept shouting Stella.

Hi ho, the tune is done,
The words don't mean a thing,
Isn't this a silly song for anyone to sing.

215

The enterprise seems to have been augmented by the enthusiasm of a generation of children who gradually began to leave the club and enter either National Service or work. Its demise around the late 1950s signalled an end to its achievements but its justification is rewarded in the amount of friendships it augmented, some of which still continue today.

Denby Carnival

In 1962 the village held a colourful carnival, perhaps the residents finally missing the long since departed feast.

A parade was organised and competitions which included fancy dress for both adults and children alike. Scenes from this occasion can be found below.

Scenes from carnival held in Denby in 1962. *Author's collection.*

Denby Dale Pie

The best known tradition within the area, has to be the baking of the monster pies. We only have space enough to briefly examine this quirky, yet world-renowned phenomenon and I would refer the reader to my book *The History of the Denby Dale Pies* for more in-depth information.

Pie 1: Tradition records that the first pie was baked in 1788 to mark the return to sanity of King George III. The King did not in fact fully recover until 1789, therefore the date is open to conjecture. Perhaps early news reached Denby, possibly from a member of the Turton family, as it is known that a Dr Turton was one of the King's advisors. The pie was cooked at the *White Hart Inn* and was served to the villagers in Cliff Style field, just behind the pub.

Pie 2: Baked to celebrate the Duke of Wellington's victory over Napoleon at Waterloo in 1815, this pie probably reflected the relief felt by most of the country as fears of an invasion were dispelled. Waterloo veteran, George Wilby of Pogstone House, Denby Dale, may well have had the honour of ceremonially cutting the pie, if he did not, he must at least have added a special dimension to the day.

Pie 3: This was the first real 'monster' pie at, 7ft 10ins in diameter and 22ins deep, it contained: 44$\frac{1}{2}$ stones of flour, 19lbs lard, 16lbs butter, 7 hares, 14 rabbits, 4 pheasants, 4 grouse, 2 ducks, 2 geese, 2 guinea fowls, 4 hens, 6 pigeons, 63 small birds, 5 sheep, 1 calf, and 100lbs beef. It celebrated the repeal of the hated Corn Laws, which had kept the price of corn, and therefore bread, artificially high and had become a symbol of the repression of the poor. On 29 August 1846, after ten and a half hours of baking, a procession made its way to Norman Park where the pie was put on to a temporary platform. Unfortunately as the number of people on the platform increased, the weight became too much. The platform collapsed and 15,000 people surged forward. Riot and turmoil saw to the demolition of the pie and what was left of the stage.

Pies 4 and 5: It took 41 years after the fiasco of 1846 before the 'Dalers' baked another pie. The date was set, 27 August 1887, this time to celebrate Queen Victoria's Golden Jubilee. At 8ft in diameter and 2ft deep, a special oven had to be constructed behind the *White Hart Inn* which was 14ft square. A stewing boiler adjoined the oven, this being made by Joseph Barraclough, the Upper Denby blacksmith. A firm of professional bakers from Halifax supervised the creation of the pie. Meat, which had been displayed in the butcher's shop was cooked and put into the pie in batches. This meant that at regular intervals hot food was being added to meat that was cooling rapidly. Including forty-two stones of potatoes and the crust of the pie it weighed in at 1$\frac{1}{2}$ tons. On the night before pie-day, the professional bakers left town! As with the last pie, the procession made its way to Norman Park, bedecked with flowers and pulled by nine horses. As Chairman of the Pie committee, Mr H J Brierley stood to make his speech, the crowd numbering thousands, once again surged forward. As the pie was opened a terrible stench emanated from it. To say it was 'off' would be a huge understatement, although according to one eyewitness, the carcass of a skinned fox cannot have helped matters. Rioting again ensued, tents and marquees were damaged before the crowds finally disbursed. The remains of the pie were taken in a mock funeral procession to Toby Wood where they were buried in a pit in quick lime. To satisfy the people of Denby Dale the ladies of the village baked another pie which was eaten on 3 September 1887, at Inkerman Mills, which was a success.

The scene, looking towards Wakefield Road, at the Jubilee pie-making of 1887. Springfield Mills are on the right, and Inkerman Mill is at the back of the picture on the skyline. *Author's collection.*

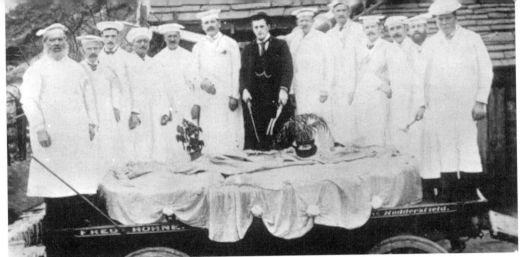

The 1896 pie and the cooks who baked it. *Courtesy of Leach Lithoprint, Brighouse*

The 1896 pie in front of the White Hart public house on Wakefield Road. *Author's collection.*

Pie 6: After a gap of only nine years it was decided that the fiftieth anniversary of the Repeal of the Corn Laws was an important enough occasion to warrant another pie. The old dish was scrubbed out, an oven was built behind the corn mill in the village and game and poultry were omitted from the ingredients! Barricading surrounded the platform in Norman Park and was erected in the field itself to stop any possibility of the crowds rushing forward. The procession to Norman Park was headed by two boys, one in rags, one in good clothing to represent the difference the repeal of the corn laws had made to the people. At 4.30 pm on the 1 August 1896, the Medical Officer of Health certified that the pie was good and fit to eat, and finally, lessons all learnt, 2000 portions were issued by twelve servers at a shilling a piece.

Mr William Wood making the first ceremonial cut into the 1928 pie. *Author's collection.*

Pie 7: To help raise funds for Huddersfield Royal Infirmary and also celebrate belatedly, the end of the First World War the seventh pie day was dated 28 August 1928. It was decided to make this the biggest pie ever and so a new dish was constructed measuring 16ft long, 5ft wide and 15ins deep. It contained 4 bullocks, 600lb beef, 15cwts potatoes, 80 stones flour, 2cwts lard, and 2 stone of baking powder. Five local butchers and eighteen local ladies cooked the pie. All went well and at 1.00 pm on Saturday 28 August 1928, it was adjudged to be well done, then the problems began - it was stuck in the purpose built oven. Men armed with crowbars moved in, eventually ten foot tram rails aided by jacks proved effective, as well as knocking down part of the wall! A half mile long procession made its way around the village to Norman Park where long queues kept servers busy all day. The infirmary benefited to the tune of £1147 3s 5d.

Pie 8: A committee decided to bake another pie on 5 September 1964 with a view to building a new community hall. Luckily, four Royal babies were also expected within the next year and the tradition of celebrating a national event could be maintained. A new dish was made, 18ft x 6ft x 18ins deep to continue with the tradition of breaking last times record. It was to contain three tons of beef and 1½ tons of potatoes and ½ ton of gravy. Publicity was enormous, even the BBC were involved. Tragedy struck when four committee members were killed in a car crash whilst returning north from recording a programme with Eamonn Andrews in London. Pie day went on in their memory. At 2.00 pm it left Hector Buckley's milking parlour at Lower Denby and made its way to Norman Park where it was served to 30,000 people. A funfair, dance, fireworks, professional wrestling and many other attractions helped make the day a great success. Profits from the event were used to purchase Birkwood House in Denby Dale in 1969, it was then converted into a village hall which opened on 5 September 1972, now known as the 'Pie Hall'.

Pie 9: Many changes took place between 1964 and 1988, not least the influx of new people living in the area. To celebrate 200 years of pie making and to give these newer arrivals the chance to sample the old tradition the Bicentenary pie was baked on 3 September 1988. Yet another new dish was constructed, 20ft x 7ft x 1½ft deep. It weighed half a ton and was designed to hold seven cubic metres of pie. Stringent health and hygiene guidelines meant new, though not insurmountable problems for the organisers. Publicity was again enormous, but the weather was causing a number of headaches during the run-up to the big day as the pie field on Barnsley Road was waterlogged. The committee were lucky – the sun came out and shone on around 100,000 visitors who invaded the village for the day. The 1964 pie had been pulled by a traction engine,

The 1964 pie at the bottom of Miller Hill at the side of the Corn Mill. Notice the now long since demolished BP petrol station towards the top left of the picture. *Author's collection.*

The 1988 pie in procession, passing the Prospect public house (now the Dalesman) on Wakefield Road. John Cook oversees matters via a walkie talkie. *Author's collection.*

as horses were now insufficient to manage its great weight. The 1988 pie had to be placed on to an articulated lorry! After being paraded around the village, the pie arrived in the field and was distributed by an army of 170 servers to the waiting thousands. Helicopter flights, a fun-fair, stalls, crafts, army bikes, a parachute drop and a Radio One Roadshow, were amongst the many entertainments available.

Pie 10: A plan was hatched during February 1999 to celebrate the millennium by baking the biggest pie yet on 2 September 2000. Howard Gamble, one of the chefs involved in 1988 was appointed to oversee the cooking which took place at Dry Hill farm, Lower Denby. Hector Buckley, the owner of the farm, also allowed the organisers to stage the event on his land. At 12 tonnes, 12metres long(40ft), 2.5 metres (8ft) wide and 1.1 metres (3ft 8ins) deep it broke the world record and entered the Guiness Book of Records as the world's biggest pie. Entertainment was also provided which included a pop concert featuring tribute acts to Queen, the Bee Gees, Robbie Williams, George Michael and Abba.

The traditions of pie-making in Denby Dale live on. It is only a matter of time before yet another monster pie will be conceived, cooked and eaten in the village.

The 2000 pie making its way up Miller Hill towards the pie field. *Author's collection.*

Chapter Eleven
The Early Twentieth Century

TYPHOID IN DENBY DALE

On the 17 September 1932, a case of typhoid fever was identified. A land drain at Square Wood reservoir became contaminated with the disease culminating in the infection of almost every household in the village, and within two weeks seventy-two people had been infected. They were taken to isolation hospitals at Kirkburton, Mill Hill, Penistone and Meltham and newspapers printed regular updates of their condition. The mains water supply was cut off for months and water had to be fetched from wells and springs in buckets. Schools were closed, and on re-opening only thirty out of 166 children attended. The Denby and Cumberworth Urban District Council organised an appeal fund, the subscriptions of which range from businesses to private individuals. Though many people were seriously ill for some time only eleven died, the reservoir still exists but remains only as a monument to those who suffered from the lethal water it supplied.

Denby Dale Typhoid Appeal Fund - subscriptions.
Author's collection.

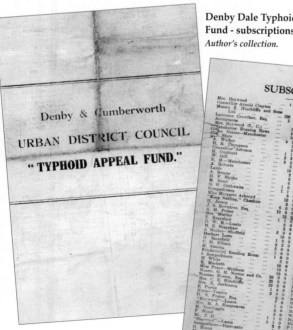

Regular information in the local press provided updates on the condition of sufferers.
W H Senior.

Snow in 1933 on Barnsley Road, the *Dunkirk* pub is to the right. *Author's collection.*

Shire horses were used to help speed up the clearing operation in 1933. A community effort was required to clear blocked roads including in the picture above, the author's grandfather, Ernest Heath, third from the right. *Author's collection.*

Denby's 'Big Snow'

Often, amongst the older residents of the village a reference will be made to the 'big snow' of 24 February 1933. It was, at the time, the deepest snow recorded for fifty years. Hence the fact that these people will acknowledge, what today is regarded as a heavy snow fall, with only a mild, 'the's nobbut a coverin'. Another bad year for snow was 1947.

The Second World War (1939-1945)

Denby was lucky to escape damage from bombs dropped by enemy air-raids. ARP Wardens such as W.H. Senior and Joe Willie Heath had the duties of enforcing blackouts and assisting in maintaining services after raids. On the night of 12 December 1940, two bombs fell in the fields at Upper Denby which were dealt with by ARPs, one of them even covering a bomb with his steel helmet! A further 2kg incendiary bomb landed at the bottom of Bank Lane in Denby Dale which was rendered harmless by two ARP wardens who covered it in ashes from the side of the road. The planes that carried them flew on to Sheffield and continued their intended wholesale blitz of the country, the flames as the City burned, could be clearly seen from Denby. Sixteen air raids took place altogether over Sheffield which included two blitzes which killed 631 and injured 1817 people.

Pamphlets were issued for villagers concerning air-raids advising them to look after their respirators, to be prepared and to keep calm. They

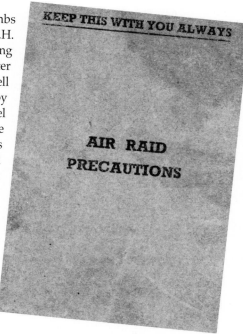

KEEP THIS WITH YOU ALWAYS

AIR RAID PRECAUTIONS

Air Raid Precautions Handbook. One of a series issued to every household within the township. *Author's collection.*

This will help you to remember . . .

TEAR AND OTHER GASES
(Without Tears)

TEAR GASES

Tear Gases—First comes C.A.P.
Then K.S.K. and B.B.C.
If you smell peardrops then beware,
For K.S.K. is in the air.
These gases too, affect the mind,
Explain they will not make one blind.
Remove and reassure. You 'Oughter
Wash out eyes with saline water.

NOSE GASES

Nose Gases—D.A., D.M., also D.C.
You cannot smell, you cannot see.
This makes it harder still to tell,
There's arsenic in them as well.
They make one sniff and sneeze and blow.
They make one very sad and low.
Non-permanent, so won't endure,
Pop on a mask and reassure,
Be cheerful and remove patient quick,
Don't be surprised if she is sick.

CHOKING GASES

Phosgene and Chlorine are, alas,
Chloropicrin, too, a deadly gas,
Affects the lungs, affects the breath,
And very soon may lead to death.
The only hope is perfect rest,
Remember this, and do your best.
Pop on a mask and quickly fetch her
Without the least delay a stretcher.
Don't let her move, give her beef tea,
Keep her as warm as she can be,
Don't give the alcoholic drinks,
Persuade her to have forty winks,
And don't in spite of great temptation,
Try artificial respiration.

BLISTER GASES

When you have heard the warning sound,
That Mustard Gas is on the ground,
Put on the mask that you possess,
All helpers have protective dress,
Remember 'tis persistent gas,
Will last for weeks on roads or grass,
The smallest splash upon your hand,
Will quickly to a sore expand,
If on a person there's a trace,
Rush him to the appointed place,
Take off his boots and clothes and suit,
And scrub him well from head to foot,
Then in another room he'll find,
Fresh clothes and boots, assistance kind.

DECONTAMINATION

SKETCH OF PROCEDURE

After a Gas Raid the following general principles will come into operation :

(a) The identification of the gas.

(b) The severity of the contamination.

(c) The urgency of the decontamination having regard to the danger to public.

(d) The materials and facilities available for decontamination work.

Mustard Gas is the most important among the contaminating gases, and if this gas is used, decontamination can be achieved by using one or more of the following methods :

1. Chemical destruction of the gas.

2. Physical removal of the gas.

3. Sealing in the gas.

4. Allowing the gas to weather away.

Fireguards Handbook. *Author's collection.*

(vi) Methods of Dealing with Fire Bombs

The quickest method of extinguishing a kilo magnesium fire bomb is to apply a jet of water from as close a range as possible. By this means the bomb can be disposed of in less than one minute, and where speed is the governing factor this method should be adopted. Although a jet of water applied to the bomb will cause

When a Bomb falls in the open....   Hold a Sandmat in front of your face....

Place it on the Bomb....   and get away quickly.

FIG. 4.—TACKLING AN INCENDIARY BOMB IN THE STREET.

advised on how to deal with noxious gasses and even on how to deal with an incendiary bomb.

Denby and its near neighbours made strenuous efforts to provide for the war effort. The 1887 Denby Dale Pie Dish was sold on 20 September 1940 for £72 17s to provide scrap metal.

Denby Dale Urban District held a Warship Week from 27 February to 7 March 1942, the programme heralded the minimum objective of raising £70,000 for a Motor Torpedo Boat. The actual sum raised was £298,596. A similar scheme was organised in May, 1943 this one entitled, 'Wings For Victory'. The objective was to provide £80,000 to supply the air force with a plane. The eventual total raised was £182,808.

National identity cards were issued to the populace as a precautionary measure and food rationing was introduced in January 1940 for foods

a motor vehicle which has petrol in its tank. For the same reason, a fire caused by a bomb should usually receive attention before the bomb itself, although this cannot be made a hard-and-fast rule since it will depend on the state of the fire. Water should be applied to the bomb as early as possible where there is any danger of its burning through the floor.

The fire should be tackled with the jet and it is essential that it should not be allowed to get out of control.

How to enter a Burning Room   The pump operator stays outside Room

Keep under cover as you attack Bomb   First check fire caused by fire bomb.

FIG. 5.—TACKLING AN INCENDIARY BOMB IN A ROOM.

Warship Week, Souvenir programme cover, 1942. *Author's collection.*

Wings for Victory, Souvenir programme cover, 1943. *Author's collection.*

which included, butter, bacon and sugar. A points system was introduced for clothes in June 1942. Although the war ended in 1945, rationing continued, under Attlee's government until the 1950s, tea was de-rationed in 1952 and sweets in 1953.

The roads and fields behind Inbirchworth reservoir were used for storing bombs, some of which were gas orientated, as traffic was regularly halted by a sign which said 'No Entry - Gas Leak'. Just above the *George* public house and heading slightly for today's Fairfields council estate was a search light station, which may have had a gun fitted. A shelter for the soldiers who operated this was built in the second field down Coal Pit Lane. If you look at the walls as you walk down this public footpath it is still possible to discern sandbags, hardened with age mixed up with the rest of the dry stone walling.

Of course, local enterprise was not found lacking during these difficult years. A man called Benjamin Beever adapted an old Model T Ford (Tin Lizzie) into a mobile fish and chips vehicle at this time. Apparently it was mostly chips and very little fish that he sold in Denby, Gunthwaite, Ingbirchworth and the district. As the war raged on and rationing started to bite he substituted potatoes, which had become scarce, for turnips and tried to continue. Needless to say, the business folded shortly afterwards.

Government Evacuation Scheme

As the war with Germany loomed in 1939 a huge operation was mounted to evacuate children from Britain's cities and towns, moving them to safe areas in the countryside. Each child was labelled and allowed to take little in the way of personal possessions with them, most had their own gas masks, usually some spare clothing, toothbrush, comb and a handkerchief along with a bag of food for the day. As children began to arrive at their temporary homes reports began to come in from country folk, shocked by the condition of children from city slum areas. Equal shock was expressed by the children at their new surroundings. For many it was their first sight of cows and other farm animals.

Joe Price was sent from his home in Woolwich in 1941 to a temporary home whilst waiting to be placed with a new family. His most vivid recollection of this time was the pungent smell of carbolic soap, used at the home on the kids as soon as they arrived, aged only three, he little knew that his life was about to change forever.

He arrived by train and was met at the station by a Mrs Norton of Bagden Hall. Mrs Norton was responsible for the 'distribution' of the evacuees and escorted young Joe by car, to the home of Rob (Robinson) and Amy Graham at Croft Cottages, Lower Denby.

The war dragged on, Joe now being brought up by his surrogate parents, the Grahams alongside their own family. He attended the village school and lived life just as any of the local kids. Letters from his family in Woolwich were regular as his parents tried to keep tabs on their young son.

Joe was eight or nine years old (1946/7) when his mother requested that he should go back to Woolwich. The implications for the Grahams were not only apparent but distressing as Joe was by now very much a part of their family and they did not want to lose him. In the end he did return, for just nine months. He was very unhappy and indeed became ill, he was taken to see the doctor who decided that he was fretting for Yorkshire and the Grahams. More letters were sent between Woolwich and Denby, which eventually concluded with Rob and Amy Graham fetching Joe back to the village.

When he was eighteen, due to enter the army, and travelling south anyway, Joe became curious to meet his real family and though the visitation occurred he felt no particular emotion towards them, his family now being the Grahams, his home Denby, Yorkshire, in this he would never change. Joe now lives with his wife Monica at the old schoolhouse in Lower Denby, only a few yards from where he was brought up by the Grahams. He is a successful building contractor and is involved in local environmental projects and is as much a part of Denby as the *George* public house.

Other evacuees to the village of Denby included, Muriel Towers, who

GOVERNMENT EVACUATION SCHEME

A YEAR AGO I appealed to householders in the safer areas to help in time of war by receiving school children from the big cities. Since then our evacuation scheme has been carried out and we are preparing further plans to be put in force if air attacks develop.

THE TASK AHEAD

At the moment we are faced with a double task, to prepare for the future and to keep in the safer areas all the children who are already there. The first piece of work must be done by the Government and the public authorities. The second can only be done by the children's parents and the householders in the receiving areas.

SHARING THE BURDEN

There are over 400,000 evacuated children now in the receiving areas, and this is an important contribution to our national defence. But the burden of this most valuable work has fallen almost entirely on the half-million or so householders who have had children in their houses for an appreciable time.

In response to the Government's appeal last year offers were made to receive 2,300,000 children. Only about a quarter of these offers have been taken up. Is it fair that the whole burden should fall continuously on one man—or rather one woman—in four ?

I do not want to suggest that billets should be disturbed unnecessarily. It is far better for the child to have a settled home. But many householders

Government Evacuation Scheme Application.
Author's collection.

lived with Fred Fawcett and his family, Lavender Garner, who lived with Ronnie White and his family and Maureen Tickner, who lived with Mrs Town and her family.

Dunkirk and the Evacuation of the BEF

'Allied Forces Evacuated from Dunkirk' screamed the national dailies, as nearly 340,000 troops, made up of the British Expeditionary Force and French and Belgians sailed across the channel in an armada made up of every available water craft. They left the beaches of Dunkirk littered with decaying corpses and massed ranks of weaponry and equipment. The advancing Germans had been held up in fierce hand to hand battles as the rearguard fought to save the lives of their countrymen. The main German assault was kept back by flooding the low lying surrounding fields and by blowing up the bridges over the canals. As the flotilla of ships with their exhausted passengers began to arrive back on the British shoreline another smaller, yet none the less important mission set sail. Heading for Cherbourg were troop transporters driven by amongst others, John Gaunt, of Upper Denby.

John was instructed how to drive the lorries at Elkington, by an experienced team of bus drivers, interestingly enough one of his co-learners was Leslie Shaw, also of Upper Denby. John became part of a twelve man team, commanded by a corporal and a sergeant, which along with others (including Les Shaw) set out from Portsmouth on their mission to Cherbourg.

As Allied troops had headed north for Dunkirk they had experienced in many cases severe casualties faced as they were with the advancing German army. Cyril Schofield of Upper Denby (mentioned on the War Memorial) was one of the many who did not make it. Some had been pushed over to the west, to Cherbourg and were now stranded, awaiting evacuation. This was where the wagons landed. Moving inland, the companies collected and ferried to the port as many of the stranded troops as possible, this was the last stage of the evacuation operation. The last to leave were, naturally, the drivers and their guards. Leslie Shaw re-embarked at Cherbourg as did all the other companies, except one. As Les Shaw's family learned of the safety of their son, the Gaunt family began to worry about theirs, as he should have arrived back in England at the same time.

Cut off by the rapidly advancing Germans, John and the other eleven drivers were forced to retreat at speed after abandoning Cherbourg. They resolved to head for St. Nazaire. With the constant fear of the nearby enemy at their backs they used the only means at their disposal to stall them, the Engineers rescued as part of the operation were hastily employed in blowing up all the bridges they crossed. The torturous retreat took three days until at last they reached St. Nazaire. Here the lorries were abandoned, supposedly set on fire and destroyed to keep them from falling into the hands of the Germans. John did not see this happen, though he does remember the local people emptying the fuel tanks as though their lives depended on it.

This remnant of the BEF finally boarded a merchant vessel after being ferried to the anchored ship out at sea on a smaller craft. They boarded the temporary troop carrier using a wooden plank, before setting out West into the Atlantic. It was not possible for them to use the usual route home as it would take them far too close to the occupied territory of France and therefore render them susceptible to missiles and gun fire. Eventually the craft turned north and then east. Flanked by its two bodyguards, a pair of His Majesty's destroyers, they made a safe landing back at Portsmouth after a three day journey. Ironically, a new troop carrying vessel had arrived in St. Nazaire just as they had left, and thus returned home empty.

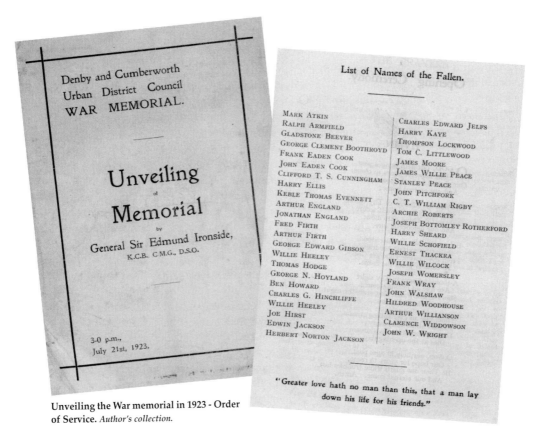

Denby and Cumberworth Urban District Council WAR MEMORIAL.

Unveiling
of
Memorial
by
General Sir Edmund Ironside,
K.C.B. C.M.G., D.S.O.

3-0 p.m.,
July 21st, 1923.

List of Names of the Fallen.

MARK ATKIN
RALPH ARMFIELD
GLADSTONE BEEVER
GEORGE CLEMENT BOOTHROYD
FRANK EADEN COOK
JOHN EADEN COOK
CLIFFORD T. S. CUNNINGHAM
HARRY ELLIS
KEBLE THOMAS EVENNETT
ARTHUR ENGLAND
JONATHAN ENGLAND
FRED FIRTH
ARTHUR FIRTH
GEORGE EDWARD GIBSON
WILLIE HEELEY
THOMAS HODGE
GEORGE N. HOYLAND
BEN HOWARD
CHARLES G. HINCHLIFFE
WILLIE HEELEY
JOE HIRST
EDWIN JACKSON
HERBERT NORTON JACKSON

CHARLES EDWARD JELFS
HARRY KAYE
THOMPSON LOCKWOOD
TOM C. LITTLEWOOD
JAMES MOORE
JAMES WILLIE PEACE
STANLEY PEACE
JOHN PITCHFORK
C. T. WILLIAM RIGBY
ARCHIE ROBERTS
JOSEPH BOTTOMLEY ROTHERFORD
HARRY SHEARD
WILLIE SCHOFIELD
ERNEST THACKRA
WILLIE WILCOCK
JOSEPH WOMERSLEY
FRANK WRAY
JOHN WALSHAW
HILDRED WOODHOUSE
ARTHUR WILLIANSON
CLARENCE WIDDOWSON
JOHN W. WRIGHT

"Greater love hath no man than this, that a man lay down his life for his friends."

Unveiling the War memorial in 1923 - Order of Service. *Author's collection.*

The War Memorial

On 21 July, 1923 at 3.00 pm, General Sir Edmund Ironside unveiled the Denby and Cumberworth Urban District Council War Memorial, to commemorate the fallen during the First World War. After the end of the Second World War two more names were added to it. I shall use the words of the poet, Laurence Binyon printed in the pamphlet to finish this chapter, they come from his work, entitled -

For the Fallen
They shall not grow old as we who are left grow old;
Age shall not weary them, nor the years dismay:
At the going down of the sun and in the morning;
We will remember them.

Chapter Twelve

A Wander Around
Mid-Twentieth Century Denby

ithin the context of this book we have examined as much of the village's history as possible, but it would be impossible to include all the people and characters so, essential to its development and so to finish, I will try to include as many as possible by taking a metaphorical walk around Denby in the mid-twentieth century. I am sure older residents will be familiar with the names and habits that will follow and that they will be ready to correct me should the need arise.

Finally, I must admit to a little poetic licence, but of course, for a set of coincidences such as follows to occur in a couple of hours would be fortuitous in the extreme.

It is a warm and sunny Saturday afternoon, the fields roll around us, undulating squares of varying greens and browns, broken only by the dry stone walls, many of which were built at the time of the enclosure awards in 1802. We are standing at the entrance to Gunthwaite Gate Farm, sited on the border between Denby and Gunthwaite, the home of the Pickford family.

Traction engine at Gunthwaite Gate farm, circa. 1920. *Author's collection.*

Dog daisies litter the fields, which surround two agricultural traction engines that are pulled slightly off the road. We begin our walk up Gunthwaite Lane, heading away from the farm, passing the seat for weary walkers on our left. Skylarks hover above, occasionally swooping, then effortlessly climbing back up and floating gracefully in the light breeze. Across to our right are playing fields; a sandpit, seesaw and football goal entertain the local kids to great extent. Beyond is the tip of the Clay Pit, once owned by Alin Ward now used as a rubbish tip by the villagers. A little further on and the wooden band hut comes into view. A faint but audible brass tune emanates from within, due to the efforts of railway linesman, Jim Harley, conducting the Denby prize band.

As we continue we find we have to tread very carefully around hot tar as the road is being repaired. Jim Slater with his steam engine and Burdett Haigh with his red, Bedford lorry, loaded with sand and pebbles are sweating profusely in the sun as both lend a hand in using the tar sprayer. A gang of local kids, gradually getting splattered with tar add to the proceedings. The hot tar is sprayed onto the road, completely covering it, pebbles are then thrown on, as evenly as possible with shovels. Jim then starts up the roller, black smoke pluthering from the chimney and moves backwards and forwards over the new area until it is flat and hard. Once completed the team will move forward and repeat the procedure until the job is done.

A few assured strides further and we are at the end of the lane, where we find a bus turning round, backing into Gunthwaite Lane to return back up the village and on into Huddersfield. To our left is the home of Mirfield school teacher, Norman Peace, a historian of some note. The house

Bank Lane, Upper Denby, just beyond houses on Ratten Row around the early twentieth century. *Courtesy of 'Old Barnsley'.*

now known as 'Poplar Villa' was once called 'Spion Cop'. Spion Cop was a peak in South Africa, which was captured by British troops at the orders of General Buller. Once attained the troops were subjected to heavy attack from the 'Boers', the date was 24 January 1900. Many hundreds of soldiers died on both sides, which resulted in a temporary armistice, which allowed both armies to collect and bury their dead. The British forces then withdrew. How the house became so named is unknown, though one presumes that a veteran of the battle would be the most likely author.

Across the road we can hear chatter from the patrons of the *New Inn* as workers quench their thirsts with the golden brew. As we draw nearer we pause to examine the notice board on the wall, detailing the selection of the cricket team for today's match in the Red Triangle League.

1. Dennis Pell
4. Joe Price
7. Percy Wadsworth
10. Oliver Marsh

2. J Jones
5. John Gaunt
8. Fred Barden
11. Colin Crossland

3. David Flack
6. Frank Burdett
9. Keith Herbert

It is to be hoped that wicket keeper, Barden, has finished his milk deliveries, which he achieves on a bike with a basket attachment! As we round the back of the pub, on Rattan Row we see a lorry marked Hammonds Ales delivering its weekly stock, Hammonds having taken over from Seth Seniors Breweries. Percy Cartwright, the landlord is supervising the unloading. The first house after this is occupied by Mrs Smithson, on a whim we call in and buy a quarter of Dolly Mixtures from her kitchen table. Groceries can also be bought further on at the Co-Op, run by Teddy Higson, and also at the other side of the road, at the red brick house owned by Arthur Turton, who sells vegetables and salad, although be careful to ask for a 'bob' of lettuce rather than a bob's worth or your arms will be full. Having finished our sweets we call up the entry on our left to see Clance Morris where we buy some more sweets, boiled ones this time and spend a moment or two whilst he reminisces about his mining days, abruptly ended by an accident which broke his back. We leave Clance listening to the wireless and continue past the homes of Horace Knowles, an auctioneer, Edward Hudson, butcher at the Co-Op, Arthur Laundon, Norton's textiles, and Bob Pontefract a baker, with his bread wagon parked outside. At Kilncroft House we turn and wave cheerily to Harry Battye, a part time wireless repair man and look up the lane to Manor Farm, where we see Colin Crossland's horse drawn milk float parked in the yard. A couple of milk churns are still aboard it, though the milk was transferred from these into smaller ones for taking into the houses, where long handled jugs measured out pints or gills at the customers request. By chance the owner of the farm, Math Webster, is coming towards us, herding his cows in for milking, back from Long Lane. Distinctive in his smock, he brandishes a walking stick, gently persuading the cows to behave and move in the right direction, he greets us as we pass.

We continue down Long Lane, passing Joe Turton, having a day off from Naylor's clay pit, hard at work, proudly mowing his beautiful lawn at Rock House. Approaching us from Lemon Acre are the Pickfords, with a full cart of freshly cut hay, drawn by their giant cart horse, George. We now turn back on ourselves and cross the style into Tom Seniors field where we are suddenly under attack from a gander and so a short run is necessary to avoid its eager beak, we should have brought the dog with us!

We come out into Back Lane, opposite the house once owned by Sam (Racket) Rawnsley, a name, apparently, thoroughly deserved! To our left is Coal Pit Lane, now silent and overgrown as the more familiar sound of hob-nail boots tramp its course no more. We continue down to the joiners and undertakers run by Joe Willie Heath. Entering the yard before us is 'Owd Bennet', of 'Fagin' like appearance. His scruffy dog yaps chirpily by his side. The shop is a regular meeting place for locals and he regales them with a tune on his tin whistle. Three or four more people can be glimpsed inside 'calin' with each other.

As we reach the end of the lane we turn into Post Office Row where we see two people going about their business. One is Lena Heath, holding a wireless battery on her way to see George Rotherforth to have it re-charged, so there must be something good on the wireless tonight. The battery, known as an accumulator was like a car battery in appearance, made of glass, about four inches square and ten inches tall, filled with acid and distilled water, with red and black terminals on top. The whole fitted into a metal carrier for transportation to someone with a charger and, obviously, electricity. Not many homes had electricity and they were lit by gas or oil lamps.

The other figure is that of Joe Willie White, just leaving his cottage with his trusty rabbitting dog and 12 bore shotgun broken over his shoulder, wearing his familiar loose collar shirt, minus collar with a scarf tied round his neck, cowboy style. He's probably going down Gunthwaite Lane to the railway banking.

A little further on and we see two vans parked outside the post office and grocer's. The first, which is just pulling away, belongs to the post office, the red Morris Minor driven by Milton Morris has the familiar double back doors with a bar lock on the outside. The second is that of J. Wood Ltd, confectioners, delivering to the shop. We enter the shop to buy some stamps and are greeted by Annie Heath. She stands behind a long counter, perched on it are a set of scales and a small display cabinet. The walls and floors and even shelves suspended from the ceiling are arranged with foodstuffs. A free space on the wall by the door is covered by a poster advertising a:

Whist drive and dance in Denby school, proceeds to the Church, at 8pm tonight, where the Serenaders band will be playing.

There is also a bill for Penistone pictures, where entry to see Johnny Weismuller in *Tarzan* costs - 1s 3d (7p), 1s 6d (7 ½p), and 2s 6d (12½p) for the balcony. We buy our stamp and bid Annie good day as she turns to deal with the van driver.

Turning left out of the door we pass what used to be the *Star* public house, now occupied privately by Mrs Town and on past the *George* public house where we can see through the windows, Frank Widdowson serving customers from behind the bar. The wooden doors into the barn at the top of the pub yard are open and a large dog lays in wait for over eager patrons. A little further on and we can see one of the former sites of the now abolished Denby feast. To our right, on Milnes Row, Fred Nicholson, retired farmer, and now caretaker of Denby Band hut, is hard at work in his allotment. He is watching warily at the antics of a group of noisy children playing under the gantry of the clay pit, he shakes his head in resignation at me and smiles his good-day. Beyond this is the ramshackle caravan used as a lodging by 'Owd Bennet', whose real name may have been 'Kettle' housed on land belonging to the Pickfords of Denroyd Farm.

Even further down the hill is Pinfold House, built in 1795 on the site where there were actually two pinfolds for rounding up stray cattle, but we turn and travel back up the main road past Milnes Row, noticing Mrs Grange smoking a clay pipe, sitting outside with her daughters, Ginny and Emma.

At the end house, Rafe Barber is tending his poultry. Looking across we can see the club, housing a billiard table for its patrons, walled in with the residence of Jimmy 'Pump' Gaunt, on the triangle of land, opposite the former site of the Barraclough blacksmith's shop, next door to

Mrs Grange seated, with her family including daughters, Ginny on the left and Emma on the right on Milnes Row, circa. 1941. *Author's collection.*

the post office, now demolished to make way for the residence of Ernest and Dorothy Heath. Oh, and a piece of advice, if you meet Jimmy Gaunt, remember not to call him 'Pump'!!

Above the club is the building, which was used as a Wesleyan Chapel, now converted into a home by Joe Willie Heath. The gate up to the house is supported by two large stones, reputed to have once been the Denby stocks. On the road in front of them is Henry Broadhead sorting out his newspapers before setting off on his rounds. The local bobby, Mr Glazebrook, comes past us up the lane and turns into his path, ready for his lunch. Also on our right as we continue up Denby Lane is the monumental mason's, and Jack Hanwell himself is outside putting the finishing touches to a gravestone.

We make our way on past the home of Joe Windle and on to Highfield Farm, residence of the Charlesworths where we decide to take a short cut through the yard to check on the cricket scores. In the field beyond we see the scoreboard on the pavilion reads that Denby are struggling on seventy-seven for seven, no change there! Play has in fact stopped as a rather lusty blow has sent the ball into the orchard and half the team are searching for it, still its better than landing it in the graveyard!

Advertisement placed in the 1954 *Penistone Almanac. Author's collection.*

Annie Heath and friend fetching water from Haley Well, 1940. *Author's collection.*

Denby school children outside the long window before it was extended to playground level, circa. 1946. Standing left to right, ?, Kenneth Jackson, Ronald Heath. Seated, left to right, Pat White, ?, Aurial Stevenson. *Author's collection.*

We nip out of the cricket field and carry on past the slaughter house and butcher's belonging to Norman Naylor. Coming out of the entrance to Tom Priest's farm on the left is Tom Moxon. He is driving what appears to be a full load in his cattle wagon, probably on his way to Penistone.

Approaching us, coming down the lane is Fred Bower in his wagon, shouting his familiar cry, 'lampoil' referring to the large drum of paraffin attached to the back of his vehicle. As we near the Church we see Rev. Moore crossing the road from the vicarage to attend to some matter in the Church, and we hear someone testing the school bell, normally rung by Miss Thompson, the headmistress, or Miss Close to signal the beginning of school for the day when both would be outside to make sure the children were lined up ready to enter the building. The bell just outside the front door is attached to a black rope inside the classroom and is rung at the start and end of each day and also at playtime, scholars are usually permitted to ring it by the teachers. Miss Close teaches baby and standard one classes, Miss Thompson standards two, three and four all in the same room, where students may use ink or pencil to make notes in their jotters.

Just past the school we reach the small reservoir, a little way up the common. Here again we cross the fields, past the farm belonging to Reg Mosley and over towards Mosley Roughs, on to

Math Webster of Manor Farm, Upper Denby, seated on the cart. His son-in-law, Colin Crossland can be seen standing behind cart horse, Duncan at the bottom of the lane leading up to Manor Farm, circa. 1946. *Author's collection.*

Math Webster (left) with his carthorse, Plunger, waiting to load up with hay. Note the tower of Denby church in the distance. *Author's collection. c.1935.*

The day is done! Math's daughter, Stella is sitting on the hay in the cart. *Author's collection. c.1935.*

the top of Broom fields. Briefly we take in the stunning rural landscape, looking out over Cumberworth, forty steps, High Flatts and Denby Dale before heading back into the village through Long Lane Wood. Looking left we can see Breeches field or close where the kids go sledding in winter snows and as we walk up the actual lane we notice the hollow known as the 'basin' which was dug out at the time of the building of the railways and used as filler for the viaduct. Quite a way behind this, in the middle of a field is Haley Well, used by the villagers in time of need.

We come back into the village via Bank Lane turning down by the green and past the cottages on Northgate or 'Flying Poker Street' as it was affectionately known! We would have continued the walk by using the snicket known as 'Shedley' just before reaching Ratten Row, but unfortunately thirst has overtaken us and so we nip down the snicket between the joiner's low shop and the cottage adjoining what was the *Star*, which brings us out, almost to the entrance to the *George*, where we finish with a pint of best.

Rev. Sheard fetching water from Haley Well, circa. 1940. *Author's collection.*

Aerial view of Upper Denby showing, in the centre, the *George* public house and to the left, Milnes Row, circa. 1960. *Author's collection.*

Postscript

✦

Our journey is now over and we have forged a path through over 2000 years of history and traced the development of Denby and its district over the centuries. The evidence survives in many forms, in the landscape, place-names, ancient documents, folklore and living memory. Utilising as much of what remains, the story, for the moment is complete. The twentieth century has probably seen more radical change than any other, today's technology, communications, transport, living standards and entertainment would be simply unbelievable to a nineteenth century Denbier.

Since the war years many of the families and buildings so familiar to the older residents of the district have disappeared. The 'old Denbiers' and 'Dalers' have dwindled in number, being replaced by newcomers, attracted by the site and situation of the area. Its close proximity to Barnsley, Wakefield and Huddersfield, alongside its easy access to the M1 motorway make it an ideal place to live in this commuter age.

New housing has been built in Upper Denby, the council estate, named Fairfields and the Southcroft housing estate alongside many other detached and semi-detached abodes.

Denroyd Farm before re-development, 1997. *Author's collection.*

Denroyd Farm after re-development, 2000. *Author's collection.*

Only one shop remains in the village, that of Peter Homes the butcher at the top of Gunthwaite Lane, there is no Post Office or general store nor even a newsagent. Harry Heath, the last in a long line of joiners is now semi-retired and the working farms have grown fewer in number as barns and outbuildings are re-developed into private properties. After the conversion of Denroyd farm into luxury homes at the end of the twentieth century, only Manor farm remains to remind us of the foundations and economy of the villages past.

Down in the valley, Denby Dale continues to grow, though only the mill of Z Hinchcliffe & Sons remains as a testament to the heritage of the village. Kenyon's buildings having been demolished to make way for the 'Kenyon Bank' housing estate and Springfield Mill now playing host to a number of retail outlets. The new industrial park on Wakefield Road, close to the viaduct is also home to various and increasingly numerous new businesses. Denby Dale has now become an important resource for the neighbouring villages up on the hills, the situation has turned full circle, as the baby of Denby Dykeside has become the mother to its older and in the past, far more important counterpart, Denby.

The district is still alive because of these changes, most of which would confound former occupants from the nineteenth century and before. Denby was considered to be one of the most beautiful villages in Britain, a few years ago, an accolade achieved from its high placing in the annual competition to find the same.

Bonfire Night is still observed in the playing fields at Upper Denby, the Rockwood Harriers still meet on Boxing Day morning at the *George* and Denby Ladies hold a harvest festival every October, to help pay for the old folks annual social. The fish and chip shop run by Mr and Mrs Bert Fisher on Denby Lane, across from today's village green was closed in 1939 and the street sellers and gypsies have long since gone, leaving Denby Dale as the nearest centre for local amenities. Mobile grocers and a library still entertain at least the older folk in the village.

Cricket and football teams still play at the back of Manor Farm though the tennis courts are gone. The footpaths and bridle ways, once so central to the travel and communications of the village are still much used by ramblers and dog walkers, though many know the routes the names may be unfamiliar to some ie: Gladehouses, Daffy Wood and Forty Steps.

The relatives of the old Lords of the Manor are still here, though of their powerful neighbours the Bosvilles, nothing remains. It would be interesting to know what Aymer Burdet II, would have thought of the village and its occupants now.

All the people of today's village are in debt to their predecessors, considered in these few pages, for the shape and station of the village today. Many will be oblivious to its rich and diverse history, though it is a history repeated throughout the country, only the characters are different.

Italian historians coined the term 'microhistory' for the study of local history, they saw it as 'attempting to see the world in a grain of sand'. Most villages were caught up in national events, the problem is finding evidence of this. For instance, at present I do not know whether the Burdets played any part in the 'Wars of the Roses', whether the civil strife in the twelfth century between Stephen and Matilda had any effect on Denby or indeed many other interesting scenarios.

In most cases the evidence has not survived and the truth will never be known. The statement taken at the trial of Susan Hinchcliffe and Ann Shillitoe in 1674 has disappeared, as has the muster roll for the defence of the country at the time of the Spanish Armada. The details of Bishop Longley's visitation to the church and his well known thought, that it was 'in such a filthy and ruinous state' may well never have been written down, as the Reverend Joseph Hunter was writing about Denby only a year or two later, the evidence may well have been oral only.

Therefore we are left with written accounts of these developments by historians of the past, their interpretation is in many cases all that remains and it is upon these facts that I have tried to build.

There are limits as to how much information can be produced in any single volume work. The families and individuals contained within these pages are simply the ones which have cropped up most often during my research. They are hopefully representative of the populace as a whole but they are by no means all encompassing. Interestingly, if one researches far enough back, most local families are inter-related with the others. My own family tree includes the Burdets, Hanwells, Rusbys, Milnes, Inghams, Hawksworths, Barracloughs, Whites, Gaunts, Turtons, Bosvilles, Ellis, Moores, Eyres, Haighs, Blackburns, Firths, Lockwoods, the list goes on and on! Most rely on a single marriage, though it must be said that the Burdet family provide links to the kings of England, Ireland, Wales, Scotland, France, the Roman Emperors, Charlemagne and many other famous dynastys, albeit via an illegitimate descent.

The pursuit goes on, though with reluctance I cannot envisage a new edition of 'Denebi' being published for a good number of years.

My efforts to glean a better and more substantial picture of the village, either due to my own efforts or perhaps via to the efforts of others will continue and it is to be hoped that more contacts will be made with other amateur historians which will continue to flesh out the history of this fascinating area.

The present day village green in Upper Denby, pictured in 1922 when it was heavily built upon. Note the stile and footpath to the bottom right. This led to the workhouse which by this time had become ruinous. *Author's collection.*

Appendices

APPENDIX 1 - Select listing of regular Denby surname meanings:

(Many surnames were spelt in a variety of ways)

ARMITAGE	derived from hermitage, place in Staffordshire.
BARRACLOUGH	dell with a grove.
BEAUMONT	lovely hill, of Norman origin.
BEAVER OR BEEVER	beautiful view, compare with town of Beverley.
BLACKBURN	black stream, and a number of places.
BOOTH	hut, shed or shelter.
BOOTHROYD	a clearing with huts or sheds.
CHALLENGOR	plaintiff, challenger, accuser.
CHARLESWORTH	2 parts, 'Charles' derived from Germanic Emperor, Charlemagne,'Worth' is an enclosure, fence or homestead.
CLAYTON	place in the clay, or place with good clay for pottery, or derived from place - Clayton (West).
COLDWELL	cold spring or stream.
CROSSLAND	one who owned a strip of land by a market or roadside cross or crossroads.
CROWTHER	fiddler, from the Welsh 'crwthl.
DICKINSON	son of Richard, comparative with Dixon.
DYSON	follower of Bacchus, or son of person whose name began with D.
ELLIS	form of Elias, in Welsh, charitable, benevolent.
FIRTH	woodland.
GAUNT	either the Belgian city, or bleak, lean and haggard.
GRAHAM	homestead of Granta, a grinner, snarler or grumbler, also a gravelly homestead.
HAIGH	enclosure, paddock, various spellings.
HANWELL	in 2 parts, 'Han', possibly derived from person named Johann, 'Well' is well, spring or stream.
HAWKESWORTH	2 parts, 'Hawks', from rapacity, or keeping hawks, or paying them as rent, 'Worth', enclosure, fence or homestead.
HEATH	dweller on the heath.
HIRST	copse, hill, wooded hill.
HORN(E)	either horn shaped hill, gable, pinnacle or land in a river bed.
HUDSON	the son of a man named Richard (hud).
JESSOP	form of Joseph, of Italian Jewish origin i.e., Giuseppe.
KILNER	worker at a kiln, lime burner.
LAUNDON	form of lavender, washer woman, launderer.
LOCKWOOD	enclosed wood and a place.
MALLINSON	son of Mary, i.e. wished for a child, Hebrew origin.
MARSDEN	boundary valley.
MARSHALL	horse servant, farmer, groom, horse doctor.
MICKLETHWAITE	big thwaite, a thwaite was a clearing, meadow etc.
MILNES	of or at the mill.
MOORE	the moor, from Latin maurus, name of sixth century Saint.
MOORHOUSE	house in a moor, or fen.
MOSLEY	in 2 parts, 'Mos' is marsh or bog, 'Ley' is wood/clearing.
MOXON	son of a person named Mog or Mogga.
PEACE	of Pace, meaning peace or concord.
POLLARD	possibly crop head, or big (large) head.

PRIEST	relates to the word, presbytr, the Greek word for elder.
ROBINSON	son of Robert or Robin.
RUSBY	possibly a bed of rushes.
SENIOR	either Lord (as in Manor), or senior as opposed to junior or swagger.
SHAW	copse, thicket, small wood.
SLATER	a person who covers roofs with slates, or sheep pasture.
SWIFT	literally swift or quick.
TURTON	Thors farm literally from the pagan God of thunder.
TYAS	of German origin.
WOOD	wood, or of the wood etc.

APPENDIX 2 - Local Place Meanings

BIRDSEDGE	Probably from Danish word 'burr' a ridge of land, and 'sedge' coarse grass. Or *Bridd ecg*, the bridge area.
CAWTHORNE	Cold, i.e. exposed, thorn tree, in old English Cald + Thorn. In 1086 spelt Caltorne.
CLAYTON	Farmstead on clay soil, in 1086, *Claitone*.
CUMBERWORTH	Enclosure of a man named Cumbra, or of the Britons, similar with Welsh - Cymru. In 1086 spelt *Cumbreuurde*.
DARTON	Enclosure for deer, deer park. In 1086 *Dertun*.
DELPH HOUSE	A delph was a quarry so, Quarry House.
DENBY	Farmstead or village of the Danes.
DENBY DALE	Identical in origin with previous name, with the later addition of dale - (valley). In 1086 spelt *Denebi*.
EMLEY	In 1086, *Ameleie*, woodland clearing of a man called Em(ma)a. Origin of ley, leah, woodland clearing, or glade, later pasture or meadow.
FALLAGE	Area of felled trees, 'folage' in 1771.
GUNTHWAITE GATE	From 'Gata' which means a road, so 'Gunthwaite Road'.
HIGH FLATTS	From the Norse 'flair', level ground, high up.
HOYLAND	Cultivated land on or near a hill spur. High Hoyland was spelt *Holand* in 1086, *Heyholand* in 1283. Hoylandswaine was *Holande* in 1086, and *Holandeswayn* in 1266. Manorial affix from possession in twelfth century of Sweinn, Grandson of Ailric.
INGBIRCHWORTH	Enclosure where birch trees grow, i.e. birce + worth (enclosure or enclosed settlement) with later addition of eng (meadow). In 1086 *Berceeuuorde*, in 1424 *Yngebyrcheworth*.
KEXBROUGH	Probably the stronghold of a man called Keptr, spelt *Cezeburg* in 1086, and *Kesceburg* c.1170. Brough and its derivatives mean a fortified place or stronghold.
KIRKBURTON	Farmstead, near or belonging to a fortification. In 1086,*Bertone*, kirkja meaning church was affixed from the sixteenth century.
OXSPRING	Spring frequented by oxen. In 1086 Ospring, in 1154 Oxspring.
PENISTONE	Probably farmstead by a hill called Penning, from Celtic, penn hill, + ing + tun (enclosure or farmstead or estate.). In 1086 *Pengestone*, in 1199, *Peningeston*.
ROMB TICKLE or ROMBPICKLE	From 'raw pightele' an enclosure near a row of houses.
SHELLEY	Woodland clearing on shelving terrain. In 1086 *Scelneleie*, in 1198 *Shelfleie*.
SHEPLEY	Clearing where sheep are kept, in 1086 *Scipelei*.
SILKSTONE	Farmstead of a man called Sigelac. In 1086 *Silchestone*.
SKELMANTHORPE	Outlying farmstead of a man called Skjaldmarr. Thorp is a secondary settlement, dependent outlying farmstead of hamlet. In 1086 called *Scelmertorp*.
SYKE HOUSE	In Old English 'sic hus'. the house by the swift stream.
THURLSTONE	Farmstead of a man called Thorfrithr. In 1086, *Turulfestune*.
WORTLEY	Woodland clearing used for growing vegetables. In 1086 *Wirtleie*.

APPENDIX 3 - Local *Domesday* Book Entries

(Phillimore - History From The Sources, Yorkshire part 1, 1986)

ALMONDBURY	Ketill and Sveinn had 4 carucates of land taxable; 4 ploughs possible there. Now Leofsige has (it) from Ilbert. Waste. Value before 1066, £3. Woodland pasture 1 league long and 1 wide.
CAWTHORNE	Alric had 3 carucates of land taxable; 2 ploughs possible there. Now the same man has (it) from Ilbert. He (has) there 2 ploughs; and 4 villagers with 2 ploughs. There, a priest and a church. Woodland pasture 2 leagues long and 2 wide. The whole manor 3 leagues long and 2 wide. Value before 1066, 40s; now 20s. To the same manor belong Silkstone, 1^1/2 c; Hoyland (Swaine), 6 bovates; and Clactone, 6 bovates. That is 6 carucates of land taxable; 2 ploughs possible there.
CLAYTON (WEST)	Alsige had 3 carucates of land taxable; 2 ploughs possible there. Now Ilbert has (it). Waste. Value before 1066, 20s. Woodland pasture, ^{1}/2 league long and ^{1}/2 wide.
HIGH HOYLAND	Asulfr had 2 carucates of land taxable; 2 ploughs possible there. Now the same man has (it) from Ilbert. He (has) there 1 plough. Woodland pasture 1 league long and 1 wide. Value before 1066, 20s now 5s.
HOYLAND (SWAINE)	Thorbjorn had 10 bovates of land taxable where 1 plough is possible. Ilbert has (it). Waste. Value before 1066, 8s. Woodland pasture 1 league long and ^{1}/2 wide.
HUNSHELF (HALL)	Alric had 3 carucates of land taxable where 2 ploughs are possible. Now the same man has (it) from Ilbert. Waste. Value before 1066, 10s. Woodland pasture, 1 league long and 1 wide.
KEXBROUGH	Godric had 2^1/2 carucates of land taxable; 1 plough possible there. Now Sveinn has (it) from Ilbert. He (has) there 1 plough and 2 villagers with 1 plough. Meadow, 2 acres; woodland pasture, 6 furlongs as long and as wide. Value before 1066, 10s, now the same.
KIRKBURTON, SHEPLEY & SHELLEY	Burton 3 carucates, Shepley, 2 carucates, Shelley, 1 carucate, There are 6 carucates of land taxable where 4 ploughs are possible.
NOTTON	Of this land 4 carucates are in the jurisdiction of Tanshelf and 2 carucates are inland. Nevertheless, Godric had a Hall there. Now Ilbert has there, 2 Freemen and 3 smallholders with ^{1}/2 plough. Woodland pasture, ^{1}/2 league long and ^{1}/2 wide. Value before 1066, 20s
OXSPRING & ROUGHBIRCHWORTH	Sveinn had 2 carucates of land taxable; 2 ploughs possible there. Ilbert has (it). Waste. Value before 1066, 20s. Woodland pasture, 6 furlongs long and 3 wide.
PENISTONE	Alric had 10 bovates of land taxable; 1 plough possible there. Now the same man has (it) from Ilbert. Waste. Value before 1066, 20s.
THURGOLAND	Aelfric and Gamall had 4^1/2 carucates of land taxable where 2 ploughs are possible. The jurisdiction belongs to Tanshelf. Now Ilbert has it. Waste. Value before 1066 20s. Woodland pasture 1 league long and ^{1}/2 wide.
THURLSTONE & INGBIRCHWORTH	Alric and Halfdan had 9 carucates of land taxable; 5 ploughs possible there. Now Ilbert has (them). Waste. Value before 1066 £4. Woodland pasture, 1^1/2 leagues long and as wide.
UPPER AND LOWER DENBY	Eadwulf and Godric had 3 carucates of land taxable where 1^1/2 ploughs are possible. Now Alric has (them) from Ilbert. There woodland pasture 1 league long and 1 wide. Value before 1066, 10s, now 6s. A cow pasture is there.
UPPER CUMBERWORTH	Leofwine and Alric had 1 carucate of land taxable. Now Ilbert has (it). Waste. Value before 1066, 6s.
WORTLEY	Alric had 1 manor of 1 carucate taxable; 1 plough possible. Now Richard has there 1 plough; and 3 villagers and 3 smallholders with 2 ploughs. Woodland pasture ^{1}/2 league long and ^{1}/2 wide. The whole, 1 league long and 1 wide. Value before 1066, 10s, now 8s 8d.

APPENDIX 4 - Selected Associated Genealogical Tables

Pedigree of Delariver Burdet
from his illegitimate son by Ann Hawcroft

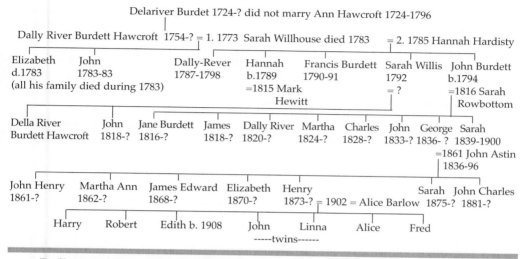

Delariver Burdet 1724-? did not marry Ann Hawcroft 1724-1796

Dally River Burdett Hawcroft 1754-? = 1. 1773 Sarah Willhouse died 1783   = 2. 1785 Hannah Hardisty

Elizabeth d.1783 | John 1783-83 | Dally-Rever 1787-1798 | Hannah b.1789 =1815 Mark Hewitt | Francis Burdett 1790-91 | Sarah Willis 1792 =? | John Burdett b.1794 =1816 Sarah Rowbottom
(all his family died during 1783)

Della River Burdett Hawcroft | John 1818-? | Jane Burdett 1816-? | James 1818-? | Dally River 1820-? | Martha 1824-? | Charles 1828-? | John 1833-? | George 1836-? | Sarah 1839-1900 =1861 John Astin 1836-96

John Henry 1861-? | Martha Ann 1862-? | James Edward 1868-? | Elizabeth 1870-? | Henry 1873-? = 1902 = Alice Barlow 1875-? | Sarah John Charles 1881-?

Harry | Robert | Edith b. 1908 | John | Linna | Alice | Fred
-----twins------

Pedigree of Delariver Burdet born 1774 from his marriage to Mary Gaunt

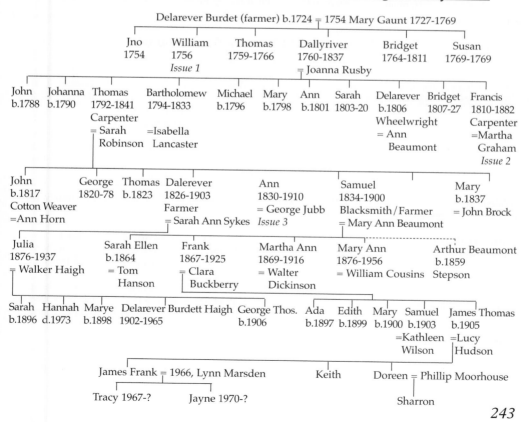

Delarever Burdet (farmer) b.1724 = 1754 Mary Gaunt 1727-1769

Jno 1754 | William 1756 *Issue 1* | Thomas 1759-1766 | Dallyriver 1760-1837 = Joanna Rusby | Bridget 1764-1811 | Susan 1769-1769

John b.1788 | Johanna b.1790 | Thomas 1792-1841 Carpenter = Sarah Robinson | Bartholomew 1794-1833 =Isabella Lancaster | Michael b.1796 | Mary b.1798 | Ann b.1801 | Sarah 1803-20 | Delarever 1806 Wheelwright = Ann Beaumont | Bridget 1807-27 | Francis 1810-1882 Carpenter =Martha Graham *Issue 2*

John b.1817 Cotton Weaver =Ann Horn | George 1820-78 | Thomas b.1823 | Dalerever 1826-1903 Farmer = Sarah Ann Sykes *Issue 3* | Ann 1830-1910 = George Jubb | Samuel 1834-1900 Blacksmith/Farmer = Mary Ann Beaumont | Mary b.1837 = John Brock

Julia 1876-1937 = Walker Haigh | Sarah Ellen b.1864 = Tom Hanson | Frank 1867-1925 = Clara Buckberry | Martha Ann 1869-1916 = Walter Dickinson | Mary Ann 1876-1956 = William Cousins | Arthur Beaumont b.1859 Stepson

Sarah Hannah b.1896 d.1973 | Marye b.1898 | Delarever Burdett Haigh 1902-1965 | George Thos. b.1906 | Ada b.1897 | Edith b.1899 | Mary b.1900 =Kathleen Wilson | Samuel b.1903 =Lucy Hudson | James Thomas b.1905

James Frank = 1966, Lynn Marsden

Tracy 1967-?   Jayne 1970-?

Keith | Doreen = Phillip Moorhouse

Sharron

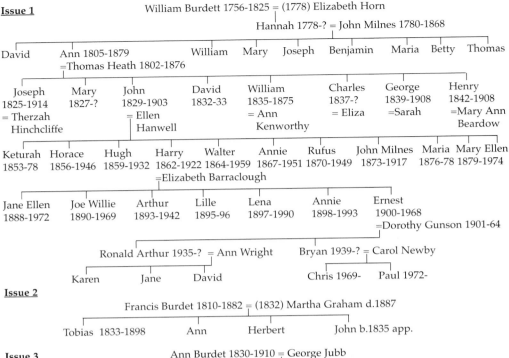

Issue 1

William Burdett 1756-1825 = (1778) Elizabeth Horn

Hannah 1778-? = John Milnes 1780-1868

David   Ann 1805-1879   William   Mary   Joseph   Benjamin   Maria   Betty   Thomas
=Thomas Heath 1802-1876

| Joseph 1825-1914 = Therzah Hinchcliffe | Mary 1827-? | John 1829-1903 = Ellen Hanwell | David 1832-33 | William 1835-1875 = Ann Kenworthy | Charles 1837-? = Eliza | George 1839-1908 =Sarah | Henry 1842-1908 =Mary Ann Beardow |

Keturah 1853-78   Horace 1856-1946   Hugh 1859-1932   Harry 1862-1922   Walter 1864-1959   Annie 1867-1951   Rufus 1870-1949   John Milnes 1873-1917   Maria 1876-78   Mary Ellen 1879-1974
=Elizabeth Barraclough

Jane Ellen 1888-1972   Joe Willie 1890-1969   Arthur 1893-1942   Lille 1895-96   Lena 1897-1990   Annie 1898-1993   Ernest 1900-1968
=Dorothy Gunson 1901-64

Ronald Arthur 1935-? = Ann Wright   Bryan 1939-? = Carol Newby

Karen   Jane   David   Chris 1969-   Paul 1972-

Issue 2

Francis Burdet 1810-1882 = (1832) Martha Graham d.1887

Tobias 1833-1898   Ann   Herbert   John b.1835 app.

Issue 3

Ann Burdet 1830-1910 = George Jubb

Hannah   Margaret   Ellen   Lucy   Flora

Australian Descent from Dallyriver Burdett

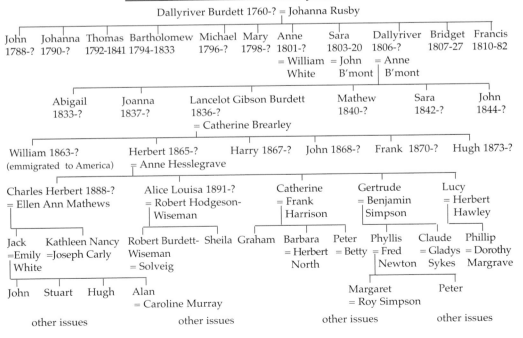

Dallyriver Burdett 1760-? = Johanna Rusby

| John 1788-? | Johanna 1790-? | Thomas 1792-1841 | Bartholomew 1794-1833 | Michael 1796-? | Mary 1798-? | Anne 1801-? = William White | Sara 1803-20 = John B'mont | Dallyriver 1806-? = Anne B'mont | Bridget 1807-27 | Francis 1810-82 |

Abigail 1833-?   Joanna 1837-?   Lancelot Gibson Burdett 1836-? = Catherine Brearley   Mathew 1840-?   Sara 1842-?   John 1844-?

William 1863-? (emmigrated to America)   Herbert 1865-? = Anne Hesslegrave   Harry 1867-?   John 1868-?   Frank 1870-?   Hugh 1873-?

| Charles Herbert 1888-? = Ellen Ann Mathews | Alice Louisa 1891-? = Robert Hodgeson-Wiseman | Catherine = Frank Harrison | Gertrude = Benjamin Simpson | Lucy = Herbert Hawley |

Jack =Emily White   Kathleen =Joseph Carly   Nancy   Robert Burdett-Wiseman = Solveig   Sheila Graham   Barbara = Herbert North   Peter = Betty   Phyllis = Fred Newton   Claude = Gladys Sykes   Phillip = Dorothy Margrave

John   Stuart   Hugh   Alan = Caroline Murray   Margaret = Roy Simpson   Peter

other issues   other issues   other issues   other issues

Descent from Mathew Burdet and Dorothy Colthurst

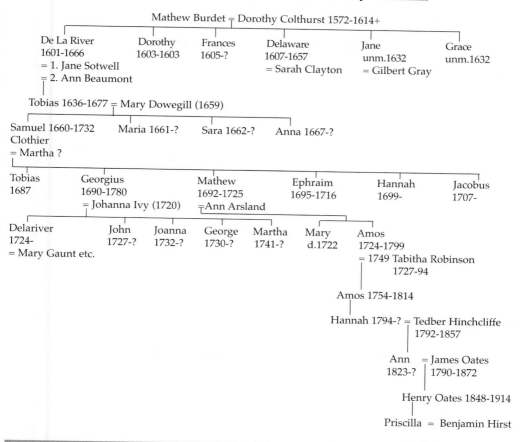

Mathew Burdet = Dorothy Colthurst 1572-1614+

De La River 1601-1666
= 1. Jane Sotwell
= 2. Ann Beaumont

Dorothy 1603-1603

Frances 1605-?

Delaware 1607-1657
= Sarah Clayton

Jane unm.1632
= Gilbert Gray

Grace unm.1632

Tobias 1636-1677 = Mary Dowegill (1659)

Samuel 1660-1732 Clothier = Martha ?

Maria 1661-?

Sara 1662-?

Anna 1667-?

Tobias 1687

Georgius 1690-1780 = Johanna Ivy (1720)

Mathew 1692-1725 =Ann Arsland

Ephraim 1695-1716

Hannah 1699-

Jacobus 1707-

Delariver 1724-
= Mary Gaunt etc.

John 1727-?

Joanna 1732-?

George 1730-?

Martha 1741-?

Mary d.1722

Amos 1724-1799
= 1749 Tabitha Robinson 1727-94

Amos 1754-1814

Hannah 1794-? = Tedber Hinchcliffe 1792-1857

Ann 1823-? = James Oates 1790-1872

Henry Oates 1848-1914

Priscilla = Benjamin Hirst

Descent of Robert Gaunt of Upper Denby

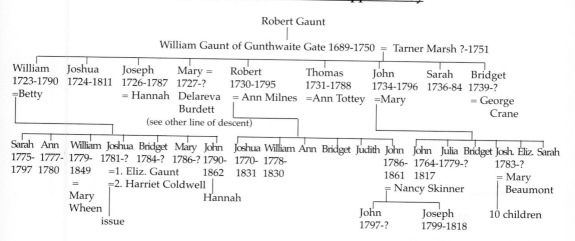

Robert Gaunt

William Gaunt of Gunthwaite Gate 1689-1750 = Tarner Marsh ?-1751

William 1723-1790 =Betty

Joshua 1724-1811

Joseph 1726-1787 = Hannah Delareva Burdett
(see other line of descent)

Mary = 1727-?

Robert 1730-1795 = Ann Milnes

Thomas 1731-1788 =Ann Tottey

John 1734-1796 =Mary

Sarah 1736-84

Bridget 1739-?
= George Crane

Sarah 1775-1797

Ann 1777-1780

William 1779-1849 = Mary Wheen

Joshua 1781-?
=1. Eliz. Gaunt
=2. Harriet Coldwell

Bridget 1784-?

Mary 1786-?

John 1790-1862

Joshua 1770-1831

William 1778-1830

Ann

Bridget

Judith

John 1786-1861
= Nancy Skinner

John 1764-1817

Julia 1779-?

Bridget

Josh.

Eliz. 1783-?
= Mary Beaumont

Sarah

issue

Hannah

John 1797-?

Joseph 1799-1818

10 children

Pedigree of Wheatley of Wooley

Thomas Wheatley, living 1612 = Margery Week

Thomas Wheatley
= DOROTHY BURDET
dau. Richard Burdet of Denby

Richard   Elizabeth   Ann   Alice

Thomas Wheatley al.1612,1674 = Elizabeth Oldfield   Richard

George   Francis   Richard   Michael   Thomas   John   Everilda   Catherine   Elizabeth   Frances
=1. Edith Rider =2. Mary Drue

Francis = 1. Emilia Hardwick = 2. Ann Devevere = 3. Jane Riccard   George   John   Thomas   Elizabeth   Prudence

Michael   Ann   Barbara   Dorothy

Pedigree of Woodruffe of Wooley

Thomas Woodruffe of Wooley, *will 1549* = Elizabeth Waterton of Walton

George
= ALICE BURDET of Denby dau. of Richard Burdet

Richard   William   Susan   Dorothy   Elizabeth   Ann

Francis d.1573 without issue
= 1. Elizabeth Nevile of Liversedge   = 2. Margaret Kaye

George = Usrula Clifton

Francis   Richard = Elizabeth Percy   Thomas = Elizabeth Cookson   Gervas
dau. of attainted Earl of Northumberland

Descent of the Wortley Family

Alanus de Wortley, (King Stephen)

Nicholas de Wortley =?

Sir Nicholas de Wortley = Dionysia (dau.of Ralph de Newmarch)

Sir Nicholas de Wortley = Isabel Heron

Nicholas de Wortley = 1. Joan Musard = 2. Matilda de Dutton

Sir Nicholas de Wortley (33 Ed I) = dau. Ralph de Horbury   Ralph

Sir Nicholas de Wortley = Sebilla Wastneyes

Sir Nicholas de Wortley (d.1347) = Lucy

Sir Nicholas de Wortley (d.1360) = Elizabeth Wannerville

John Wortley (under age 1360 living 1424) = ?

Nicholas Wortley (will 1448) = ?

Nicholas Wortley = Isabel Tunstall   Robert   Thomas   Matilda   Catherine

Catherine Fitz William 1. = Sir Thomas Wortley   = 2. Joan Balderstone   = 3. Elizabeth Fitz William

Nicholas = Alice   Isabel   Thomas Wortley = Margaret Saville

Mary Swyft 1. = Francis Wortley (d.1583)   = 2. Frances Burdet (rem.Foljambe)

Nicholas   Sir Richard   Elizabeth   John = Bridget Lynsey   5   6   7   8   9   10   11

Mary = Francis Bunney (son and heir of Francis of Durham)

The Lordship of Denby and the author's connection

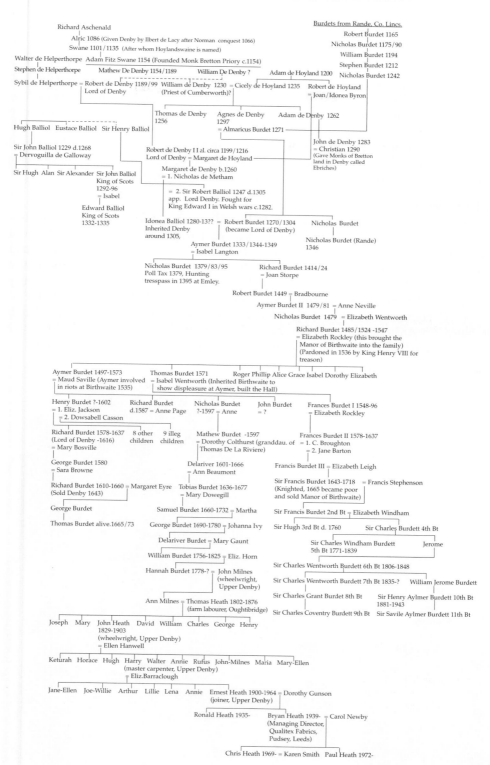

APPENDIX 5

RAND

Rand is a very small hamlet situated between Langworth and Wragby, its name meaning a ridge overlooking a valley. In the late eleventh century, Rand formed a part of the Manor of Wragby, but during the twelfth century, a separate Manor was established here by the Burdet family, who retained it until the mid fourteenth century. Under their Lordship, a planned expansion of the village took place and the population increased. From the late fifteenth century, the population began to decline, probably as a result of enclosure for sheep pasture. By 1563, there were just seven households in the village and by the early nineteenth century, just one.

THE CHURCH

Documentary evidence shows that a church has stood in Rand since at least the mid-twelfth century, dedicated to St Oswald. It has been noted that during the thirteenth century there seems to have been an open air mission station marked by a cross where worship took place. As a result of the decreasing population of the village, the church began to fall in to disrepair. The north aisle was removed in 1783, the south nave wall fell down in 1829, but was repaired the following year, and in 1863, the chancel was rebuilt along with a new vestry. The broad west tower is the exception, sporting excellent gargoyles. A date somewhere in the fifteenth century has been attributed to it. Archaelogical excavation has rediscovered the remains of the north aisle, but more importantly, a pillar capital dating to the mid-twelfth was discovered in the churchyard.

Rand Church, 1999. *Author's collection.*

Effigy of an unknown lady, lying in the recess of the north wall of the chancel, dating to the thirteenth century. She was almost certainly a member of the Burdet family. *Author's collection.*

Ancient coffin lid, dating to approximately the late twelfth century. There is again, a high possibility that it was originally associated with an early Burdet. *Author's collection.*

Underneath the remains of the north aisle, limestone footings were found which indicated the presence of an earlier north nave wall. The earlier building was considerably shorter, though at its west end large foundations of sandstone and limestone rubble indicated the remains of a tower, which was on a slightly different alignment to the present day structure. A further set of foundations, this time of sandstone, were also discovered which represented an even earlier structure though much of this had been destroyed by later burials. Two burials were found which pre-dated even this earlier structure and indicate the presence of an ancient church of which, so far, no trace has been found.

Finally, the discovery of a large domestic oven at the east end of the nave provided evidence for activity on the site prior to the first religious house being erected there. Within the oven were fragments of a limestone vessel, similar to the Saxon oil lamp in type.

MONUMENTS

There are numerous monuments in the church, most of which date from Elizabethan times onwards. Of the others, the most interesting is a thirteenth century effigy of a lady, lying in a recess in the north wall of the chancel. Her head lies on a pillow supported at each end by an angel. Her hands are placed together as if in prayer and the hem of her gown and her feet rest upon a dog, a shield rests on her middle. It is unfortunate that this exquisite effigy at present bears no name. The lady must have been of considerable importance and dated as she is to the thirteenth century must almost certainly have been a Burdet. The possibilities are endless, though just as a thought, where was Agnes de Denby laid to rest?

Fixed to the north wall at the back of the nave, is an ancient, coped coffin lid. It dates from around 1200 and was possibly found in the churchyard. At almost eight feet long, it is elaborately carved with a roundel at its base and three at the top with small foliage. There is a shaft like that of a cross, or sword, which runs up the spine. Here, again, we are in Burdet territory but without a name, the lid must go unclaimed.

DESERTED MEDIEVAL VILLAGE

Substantial earthworks survive to indicate the size and extent of the long disappeared village along with the remains of its open field ridge and furrow operation. The earliest remains are located around the church, a broad linear depression from the south side of the churchyard represents the principal medieval street and the rectangular enclosures on either side of it represent house plots. To the north west of the church is a substantial moated site measuring about thirty-five metres square, the moat was up to two metres in depth and was ten metres wide. Earthworks indicate the remains of buried buildings including that of a medieval manor house, first established in the late twelfth century and two sluices by which the water in the moat was controlled. Linked to the manor house site were a fishpond, rabbit warren, gardens and paddocks. There are also remains of a manorial watermill. The whole manorial complex dated from the late twelfth or early thirteenth centuries. Adjacent to these are the remains of an even earlier settlement, thought to have been abandoned in the thirteenth century, and then enclosed within the manorial complex which also included the church and churchyard. This earlier site has earthworks, which may have included a manorial dovecote. The whole site has been registered as a scheduled ancient monument.

The importance of this site and its relationship to the early Burdets cannot be doubted. It is to them that the foundation of most of the above can be attributed. The moated manor house was where they lived; they ate fish from the pond and rabbits from the warren. Their tenants lived around them in small plots off the two main streets. Agriculture followed the ridge and furrow design and their lives centred on their worship at the church. Why the family chose to settle here is currently unknown, though heraldic evidence may answer this conundrum. Whatever the reason, these forbears of the Lords of Denby were builders and planners and the basis of a Norman dynasty which has lived on to the present day.

Glossary

ADVOWSON	the right of presentation to a church benefice.
ANNUITANT	a person who receives an annuity, a payment which is regular and continues for a period of years or for life.
BOVATE	an oxgang, which was one eighth of a carucate of ploughland, the share attributed to each ox in a team of eight, averaging around thirteen acres.
CARUCATE	as much land as a team of eight oxen could plough in one season.
DEFORCIANT	to keep out of possession by force, a legal distress.
DEMESNE	manor house with lands adjacent to it not let out to tenants.
DISTRAINT	to seize goods for debt, especially for non payment of rent or rates.
FEAST OF ST. BARTHOLOMEW	held on 24 August.
FEE SIMPLE	land granted to an individual and his heirs. This meant that land would pass upon death to the immediate heir unless another agreement superceded it. If the line of heirs died out at any point, then ownership of the land would return to the grantor.
FEOFFMENT	to grant possession of a fief or property in land.
FIEF	land held in return for feudal service or on condition of military service.
FIEFDOM	an area of influence, autocratically controlled by an individual or organisation.
HECTARE	100 acres or 10,000 square metres.
QUITCLAIM	relinquish a deed of release to a claim or title to land.
MARTINMAS	feast of St. Martin, 11 November.
MESNE	intermediate or middle.
MESSUAGE	dwelling and offices with the adjoining lands appropriated to the household.
MULTURE	fee, generally in kind, for grinding grain, the right to such a fee. A miller was a person who would have paid multures.
PERCHES	a rod or pole, a measure of $5^1/_2$ yards (5.03 metres) or square perch $30^1/_4$ square yards (25.3 sq. metres)
PLAINTIFF	a person who commences a suit against another.
ROOD	a rod, pole or perch, linear or square, varying locally in value; a quarter of an acre, or 0.10117 hectares.

Bibliography

1. *A Further History of Penistone*, Penistone WEA History Group.
2. Abbott, Geoffrey, *Rack, Rope and Red Hot Pincers*, Brockhampton Press.
3. Bede, *Ecclesiastical History of the English People*, Penguin.
4. Belfield, Eversley, *The Boer War*, Pen & Sword.
5. Beresford Ellis, Peter, *Celt & Saxon*, Constable.
6. Bewley, Robert, *Prehistoric Settlements*, Batsford.
7. Bower and Knight, *Plain Country Friends*, Wooldale Friends Meeting.
8. *Burkes Peerage*.
9. Canon & Griffiths, *Oxford Illustrated History of the British Monarchy*, Oxford.
10. Chandler, John, *John Leland's Itinerary*, Alan Sutton.
11. *Comptons Encyclopaedia Vol.3*.

12. Cook & Stevenson, *Modern British History*, Longman.
13. Cottle, Basil, *Penguin Dictionary of Surnames*, Penguin.
14. Cuncliffe, Barry, *Iron Age Britain*, Batsford.
15. *Denbigh Castle*, CADW - Welsh Historic Monuments.
16. Dransfield, John Ness *History of Penistone*.
17. Elliott, Brian, *The Making of Barnsley*, Wharncliffe Books.
18. Hey, David, *Yorkshire From ADIOOO*, Longman.
19. Higham, N J, *The Kingdom of Northumbria*, Alan Sutton.
20 Huddersfield Local History Library.
21. Hunter, Joseph, *The Life of Oliver Heywood*.
22. Hunter, Rev. Joseph, *South Yorkshire V2*.
23. Ingram, Rev. J, *The Saxon Chronicle*, Studio Editions.
24. Kenyon, A / P.Thorpe?*A Stroll Round Denbi*.
25. Lane, Peter, *Success in British History*, John Murray.
26. Lawton, Fred, *Historical Notes on Skelmanthorpe & District*.
27. Mackay, John, *William Wallace*, Mainstream Publishing.
28. Marsden, John, *The Fury of the Northmen*, BCA.
29. Morehouse, Henry, *The History of Kirkburton and the Graveship of Holme*.
30. Morris, John, *Doomsday Book Volume 1 and 2*, Gen.Ed. Philimore.
31. Morris, John, *The Age of Arthur*, Weidenfeld & Nicholson.
32. Nicholson, Vera, *Gunthwaite and the Bosvilles* from *Aspects of Barnsley 1* , Wharncliffe Books.
33. Orton, Diana, *Made of Gold*.
34. *Penistone Almanac 1954*.
35. *Penistone Almanac 1984*.
36. Poole, A L, *Doomsday Book to Magna Carta*, Oxford.
37. Popjoy, H N, *The History of Emley*.
38. Radford, Ken, *Tales of Witches & Sorcery*, Chancellor Press.
39. Richards, Julian D, *Viking Age England*, Batsford.
40. Salway, Peter, *Oxford Illustrated History of Roman Britain*, Oxford.
41. Senior, W H, *A History of Denby Dale Urban District Council*, Denby Dale UDC.
42. Singer, Andre and Lynette, *Divine Magic*, Boxtree.
43. *The John Goodchild Collection*, Wakefield.
44. Various authors, *History Today Companion to British History*, Collins & Brown.
45. *Victoria County History Vols. 1, 2, and 3*.
46 Wakefield County Archives.
47. West Yorkshire Archaeology Service.
48. Wood, Eric S, *Historical Britain*, Harvill.
49. Wood, Michael, *In Search of the Dark Ages*, BBC.

Epitaph

Even such is time, which takes in trust
Our youth our joys, and all we have,
And pays us but with age and dust;
Who in the dark and silent grave,
When we have wandered all our ways,
Shuts up the story of our days:
And from which earth, and grave and dust,
The Lord shall raise me up, I trust.

WALTER RALEIGH

Index

Purely for reasons of space, this index is highly selective. It has been impossible to include all the personal and place names included within, and is designed to help the reader around the book rather than be fully comprehensive.